BEANS DOME
Slowtecture M Project

ENDO SHUHEI

この記録写真は2005年11月4日からの506日間を撮影したものである。
写真家天野憲一による2522枚の写真から264枚を掲載した。

These photographs were taken over 506 days, beginning November 4, 2005.
The 264 photographs included in this volume were selected from
the 2,522 that photographer Amano Kenichi shot during that period.

Table of Contents   Photographs of the work in progress   4   The Ordinary and the Extraordinary: New Issues for Public Facilities by Miyake Riichi   21

Photographs of the work in progress   28   Photographs of the completed facility   117   Memo: Slowtecture M by Endo Shuhei   137   The plans   140

2005 DECEMBER

2006 JANUARY

2006 FEBRUARY

JANUARY

2006 MARCH   2006 APRIL

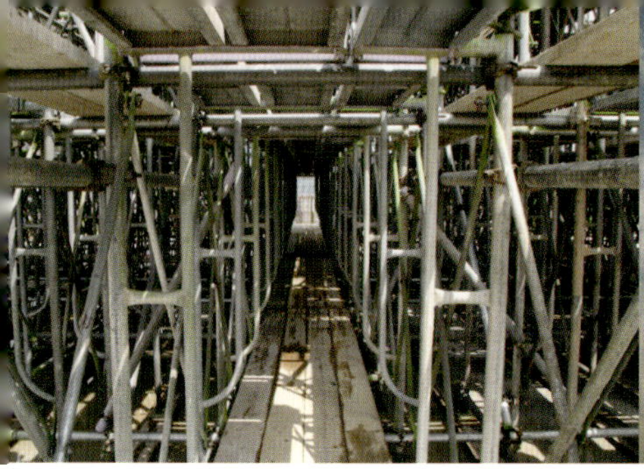
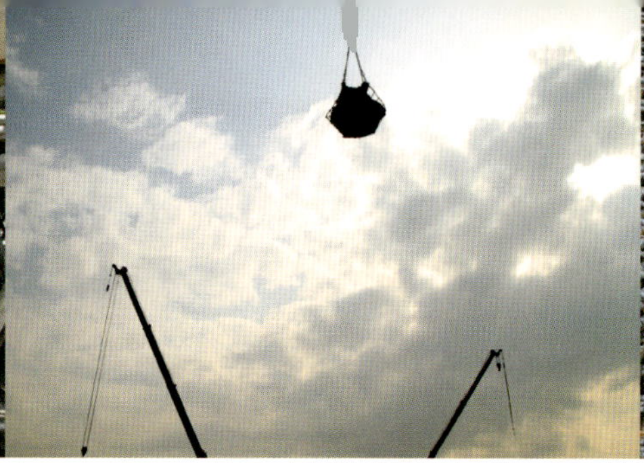
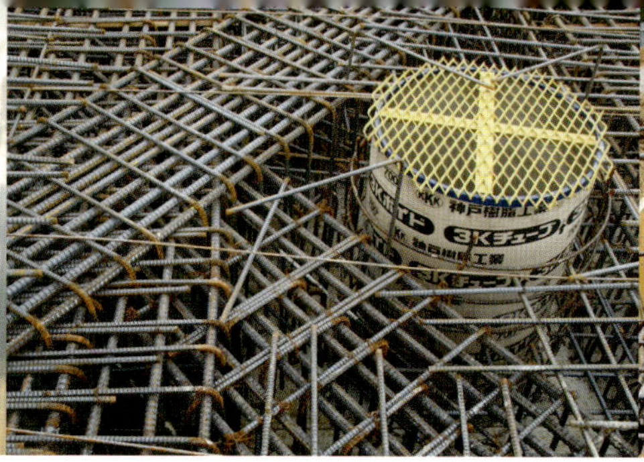
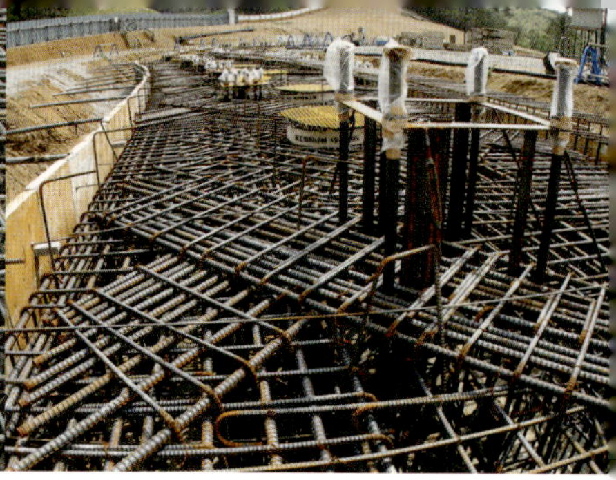
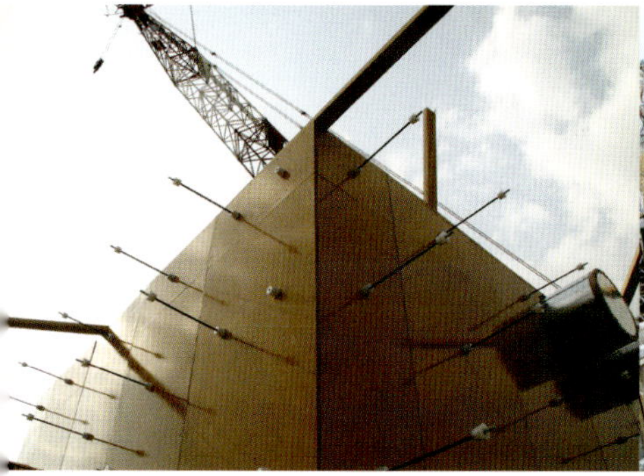
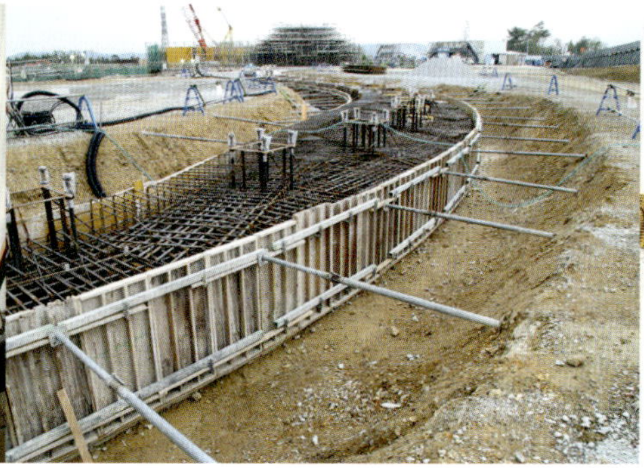
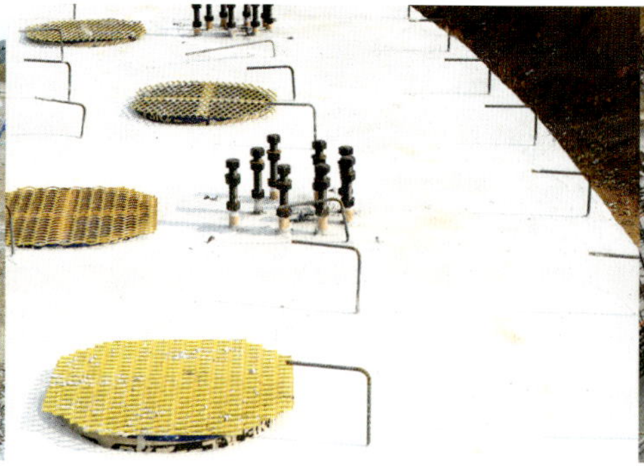
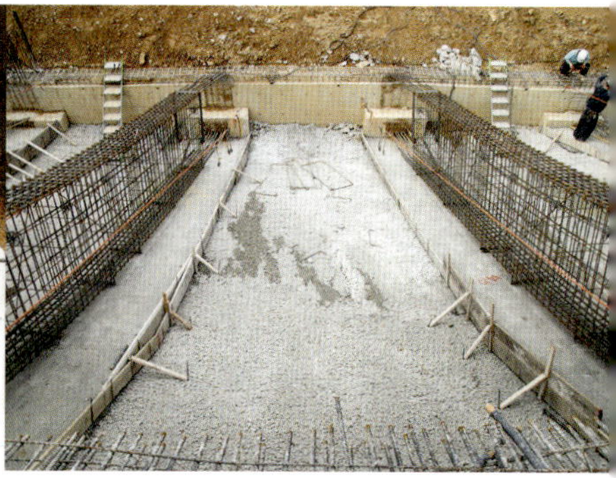
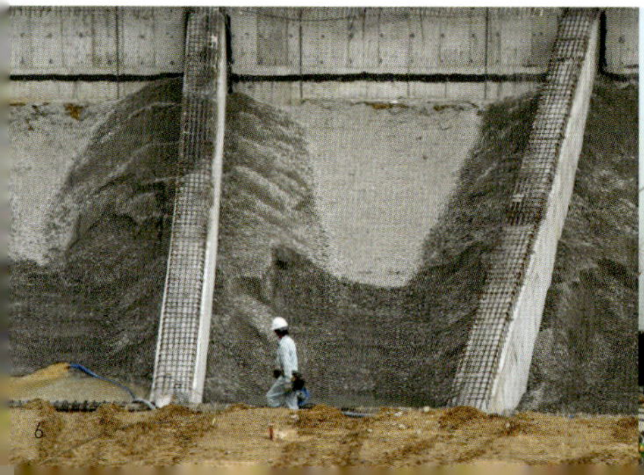
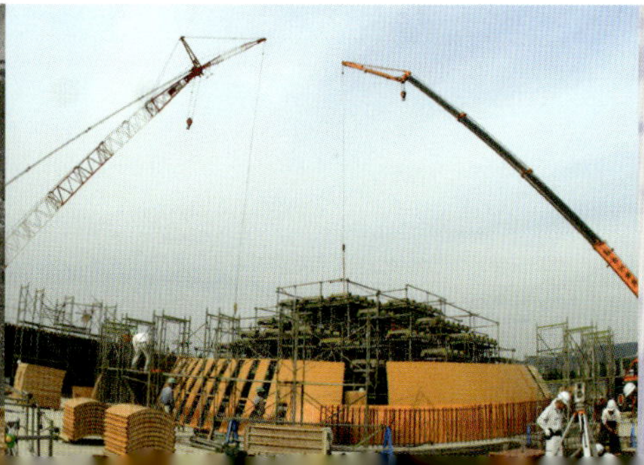
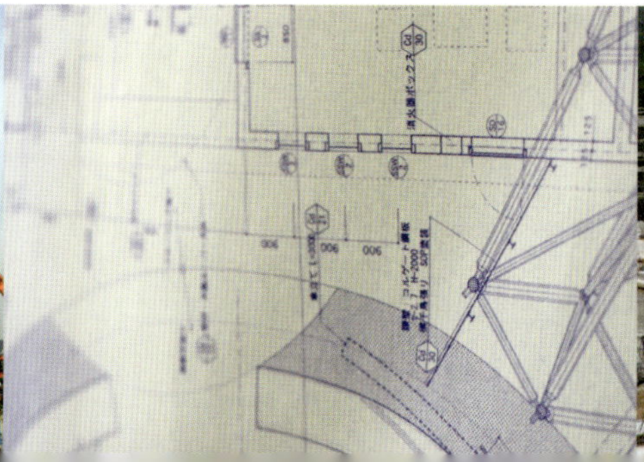
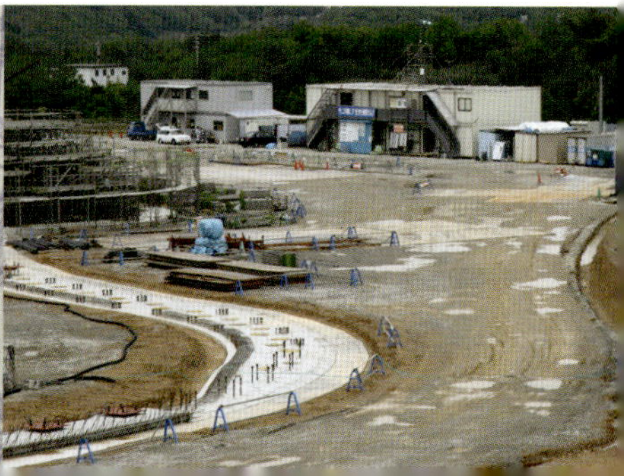

2006 MAY

2006 JUNE →

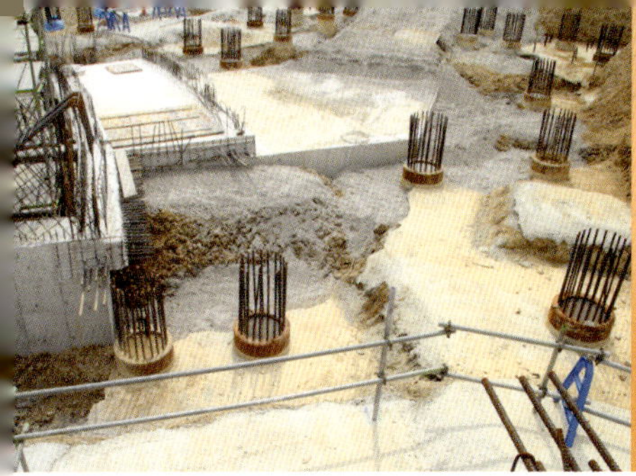
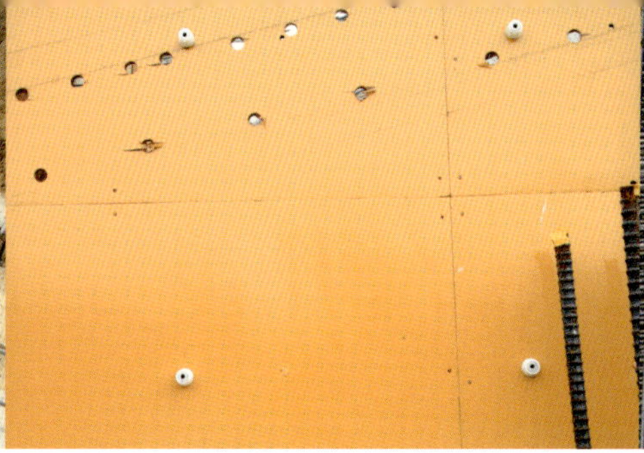
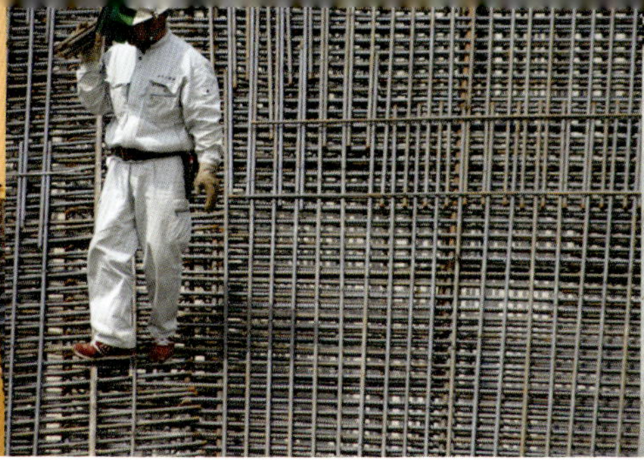
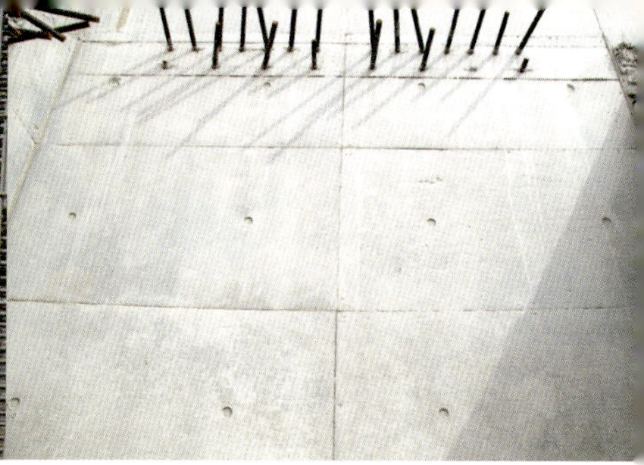
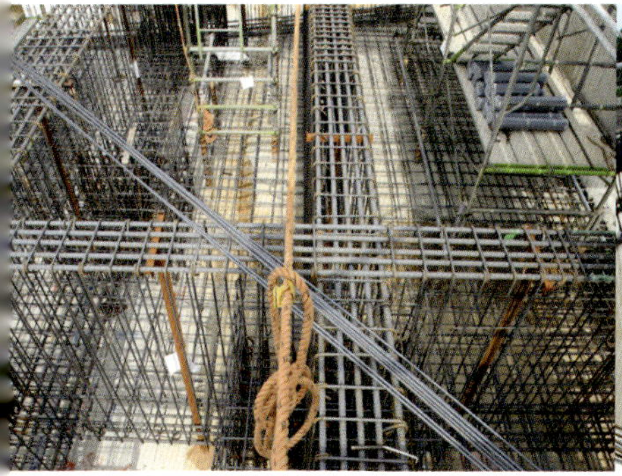
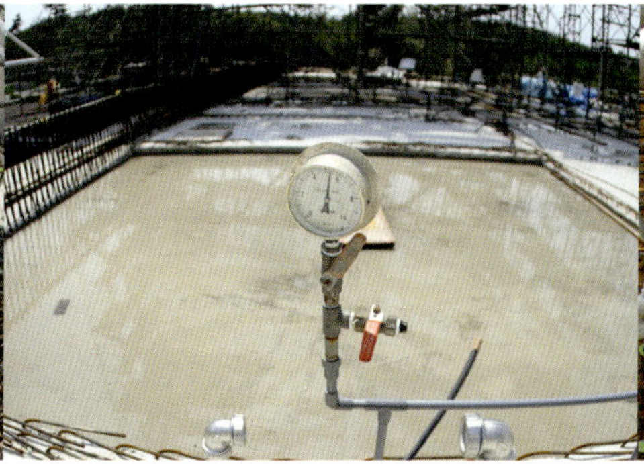
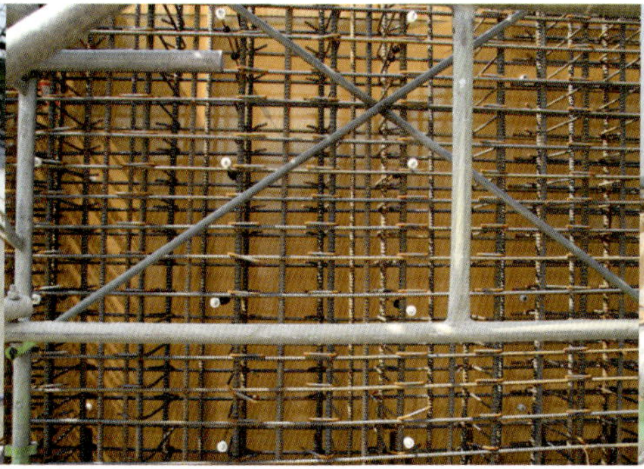
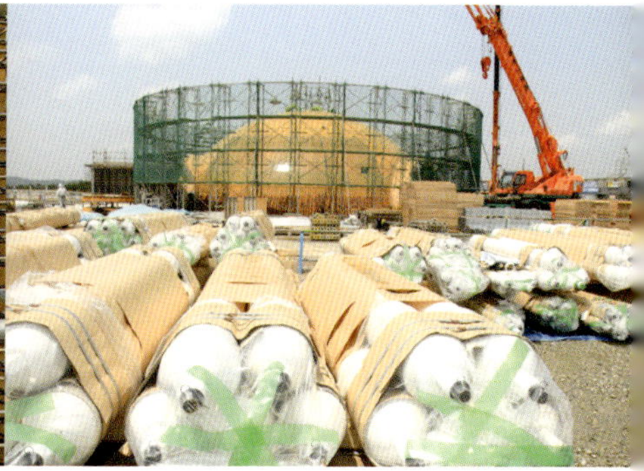
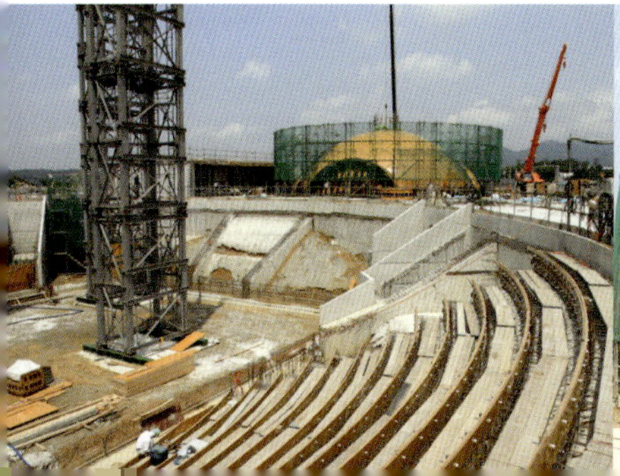
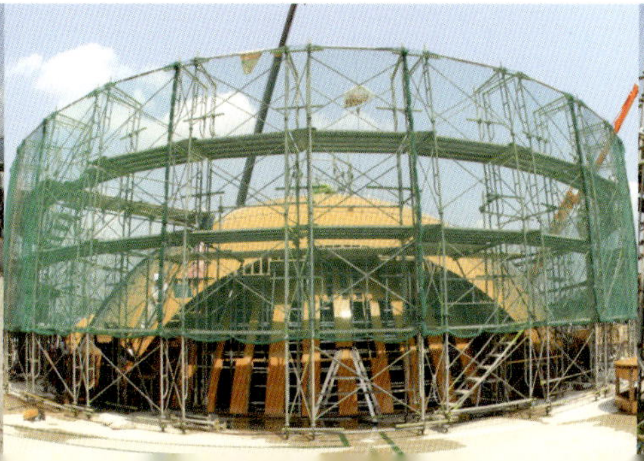
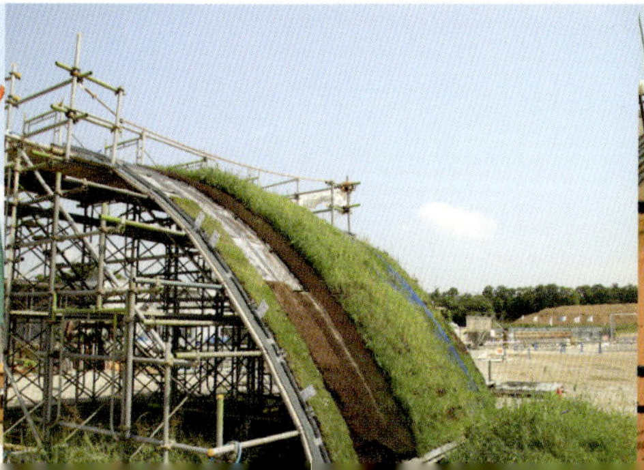
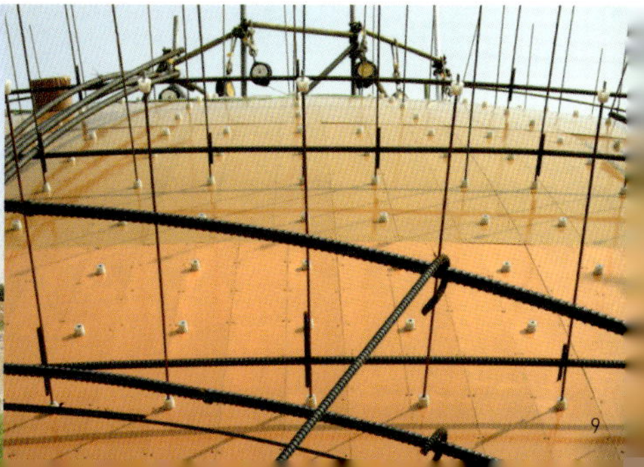

2006 JULY

6 AUGUST

2006 SEPTEMBER

2006 NOVEMBER

2006 OCTOBER

14

2006 DECEMBER

2007 JANUARY

2007 FEBRUARY

7 MARCH

2007 APRIL ⟶

2007 JUNE ⟶

19

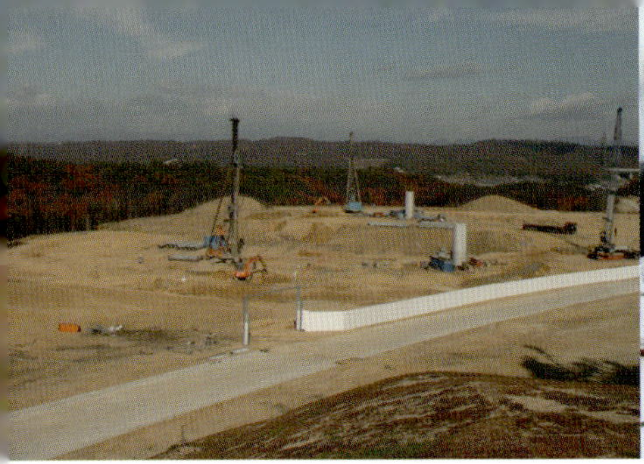
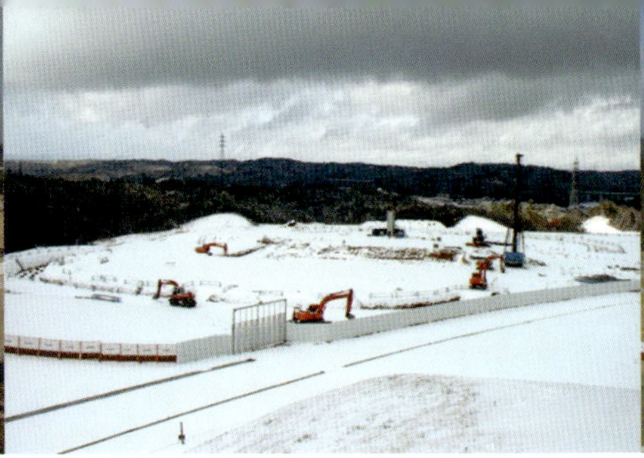
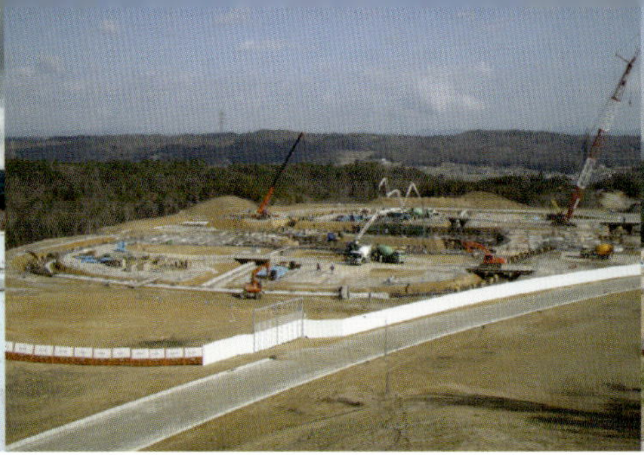
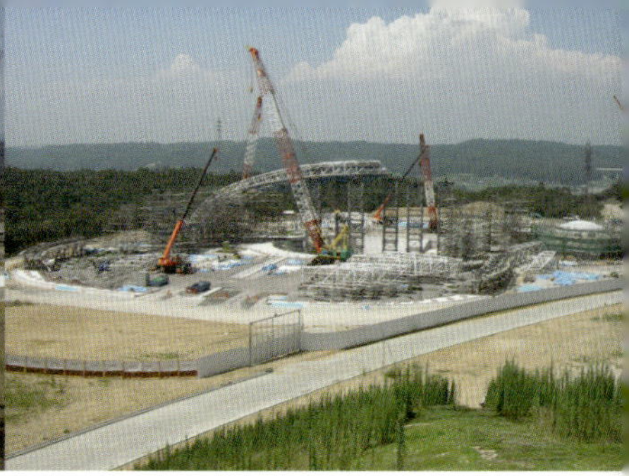
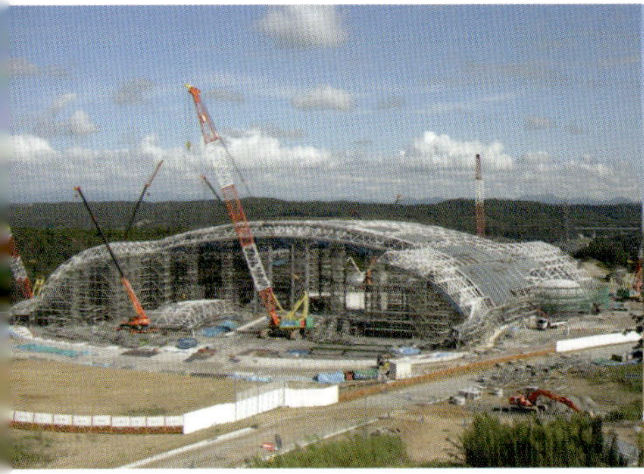
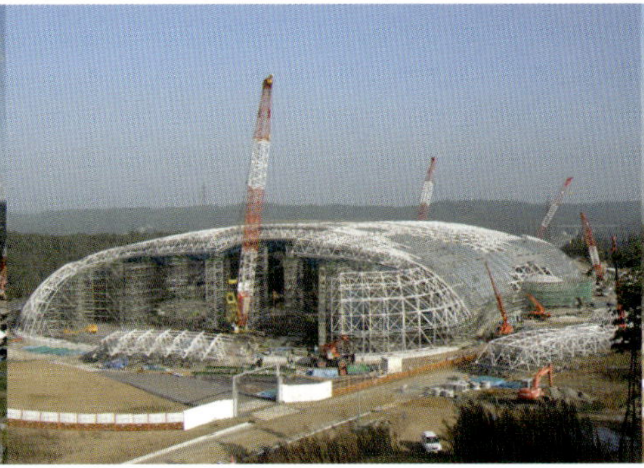
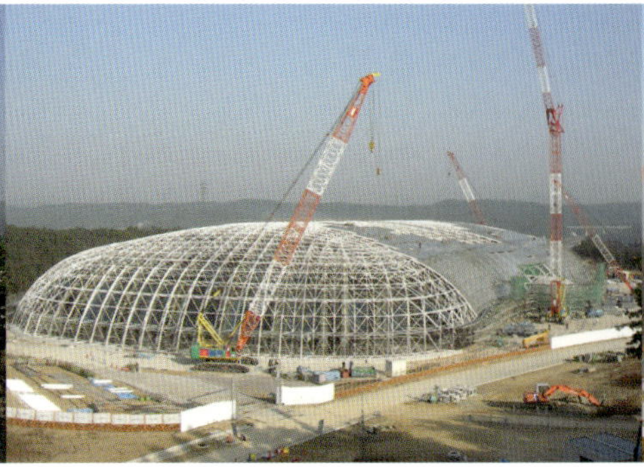
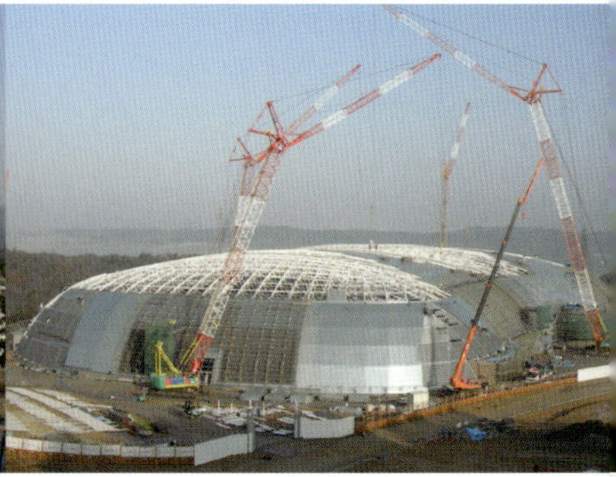
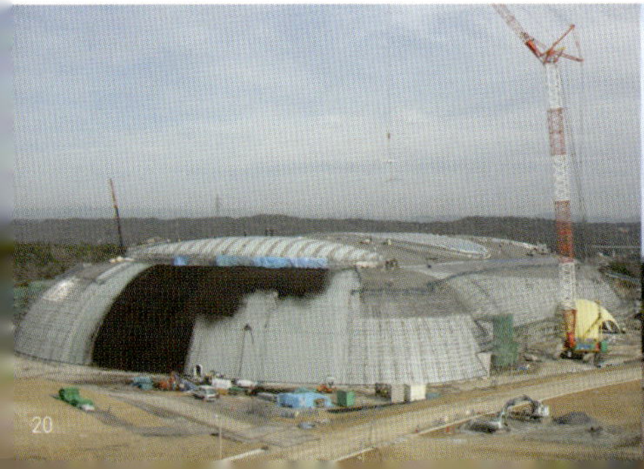
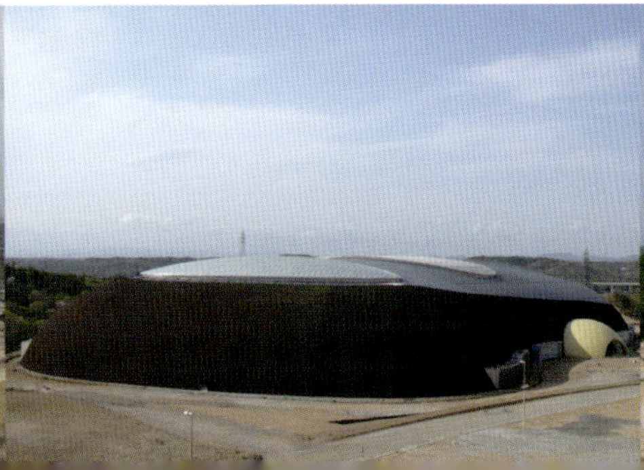
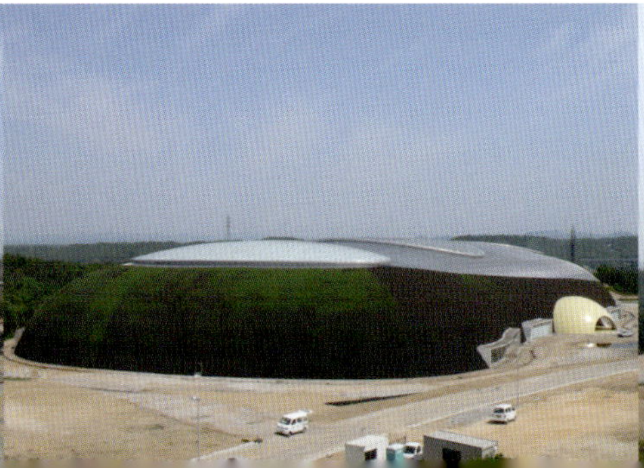
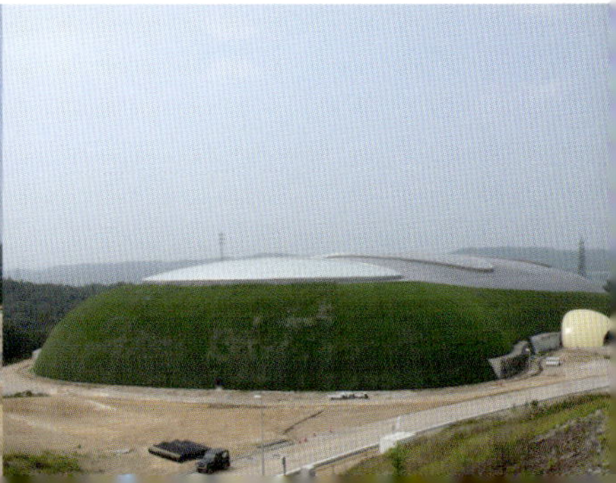

非常と日常 — 新たな公共建築の課題　　三宅理一

防災拠点としての体育施設

兵庫県といえば1995年の阪神淡路大震災の記憶が今なお生々しく残っている場所である。地震は国内到るところで繰り返し発生しているが、やはり神戸の場合は大都市を直撃したということでその被害の程度も他とは較べものにならなかった。しかも、政府の対応が後手に回ったことから救援や復興にあたって各方面からの批判があい続き、その意味で後世に悪しき評判を残す結果となった。それ以降、全国の自治体は神戸を反面教師として防災のためにさまざまな施策を打ち出し、10年前に較べて我国全体の防災水準は相当改善されたといってもよい。とはいっても、災害とはいつどこの地域を襲うかがわからない不確定の代物で、どんなに対策を講じていてもそこから漏れるケースを覚悟しなければならない。50年、100年というスパンでも対応できる計画思想が必要である。

そのような経緯で建設されたのが、兵庫県の中ほどに位置する「三木総合防災公園」である。災害時における県の防災救援拠点となるべく計画されたもので、県の防災事業に国の補助金をからめて兵庫県全域をにらんだ広域ネットワーク・ハブとして位置づけられている。全体で約200 haの面積を数え、その中にいくつものスポーツ施設を立地させた点が特徴的だ。防災とスポーツという取り合わせは一見奇異に思えるが、平時での活用、広い面積や自然との一体性に対応した利用形態などを考えると、スポーツ施設がもっとも適合しているとの判断から、そのようになったと聞く。ヨーロッパならどこにでもある核シェルターがこれに対応するものだが、残念ながら我国では国や自治体の施策にそのようなカテゴリーはなく、もっぱら「自然の攻撃」にのみ対応した施設のつくり方になっている。

この防災拠点の基幹施設のひとつとなっているのが、この公園内にある「屋内テニス場」である。いかにも平和な響きをもった体育施設であるが、いざという時

The Ordinary and the Extraordinary: New Issues for Public Facilities
Miyake Riichi

A Sports Facility as a Disaster Management Center

Memories of the Great Hanshin Awaji Earthquake that struck Hyogo Prefecture in 1995 are still raw. Earthquakes are part of life in Japan, but the Hanshin quake directly struck a major city, Kobe. The level of damage far exceeded any other earthquake in recent memory, and the sluggish government response—both in emergency relief in the immediate wake of the quake and then in the reconstruction efforts—has been widely criticized. It is now seen as an example of how not to deal with a disaster. Since then, local governments throughout the country, having learned from Kobe how not to behave, have been working on their own disaster management plans. Thanks to Kobe, the nationwide level of disaster preparedness has improved considerably over the past decade.

Disasters are, however, by nature unpredictable; we do not know when and where they will strike. We do know that no matter what measures we put in place, they will necessarily be flawed. Moreover, the planning for unpredictable but inevitable events must address a long time span, with preparations for disaster response made in terms of fifty or even a hundred years.

That need for long-term planning motivated the construction of the Miki Disaster Management Park in central Hyogo Prefecture. The park is intended to function as the prefecture's disaster response center. Built using disaster preparedness funds from the national government, the park is conceived as the hub of a vast network that covers the whole of Hyogo Prefecture.

The two hundred hectare park also includes several sports facilities. At first sight the combination of disaster management and sports may seem odd, but it came about through careful thought about how to provide an extensive area for a disaster response effort while building a facility that would be in harmony with its natural setting and be useful in normal times as well. In this sense it resembles the nuclear fallout shelters found all over Europe. (For good or for ill, no such facilities have been built in Japan by the national or local governments; the focus has been exclusively on meeting natural threats.)

The vital core of this disaster management facility is the tennis dome that encloses a set of indoor tennis courts. This sports facility resonates peace and tranquility; in an

は救援物資の配送センターになり、場合によっては避難民を収容しつつ、防災ロジスティックスの中枢を担う結節点でなければならない。高速道路に沿っているのもそのためである。この種の広域的でネットワーク型の施設の重要性はいうまでもないが、それを空間計画に落とし込んだ時に直面する設計上の難しさは相当のものであったと察せられる。何よりも大空間で、いかなる事態にも対応できるフレキシブルな建築でなければならない。しかし、緊急事態を迎えるのは長いタイムスパンの中ではほんの一瞬のことであり、その他の期間は平時の日常的な機能を収めて施設を有効に用い、維持管理をしていなければならない。ここではスポーツがその機能に対応し、スポーツ・イベントに集まる多くの来場者を前提とした施設設計を行わなければならない。

こう考えてくると、この屋内テニス場の設計者に遠藤秀平が選ばれたのはそれなりの必然性があったといってよい。彼の手がけてきた一連の建築は、どのような規模にも対応可能な架構と空間をつくり出すのに適した方法論を胚胎している

からである。これまで大空間を成立させるには、ドームやシェル、あるいはテントといった構造方式が採用されてきた。それもこの半世紀ほどの間に技術革新が著しく、大人数を集める室内競技場の類で次から次に新しい工法が開拓されている。それゆえ、技術的にみれば、現在では実質的に何でも可能であって、むしろ企画サイドの立案こそがその施設の性格と空間を大きく左右するといってよい。その点で、今回の屋内テニス場の場合は、防災とスポーツを統合するというプログラムこそが鍵であって、規模そのものはそれほどの問題ではない。

実際、内部空間は極端に大きいわけでもなく、ウインブルドンをみればわかる通り、小さなテニスコートで分節されてしかるべき体育館である。メインコートがあって、その周りに多くのコートが広がる形式が自然であり、それを字義通りにつくり込むと、今度は防災拠点としての多目的かつ段差のないフラットな平面という県の要求に抵触してしまう。そこをまとめ上げるためには、ある程度の分節性と平坦な床面という矛盾する要素を調整しなければならない。むろん技術的にこの

emergency, however, it will turn into the distribution center for emergency supplies and the hub for disaster response logistics. It will also function as a refuge for displaced people. That is why is the tennis facility has been built beside the expressway. The importance for disaster management of such a facility, the core of a network covering a large region, should be obvious.

How to translate the concept behind that facility into the design for a structure was, however, far from obvious. What was needed, above all, was a large space with the flexibility to respond to any and all situations. But emergencies will be few and far between during its long useful life. The rest of the time, the facility must work well as a space for its non-emergency functions and must be maintained on that basis. In the case of the tennis dome, large numbers of spectators will gather there for sporting events.

It was almost inevitable that Endo Shuhei be chosen as the architect for this indoor tennis facility, for the series of structures he has worked on so far are rooted in a methodology that is suitable for creating a structural framework and space that can adapt to any scale.

Historically, domes, shells, or tents have been the structures employed to form very large spaces. As part of the dramatic pace of technological innovation in the past half century, a series of new construction methods have emerged for building indoor stadiums accommodating large crowds. Technologically, then, almost anything is possible; it is the proposals from the planning side rather than technological limitations that most influence the resulting character and space of a facility. For this indoor tennis facility, the central problem is that it must integrate disaster management and sports scale itself is not much of an issue.

In fact, the interior space is not extraordinarily large. Consider Wimbledon: the tennis dome will be essentially one stadium that can be divided into several small tennis courts. The obvious format is to have a main court, like Centre Court at Wimbledon, with several other courts around it. But building them as separate spaces would contradict the prefecture's requirement for a multipurpose, flat, level, barrier-free surface to function as a disaster management center. The solution must, then, satisfy contradictory requirements: tennis demands a certain amount of divisibility into separate courts, while disaster management requires a level, open working surface.

Finding a solution may not have, technologically speaking, been especially difficult. The uniqueness of Endo Shuhei's solution is that instead of adopting a technical

問題を解決するのはそう難しいことではないか、設計者の遠藤秀平のユニークさは、技術志向からこのような大空間に挑んだわけではなく、彼独自の空間思想からこの空間に到り着いたところにある。周囲の山並みに対応するかのようなうねった空間がそこに登場し、一目でこの建築の特殊性を物語っている。なぜか。それを知るためには遠藤のこれまでの活動を参照しなければならないが、その鍵は意外なところに潜んでいた。

 998年に行った播磨科学公園都市での仕事がそれである。大変小さな建築で、それも公衆便所というささやかな建築であった。山間の土地を造成して大規模な科学技術拠点を形成したところは防災公園に似ているが、公園と都市では規模が異なる。周囲のひなびた雰囲気とは似ても似つかぬ近代都市が広がっている。もともとは山間の寒村地帯にすぎなかったこの辺りにこの巨大な研究学園都市ができると、この地域一帯の都市構造も景観もがらりと変わってしまった。著名な建築家のデザインになる建築もあい続き、磯崎新や安藤忠雄の名前がごく普通

に語られる。それらの基幹施設に挟まれて建つのが遠藤秀平の手になるさわてユニークな作品なのである。公衆便所という機能にとらわれず、むしろ公共空間のためのひとつの実験といったほうがふさわしい建築である。

建築の生成原理

播磨科学公園都市での実験は、遠藤が試行錯誤の末に到達したひとつのプロトタイプを示している。そこから発展し、徐々に規模を拡大させて今日の屋内テニス場に到り着くのであるが、基本的に両者の空間思想は共通である。両者は兵庫県繋がりということ以上に、今日の時代にふさわしい公共性のあり方を解く建築モデルといってもよい。20世紀型の公共建築というと、美術館、体育館、市民ホールであれば、いかにもそれっぽい建築をデザインすることが当たり前であった公共側もそれを求めていた。ところが遠藤秀平の仕事をみていると、公共建築といっても駐輪場や無人駅といったこれまではあまり目立つことのなかった建築

orientation to organizing this large space, he arrived at the answer by working from his own distinctive spatial thinking. The result is a meandering space that echoes and harmonizes with the surrounding hills, a space that conveys the distinctiveness of this structure at a glance. Why is that? To understand, one must consider Endo's career thus far. The answer lies in what may be a rather unexpected place.

 That key Endo structure can be found in Harima Science Park City, Hyogo Prefecture. Built in 1998, it is referred to by Endo as Springtecture H. It is, in fact, a small, structure of a retiring character: a public restroom.

 Its site resembles that of the Miki Disaster Management Park in that it is part of a large-scale park built on a site surrounded by mountains, but the scale is totally different. Harima Science Park is a modern city sprawling between the hills in utter contrast to the rural atmosphere of its surroundings. Once this huge urban research park took shape in the area, originally a lonely, rustic village in the mountains, the face of the entire district was transformed. Here Endo's remarkable structure stands in close proximity to a series of buildings designed by famous architects; here the names sozaki Arata or Ando Tadao are household words. Compared to those core structures,

providing desirable public spaces. That quality, not its function as a restroom, is what defines it.

The Generative Principle in Architecture

The experiment in Harima Science Park City was a prototype at which Endo had arrived after considerable trial and error. Extrapolating from that point, while expanding gradually in scale, has brought him to the tennis dome; tiny and huge, both share the same basic spatial thinking. Both could be described as architectural models exploring the qualities of public spaces appropriate in our times. These shared qualities are far more important than the accident that both are located in Hyogo Prefecture.

 In the twentieth century, public structures meant museums, gymnasiums, and civic centers. Their designs proclaimed their functions; that, it was assumed, was what the public wanted. But Endo Shuhei has followed a different path, creating structures that while definitely public buildings, would not in the past have been high on a list of important public structures: parking areas, and public restrooms. As the plazas and pedestrian decks that were so fashionable in the 1960s have devolved into merely

を積極的に手がけ、それを地域に根づいた建築として成立させているのである。公衆便所も同様である。1960年代に流行った広場とかペデストリアン・デッキが実は誰も用いないお飾りの公共空間となり下がってしまったのに反比例して、日常のさりげなさの中に潜むどこにでもある空間の価値が浮上してきたのに対応している。

そもそも公衆便所が建築的なテーマとなるというのは、世界の中でもおそらく日本だけと思われるが、1980年くらいから公共建築のミニ版として、交番と並んで都市の重要施設に位置づけられてきた。清潔さ、快適性が絶対に必要である結構難しい仕事である。遠藤秀平による播磨科学公園都市の仕事は、それまでのトイレという既成の観念を打ち破ったところに新しさがあった。彼の建築は、折版状になったスチール、つまりコルゲート鋼板を用いて空間を表現する。鋼板を波板状にして剛性を出すことで成立するこの材料は、普通、土木工事のための土留め、あるいは簡素さを旨とする工場建築に用いられることが多い。それを建築材料に

するという発想は、かつて河合健二や石山修武が実験的に住居として用いた例がある程度である。確かに鋼板一枚では熱伝導率が良すぎて室内気候をコントロールできず、それが住居に向いているとは思えない。しかし表面にメッキを施して耐候性を増し、野外にそのまま放り出しておいても問題のない材料だからこそ、メンテナンスに手間暇がかからなく、維持管理の労力を省くことが是とされるミニ公共施設ではうってつけの素材であった。内外の空間の一体性というコンセプトを追求してきた遠藤秀平にとっては、そのような力強い素材の存在が空間造形の上でも機能の上でも大きく寄与したことは間違いない。柱と梁、あるいはフレームと間仕切りといった従来の建築の作法にのっとることなく、回転しながら連続する一枚の板によって人間の行為を保証する場ができあがるわけで、そのダイナミズムこそが彼の建築をひも解く鍵になることを知って頂きたい。本題の「三木総合防災公園屋内テニス場」を説明するのに、この公衆便所という小空間を引き合いに出したのは、遠藤秀平が小さな単位から始まって

become apparent.

Quite possibly only in Japan are public restrooms treated as a specific architectural theme. At any rate, since 1980 or so they have been positioned, along with local police boxes, as important urban facilities, mini versions of public architecture. Designing them is not easy, especially since cleanliness, comfort, and peace of mind are non-negotiable conditions.

Endo's restroom for the Harima science park refreshingly demolishes conventional concepts of what a public restroom can be. His use of corrugated steel to generate that public space was, moreover, revolutionary. Corrugated steel, whose rigidity results from the ridges folded into steel sheets, is most often used in retaining walls or in factory buildings, where simplicity is the chief goal. Kawai Kenji and Ishiyama Osamu had used it experimentally in residential structures, but, before Endo, its use as an architectural material had stopped there.

Corrugated steel has an obvious disadvantage as a residential building material, for a single steel sheet conducts heat too well, making it impossible to control the internal temperature. But it also has its advantages: galvanizing or plating its surface greatly increases corrosion resistance; the result is a material that can be exposed to the

weather without worrying about the time and effort necessary for its upkeep. It is thus an obvious choice for a mini public facility, where reducing the need for maintenance would be major advantage.

To Endo Shuhei, who had been exploring the concept of integration of interior and exterior spaces, corrugated steel's strength offered a major advantage in terms of how spaces could be formed as well as in terms of functionality. Instead of being restricted to conventional construction methods, with their pillars and beams or frame and partitions, he was able to create a space suitable for human activity by twisting one continuous sheet of corrugated steel. That dynamism is the key to understanding his architecture.

I have referred to this tiny structure, this public restroom, while describing the tennis facility in the Miki Disaster Management Park, to demonstrate that Endo Shuhei seeks to create a world of continuous spaces that expand uninterruptedly from a small initial unit—just as that small restroom was the initial unit inspiring the thinking behind the tennis facility.

Architects seek to awaken human beings to experience spaces by building relationships between humans, spaces, and materials. Beautiful buildings, comfortable

途切れることなく広がる連続空間の世界を求め続けてきたことを説明するためであった。建築家がめざすのは、人間と空間、そして素材感をともなう建築を相互に関係づけて、人間の空間体験を強く覚醒するところにある。美しい建築、居心地の良い建築、心をときめかせる建築。いずれも人間が建築をどう感じどう使うかに関わっているが、遠藤の場合はやや突出していて、強いていえば認知心理学の実験を絵にかいたような建築であるといってもよい。屋内テニス場の場合は、そこで試合をするひとりひとりのプレーヤーから、周囲の千人規模の観衆を見越して空間のボリュームを分節させ、拡大していくのである。遠藤の建築に対しては、駐輪場や公衆便所が「スプリングテクチャー」や「バブルテクチャー」といったこじつけまがいの命名を行っていてどこか劇画じみた印象を受ける人もいるようだが、その根幹にあるのはしごくまっとうな発想である。空間を施設や機能に対応づけて考えるのではなく、空間が自律的に展開し、それこそひとつの点から始まって、糸玉をほぐすようにどこまでも続く無限のスパイラルをつくる可能性を秘めていることを示唆しようとしている。ル・コルビュジエであれば「幾何学」や「黄金比」がそのパラメーターになっているのが、遠藤の場合は円環やスパイラルが空間の自律構造を導くのである。コルゲート鋼板を螺旋状に回転させてスプリング（ばね）のように展開することが、そのまま新たな建築の生成プロセスとなることを意味している。従来の建築の基本である柱梁のフレームでは体験することのできない連続して流れる空間が、この螺旋から生まれるといってもよい。彼の建築を理解するためには、ほとんどオブセッションのように彼をとらえて離さない「どこまでも流れて広がる空間」を読み取り、そのデザイン原理を知っておかなければならないのである。

巨大な草の被膜

もちろん遠藤秀平は建築に要求される機能や社会性に対しては人一倍に敏感である。やみくもに「異形」の建築をつくっているのではなく、ごく当たり前に社会の中で

buildings, exciting buildings: in each case the descriptions reflect how human beings perceive and use those buildings. Endo takes the connection a bit further, with structures that might be called visual representations of experiments in cognitive psychology. In the case of the indoor tennis facility, he starts with the individual players who will be competing there, uses them as units to subdivide the volume of space in anticipation of a thousand or so spectators, and allows his vision to expand.

Endo likes to dub the public restrooms and parking facilities he has designed with somewhat peculiar names such as Springtecture or Bubbletecture. Those names may give some the impression that he's rather comic-book-like in his approach. But the core of his work is a set of extremely straightforward ideas. Instead of thinking of spaces as corresponding to their functions and facilities, he is trying to point out that spaces can develop autonomously, that they have the potential to begin from a certain point and describe an infinite spiral, like springs, like untangling a ball of yarn, on and on and on.

For Le Corbusier, the equivalent parameters were geometry and the golden section. For Endo, it is circles and spirals that lead to an autonomous structuring of space. Twisting corrugated steel sheets to form a spiral, he deploys them like springs; that in itself signifies a new generative process in architecture. His spirals generate a continuously flowing space that cannot be experienced within the pillar and beam frame that is the fundamental of conventional construction. To understand Endo's structures, it is necessary to read in them the "space flowing out forever and ever" with which he is creatively obsessed—his primary design principle.

A Giant Verdant Membrane

Endo Shuhei is also uncommonly sensitive to the functions and social qualities demanded of buildings. As is true of other progressive architects and designers as well, he does not build bizarre structures for their own sake but seeks to create structures that people will find easy to use and will come to regard as perfectly normal, not bizarre. What is fascinating about his body of work is that instead of focusing on high-density housing or community facilities, he has identified areas that are blind spots in conventional thinking about public spaces and has built a considerable track record in carefully designing those critical meeting points or nodes between human beings and society. A disaster management facility is a natural extension of that body of work in less than conventional public spaces. There were thus high hopes for Endo Shuhei's building not only a superb facility but also a new model for public spaces can be.

認知され、人々にとって使いやすい建築をめざしている点では、他の先進的な建築家やデザイナーと共通している。興味深いのは、集合住宅や社会施設といった領域よりも、従来の公共空間から取り残されてきた部分に着目し、人間と社会との結節点を丁寧にデザインしてきた実績があるということだ。防災施設という課題もその延長線上にあり、社会の遠藤秀平に対するまなざしには、新たな公共空間モデルを構築するという期待感が込められているのは間違いない。

大規模な施設を求められた三木総合防災公園では、当然ながらミニ空間とは異なった方法が必要になる。大空間をつくるにあたって、重量のあるコルゲート鋼板を用いることはできない。大地から自立して宙にスパイラルを描く鋼板に対して、屋内テニス場では逆に大地と連続して起伏する壮大な地表面を想定する。流れる空間の原型を自然地形に求め、さながら地上に置かれた巨大な繭が地下に埋まりつつあるようなイメージを喚起させている。建築の形態を規定する幾何学（ジオメトリー）という点からみると、回転体をずらして空間を構成する方法にのっとっており、その意味では一連のコルゲート鋼板と同根である。しかし、建築を宙に浮かせるのではなく、大地に沈ませようとする姿勢は、今日の環境論の視点からみて正解であり、まさに建築のランドスケープ化にほかならない。大空間のボリュームを確保するために立体トラスによってスペースフレームを組み、無柱のスペースを生み出し、防災拠点としての要件をかなえる。このスペースフレームの上を一面ステンレス鋼板で覆うことになる。ただ、外観にステンレスの銀色の輝きを期待する向きには、それを裏切ることになる。

そのためこの屋内テニス場は新たな環境技術を駆使することになった。屋上緑化がその代表で、うねった曲面全体に杉・檜の樹皮を吹き付けてつくった人工土壌を被せ、緑化のための下地であるとともに断熱材として建築全体を包むことになった。その上に草を生やすのである。結果的に外断熱方式で、空調のコストパフォーマンスを相当下げることに寄与しているが、本来この緑化技術は土木の領域に数えられていた。そういえばコルゲート鋼板も土木で用いられてきたもの

The large facility in the Miki Disaster Management Park, naturally enough, required different methods from those Endo used in building mini spaces. Corrugated steel sheets are far too heavy to use in creating large spaces. Instead of steel sheets drawing a spiral in space, independent from the earth, Endo's guiding hypothesis for the indoor tennis facility was a vast earthen surface rising in continuity with the land. Seeking natural landforms in a model of flowing space, he conceived of an image that resembles a giant cocoon placed on the earth's surface and being buried in it.

Looking at the tennis facility in terms of the geometry prescribing the structure's form, we see that his method was to structure space by displacing rotating bodies. In that sense this work is rooted in the same principle as his structures built of a continuous flow of corrugated steel. But here the structure does not rise to float in air but instead sinks into the earth. That approach turns his structure into landscape—the right answer in terms of today's environmental theories.

Endo has used three-dimensional trusses to build a space frame for the tennis facility. The space frame provides the necessary volume to accommodate the tennis courts and spectators while creating a pillar-free space. It thus meets the requirements or a disaster management center that normally functions as a sporting facility

The space frame is covered entirely with stainless steel sheets. But those who would expect to see the silver gleam of stainless outside will be disappointed. That is because Endo has made effective use of new environmental technologies here, the most important of which is greening the roof. He has covered the undulating curves of its surface with artificial soil by blowing cedar bark on it. The artificial soil is the necessary groundwork for greening the roof, and also envelopes the structure as a whole in insulation. With grass growing in the soil on the roof, the result is an exterior insulation system that will substantially improve the cost performance of the air conditioning system.

This green technology is one that might more often be encountered in the domain of civil engineering, not architecture. Corrugated steel is, of course, also used in civil engineering works; evidently, Endo is thinking on a larger scale than conventional architecture encompasses. Or perhaps he is erasing the boundaries between architecture, civil engineering, and the landscape. Certainly seen from afar, the tennis facility looks like a giant membrane covered in greenery, a new landform, rather than a man-made structure.

Greening structures is nothing new in Japanese history; in one example, shibamune plants were planted along the ridge of the thatched roofs that are traditional in Japan

で、やはり遠藤の発想は、従来の建築に較べてスケールが大きい。あるいは、建築、土木、ランドスケープの境界がなくなりつつあるということでもある。遠くから眺めると巨大な草の被膜が姿を現し、もうひとつの地形が生み出されるのである。本来、我国には伝統的な草屋根たる「芝棟」といった緑化の歴史があり、草むした建築はきわめて身近なものだった。20世紀が、近代化の掛け声の下でそのような伝統技術を消し去っていったのであり、環境の回復が叫ばれる昨今では、むしろ過去の技術やデザインが大きな意味をもつことがある。その極右に位置するのが藤森照信であるとすれば、遠藤はむしろ逆で、特に過去を振り向いて仕事をするタイプではないが、結果的には我国が培ってきた環境の技術を巧みに取り入れることに成功したようだ。

環境時代の建築はつとめてパッシブな技術を求めなければならない。エネルギー消費をできるだけ抑え、環境に対する負荷を最小限にするということである。その意味で、屋内テニス場は多くのパッシブ技術を導入し、公共建築としてそのモデルを提供している。草屋根によって断熱効率を上げ、太陽電池を用い、換気も温度によって空気の重量が異なることを利用した自然換気システムを導入した。大空間であることを利用して、熱と空気の流れをコントロールするわけである。テニスコートを利用する人たちは、地表面に沿って設けられた出入口から入出場し、施設内のコートに散って行く。大空間の中の小空間としてロッカールームやシャワールームが設けられ、屋内のランドスケープができあがることになる。全体のデザインは華美を慎み、きわめてニュートラルである。

遠藤秀平は、この防災施設のデザインを通して、新たな公共建築の手がかりを示してみせた。本来は倉庫であってもよい防災拠点に日常の機能を与え、市民公園としての務めを果たす。しかし、ある確率で迎えることが予測される非常時の備えを確保し、その空間のあるべき姿を設計の基本に乗せたということである。望むらくは、この次には我国にはまだ存在しない核シェルターの計画と設計をぜひとも行ってもらいたい。（みやけ・りいち　慶應義塾大学大学院教授）

Structures covered with growing plants were commonplace before the twentieth century drive to modernization led to the dying out of these traditional technologies. Today, with rising demand for restoring the environment, such techniques and designs from the past have taken on great significance. If the architect and architectural historian Fujimori Terunobu stands at one ultraconservative extreme in that movement, Endo Shuhei, with his approach to green structures, stands in direct contrast at the other extreme. Endo, while not confining himself to working with reference to the past, has succeeded most skillfully in incorporating historically Japanese environmental technologies in his work.

Architecture in our environmentally conscious age is asked to use passive technologies as much as possible, to reduce energy consumption, and to minimize their environmental footprint. Endo's indoor tennis facility meets that challenge by employing passive technologies and provides a superb model for their use in a public facility. The green roof increases the structure's thermal insulation efficiency. Solar batteries cut the drain on the power grid. A natural ventilation system utilizes the temperature-dependent differences in the weight of air. Endo has, that is, utilized the fact that this is a very large space in designing systems to control the temperature and air flow. The people using the tennis courts enter and leave from doors at ground level, then scatter to the various courts inside. Small interior spaces within this vast structure, locker rooms and shower rooms, help define the interior landscape. The overall design is restrained and extremely neutral.

Endo Shuhei's design for this disaster management facility presents new ideas for public structures. The facility, in its disaster management role, could simply be a warehouse, but he has enabled it to be far more, to function, in normal times, as part of a city park. But while working well in ordinary times as a recreational structure, it also stands ready for the extraordinary, devastating event that we know is likely to occur. Providing the space for that extraordinary purpose was a defining part of the design. Now, why not a nuclear fallout shelter for his next project? With that, he would truly be breaking new ground yet again in Japan.

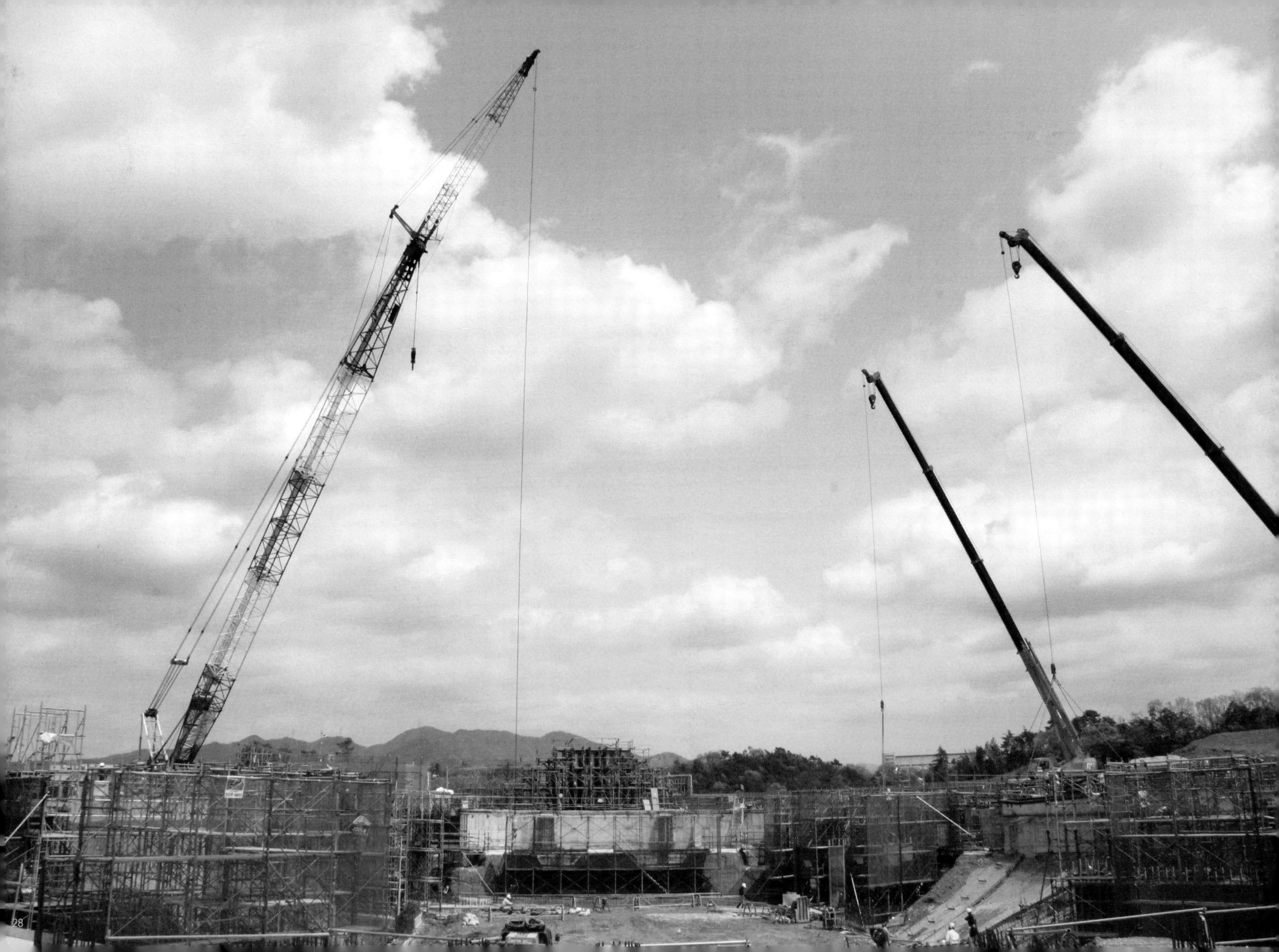

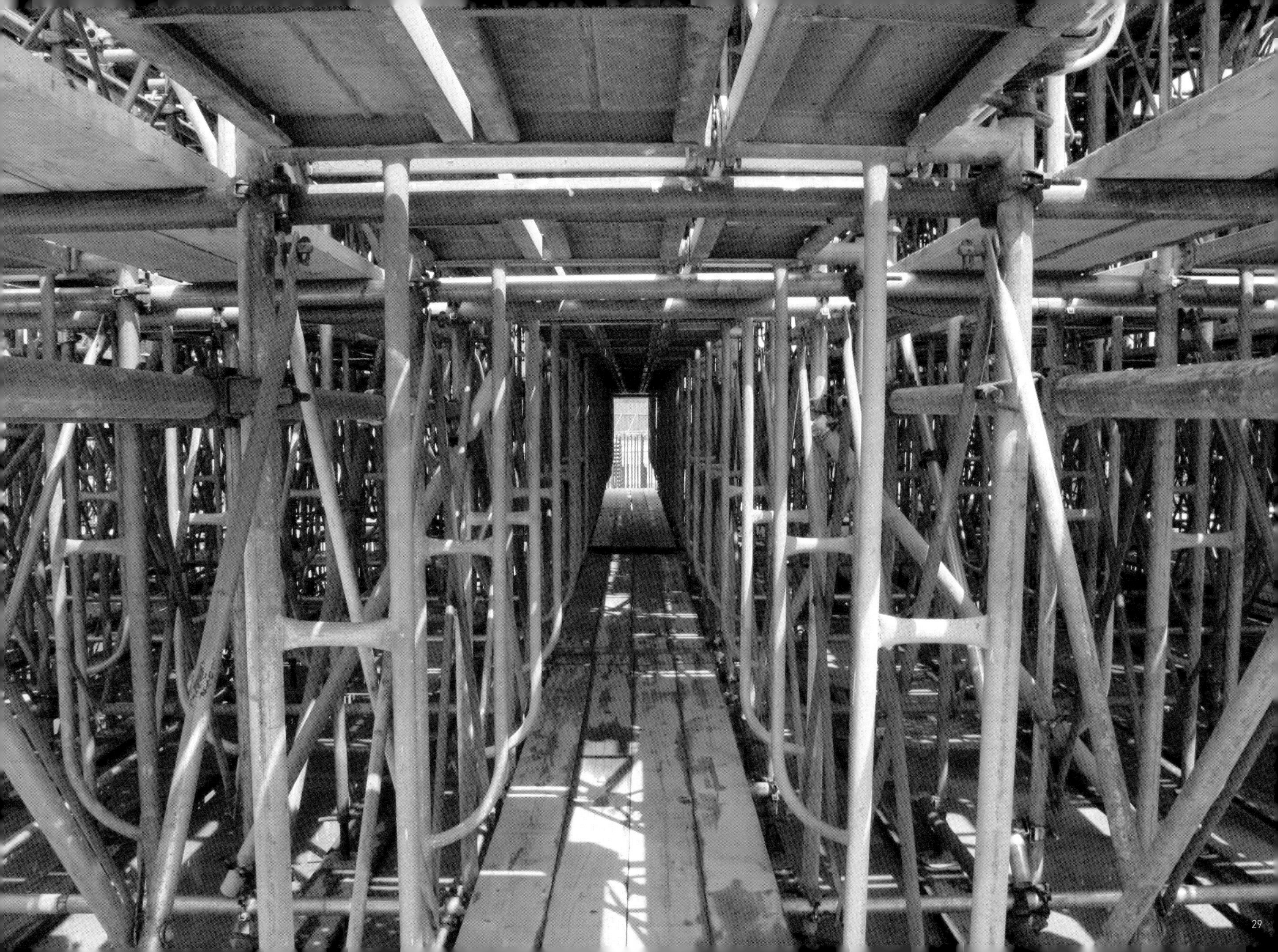

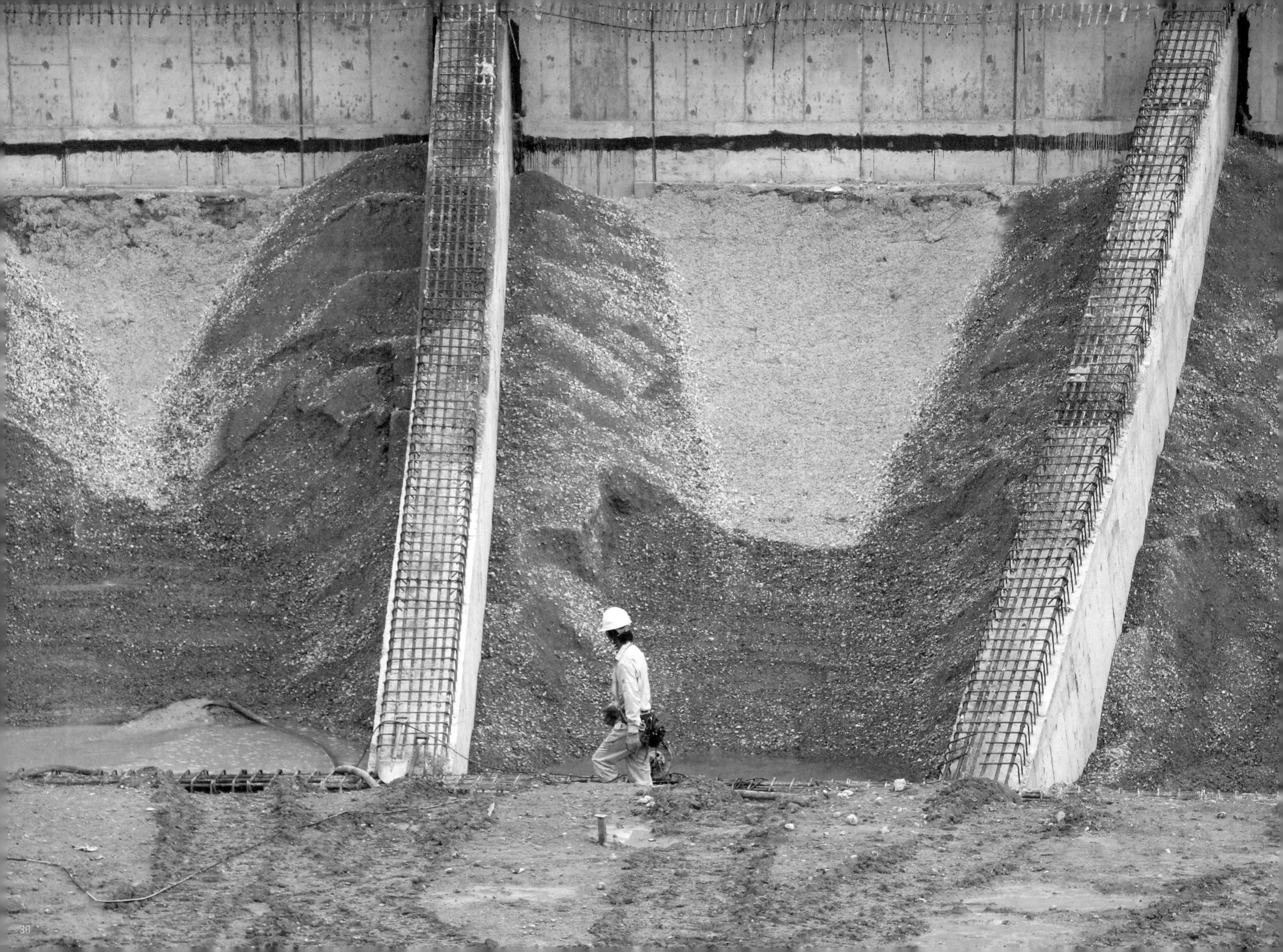

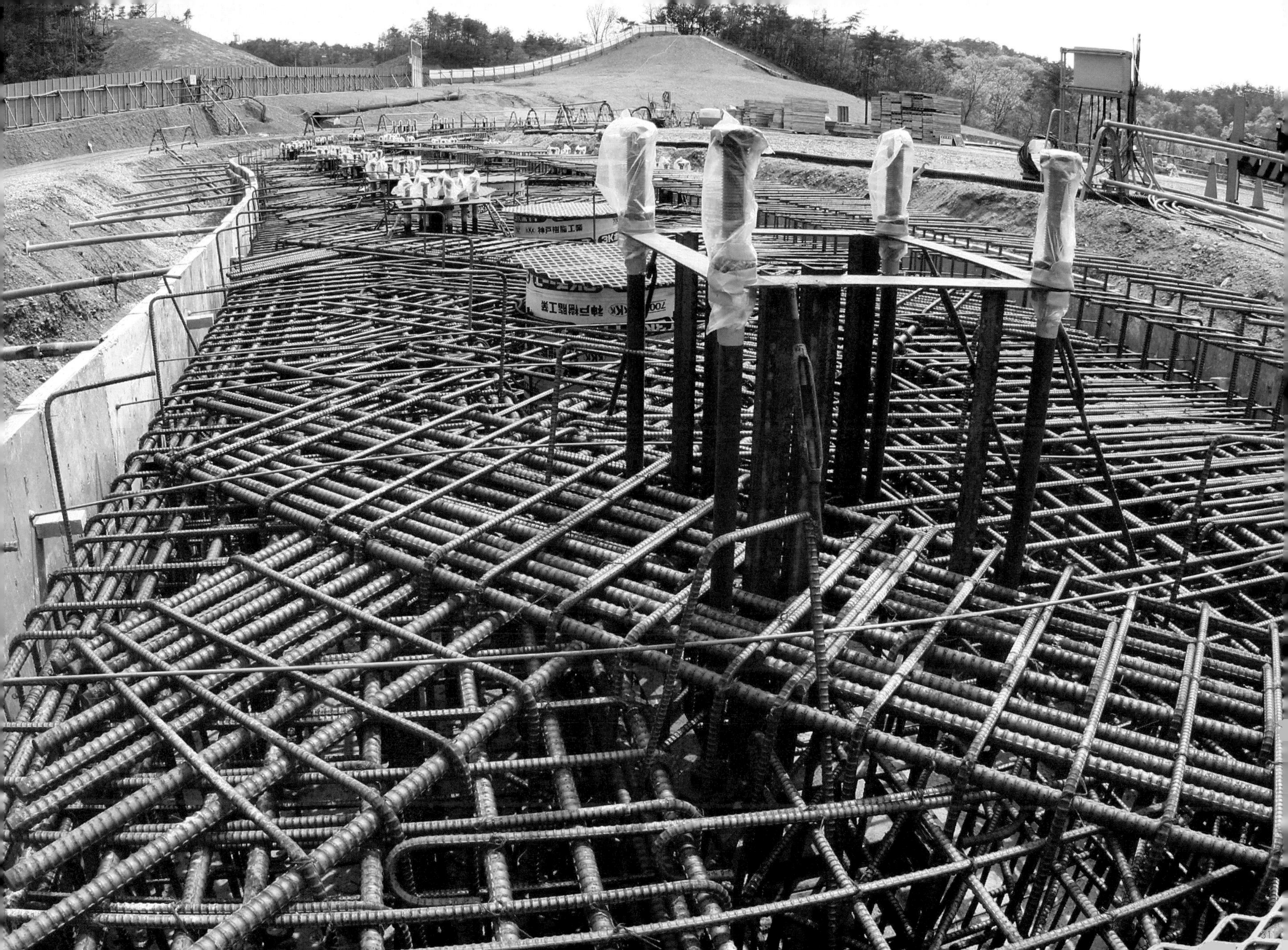
神戸樹脂工業
神戸樹脂工業

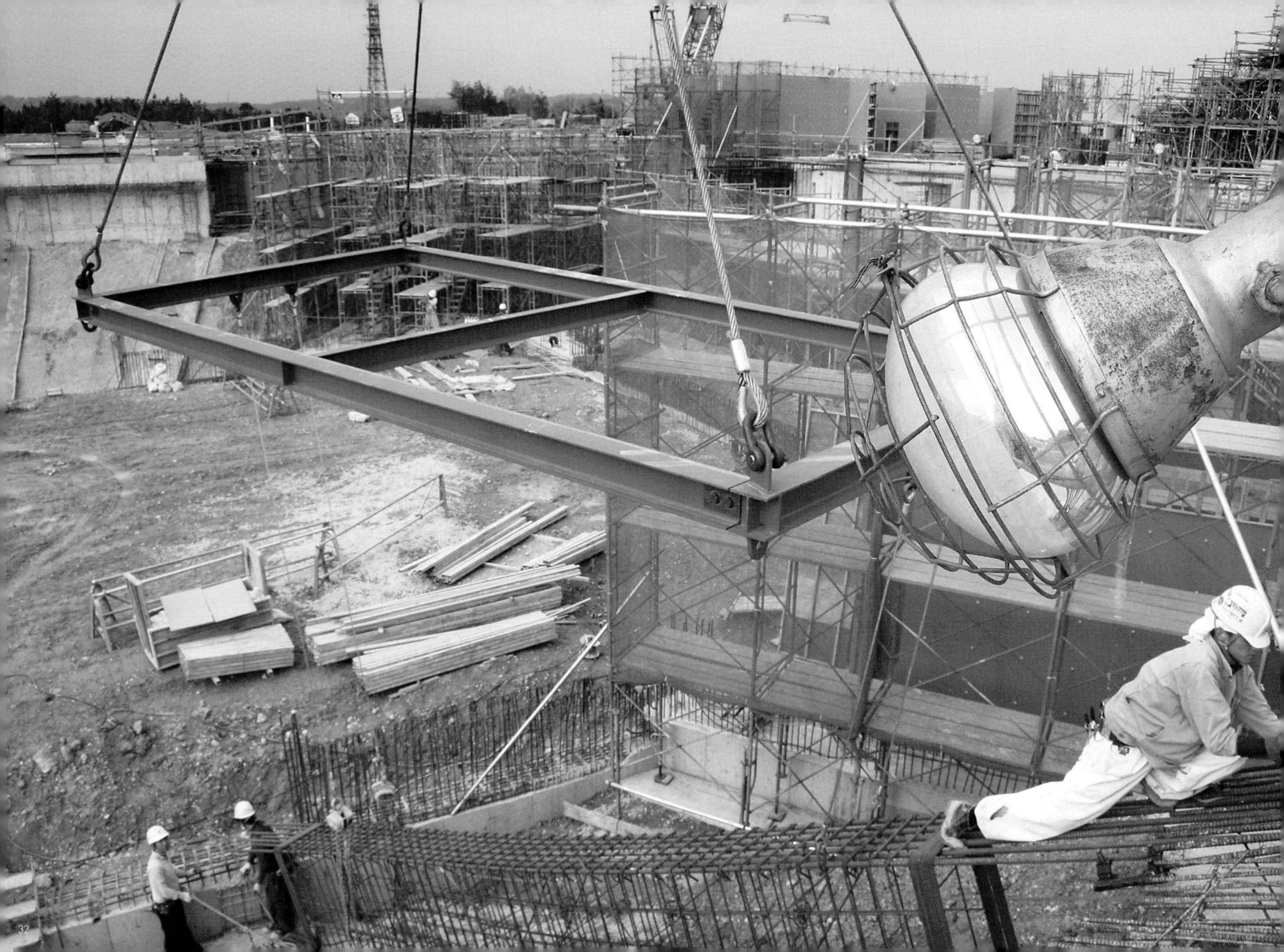

317. 1390

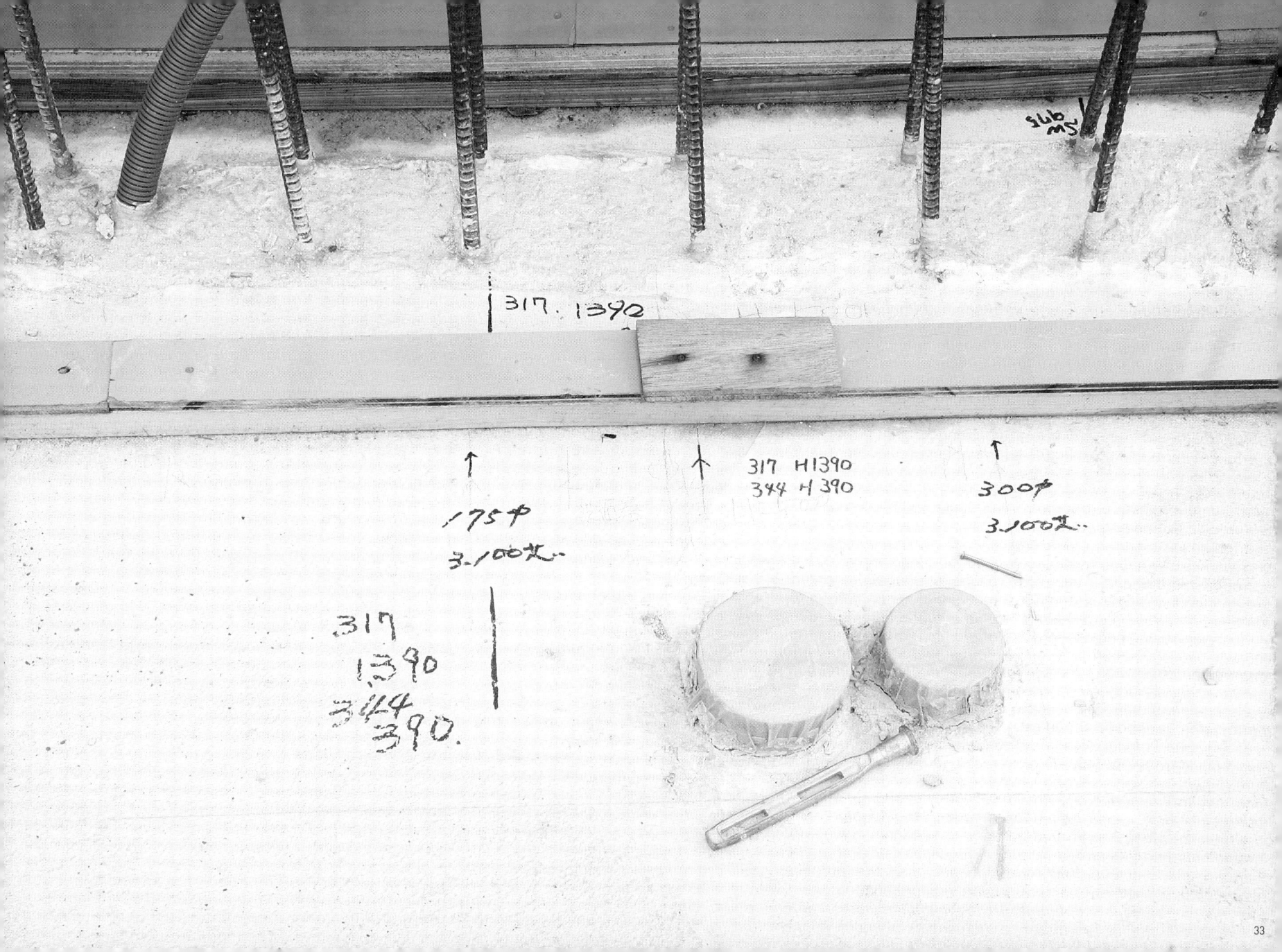

317 H1390
344 H 390

175φ
3.100%

300φ
3.100%

317
1390
344
390.

sub
ms

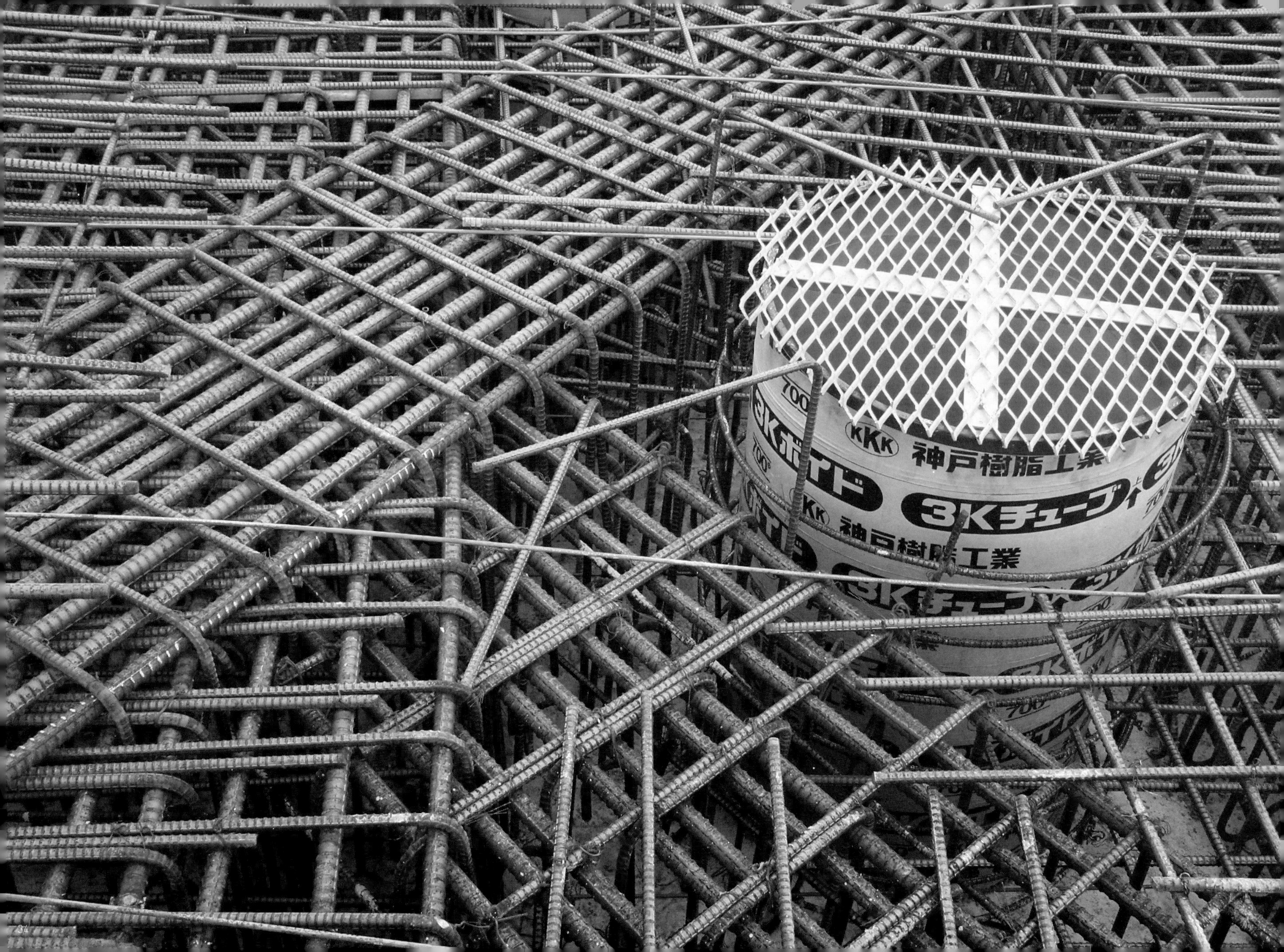
KKK
神戸樹脂工業
3Kボイド
3Kチューブ
700

35

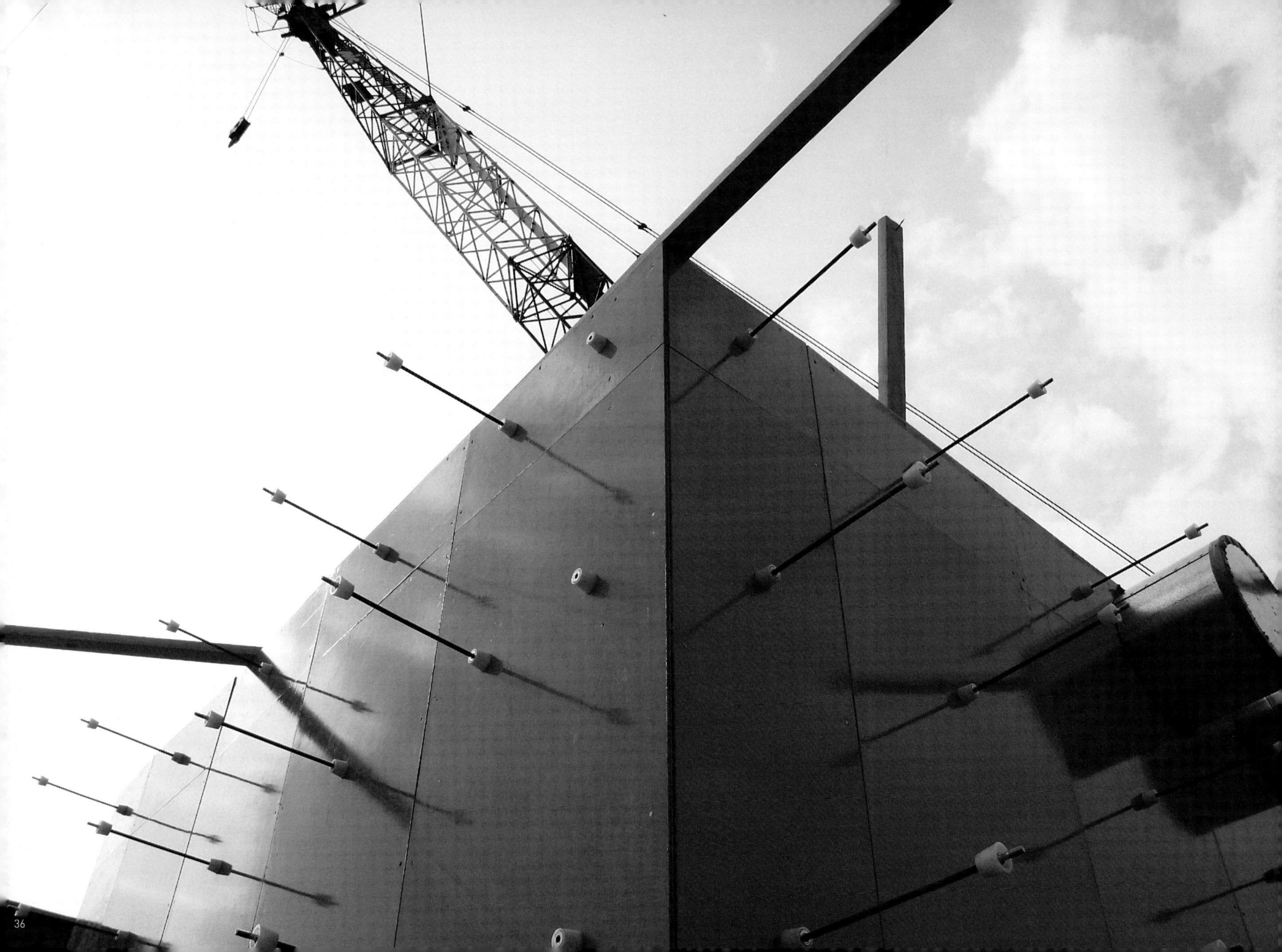

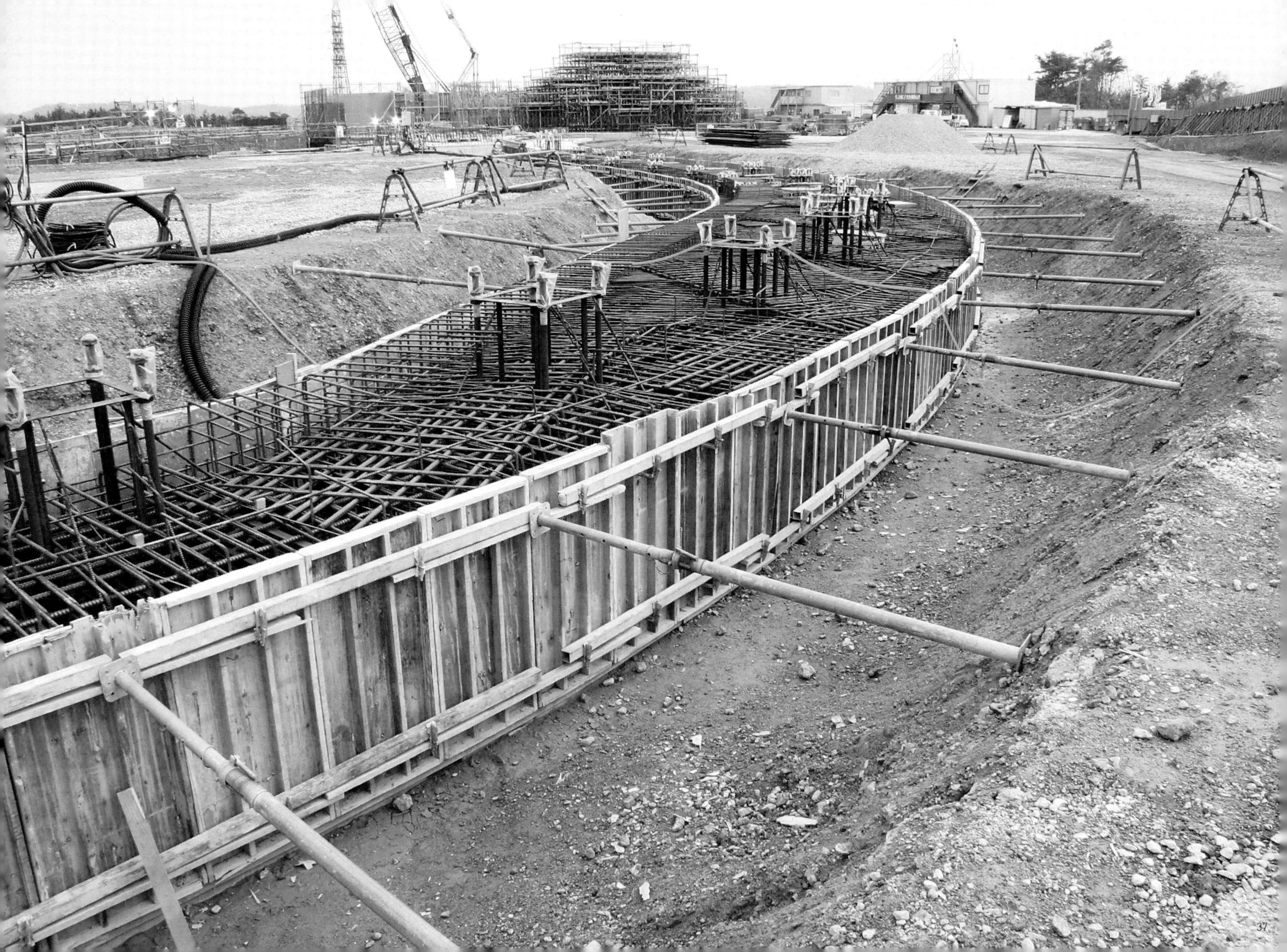

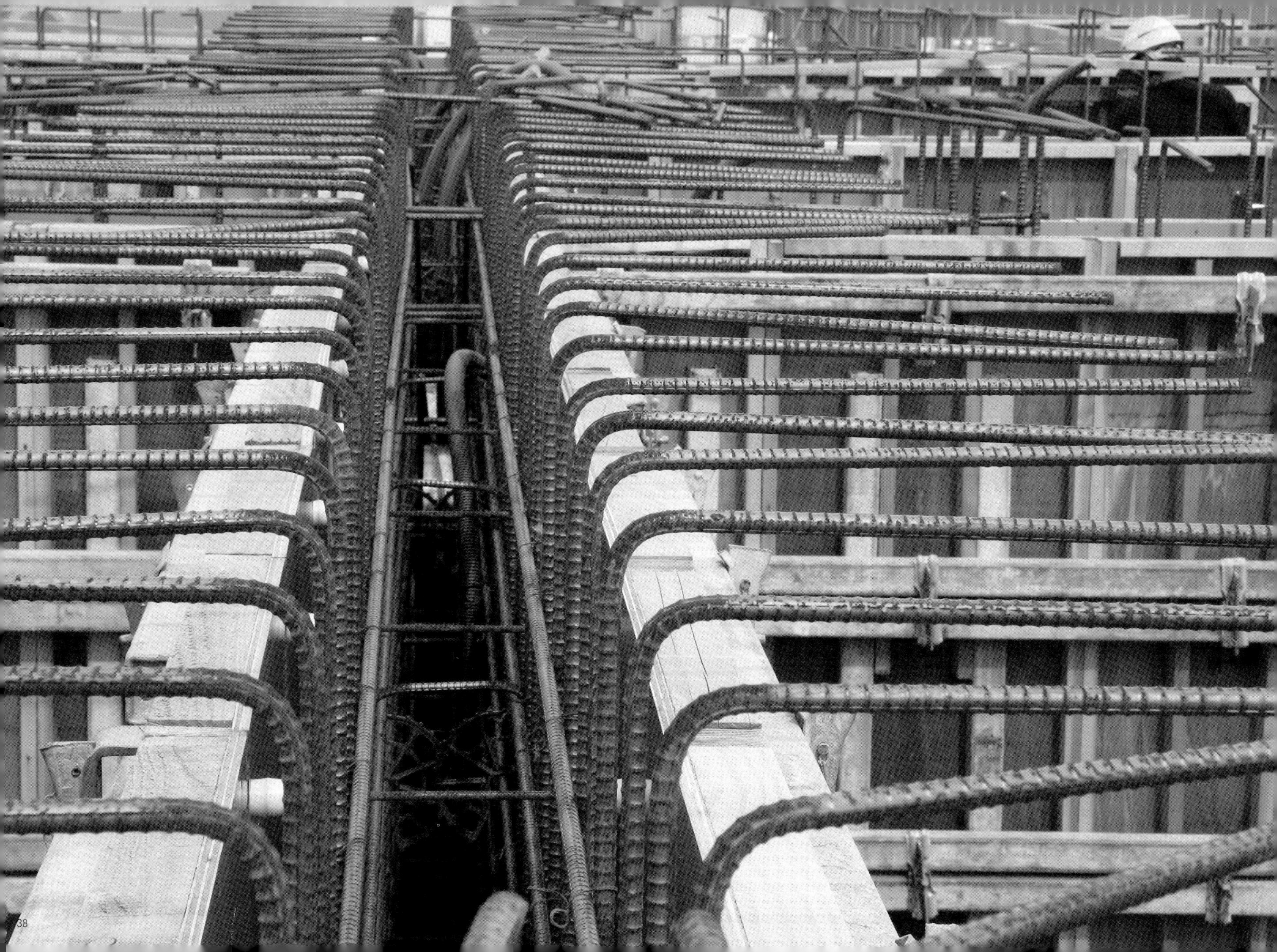

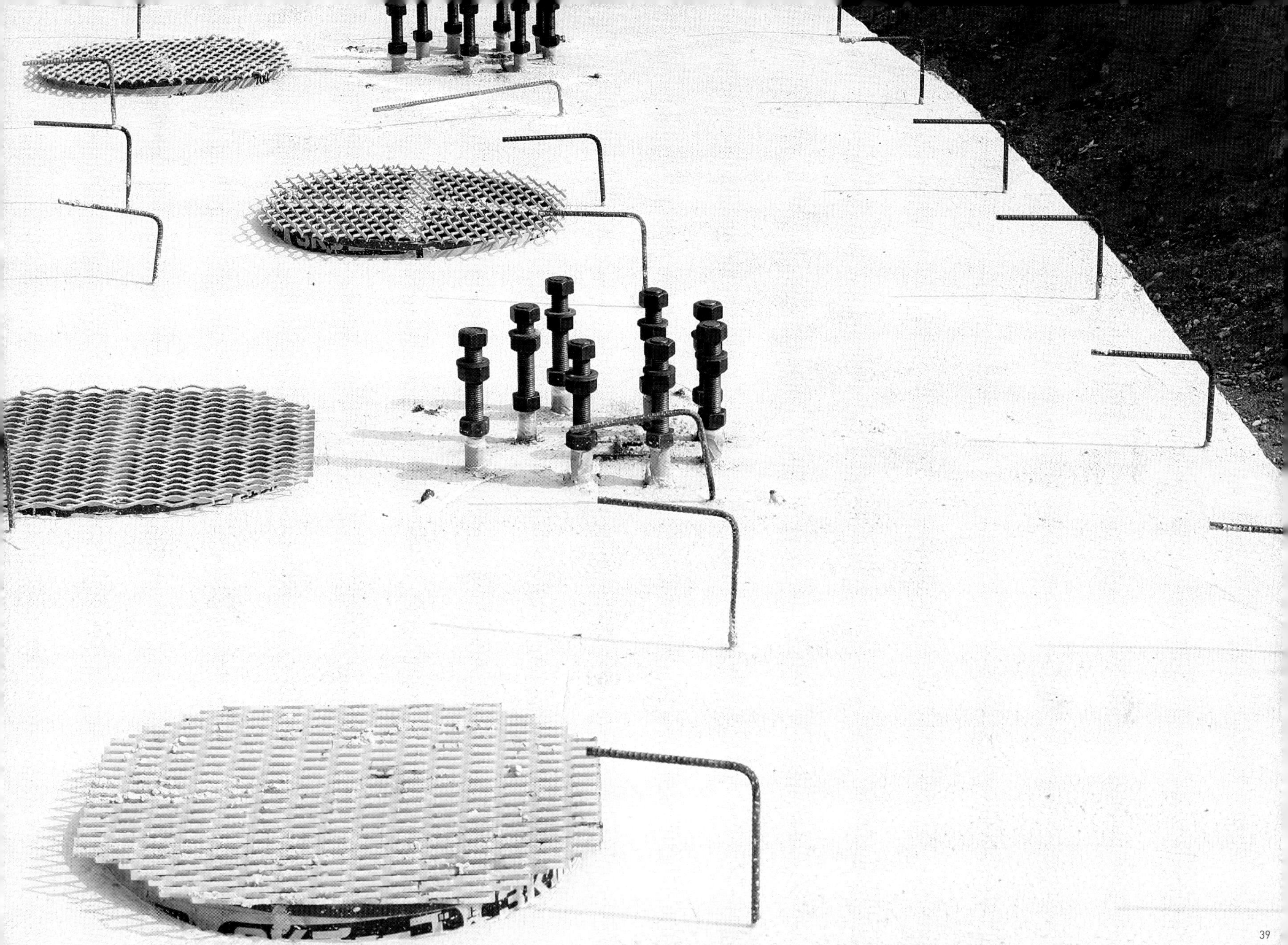

Cd 30
消火器ボックス
SD 16
SSW 2
SSW 2
Cd 21
900
900
900
コルゲート鋼板
H-2000
SOP塗装
Cd 30
125
850

41

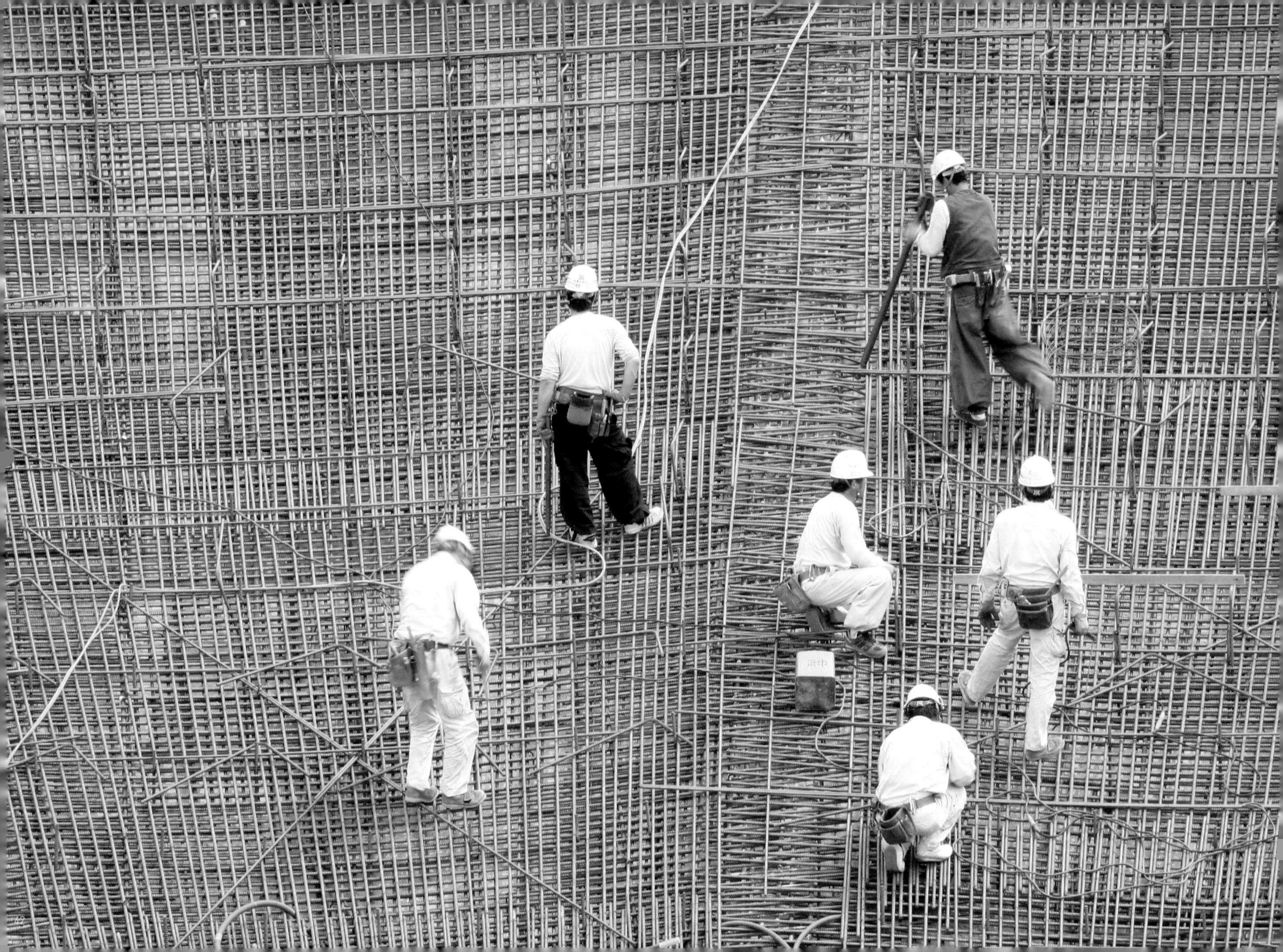

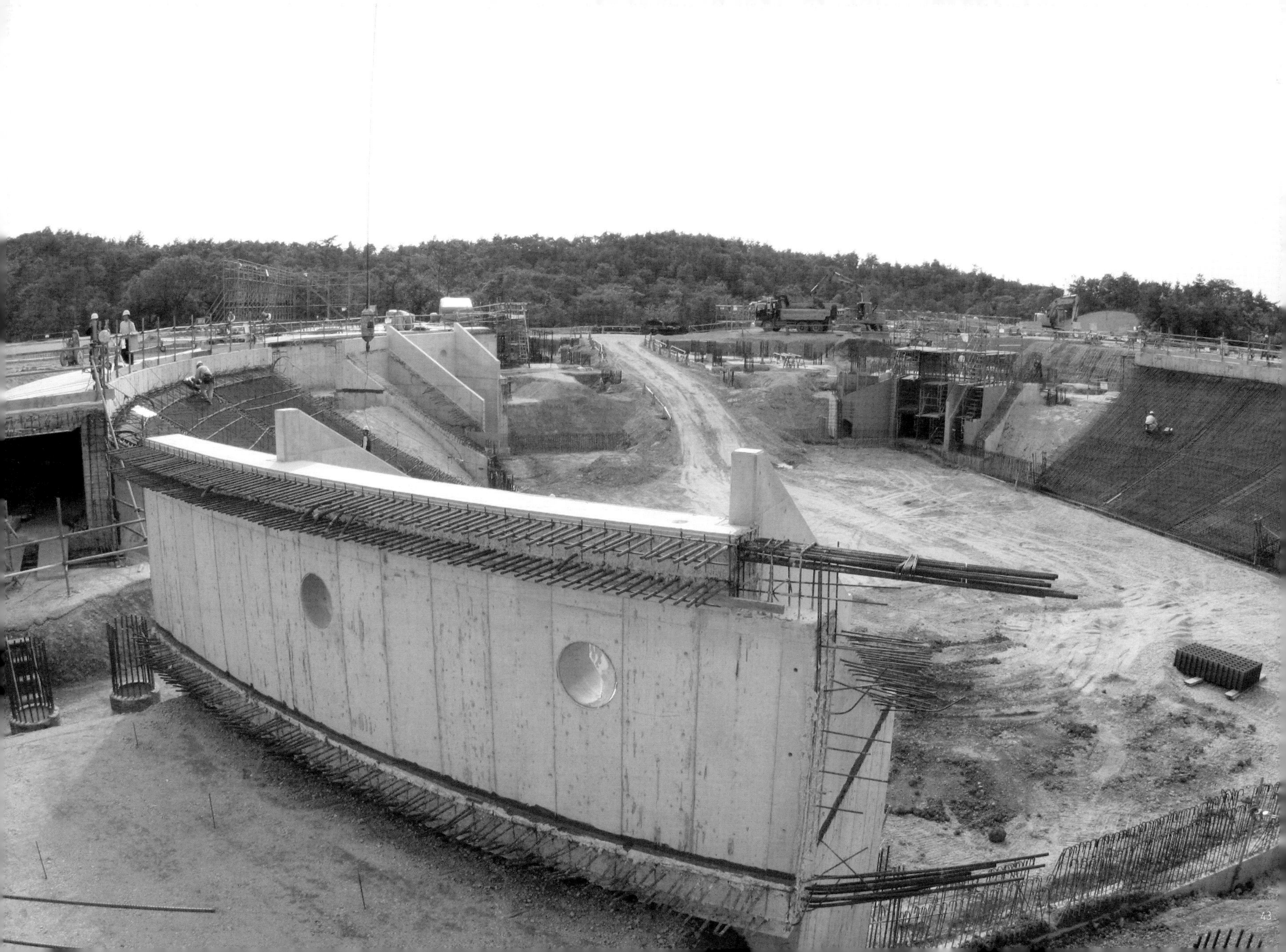

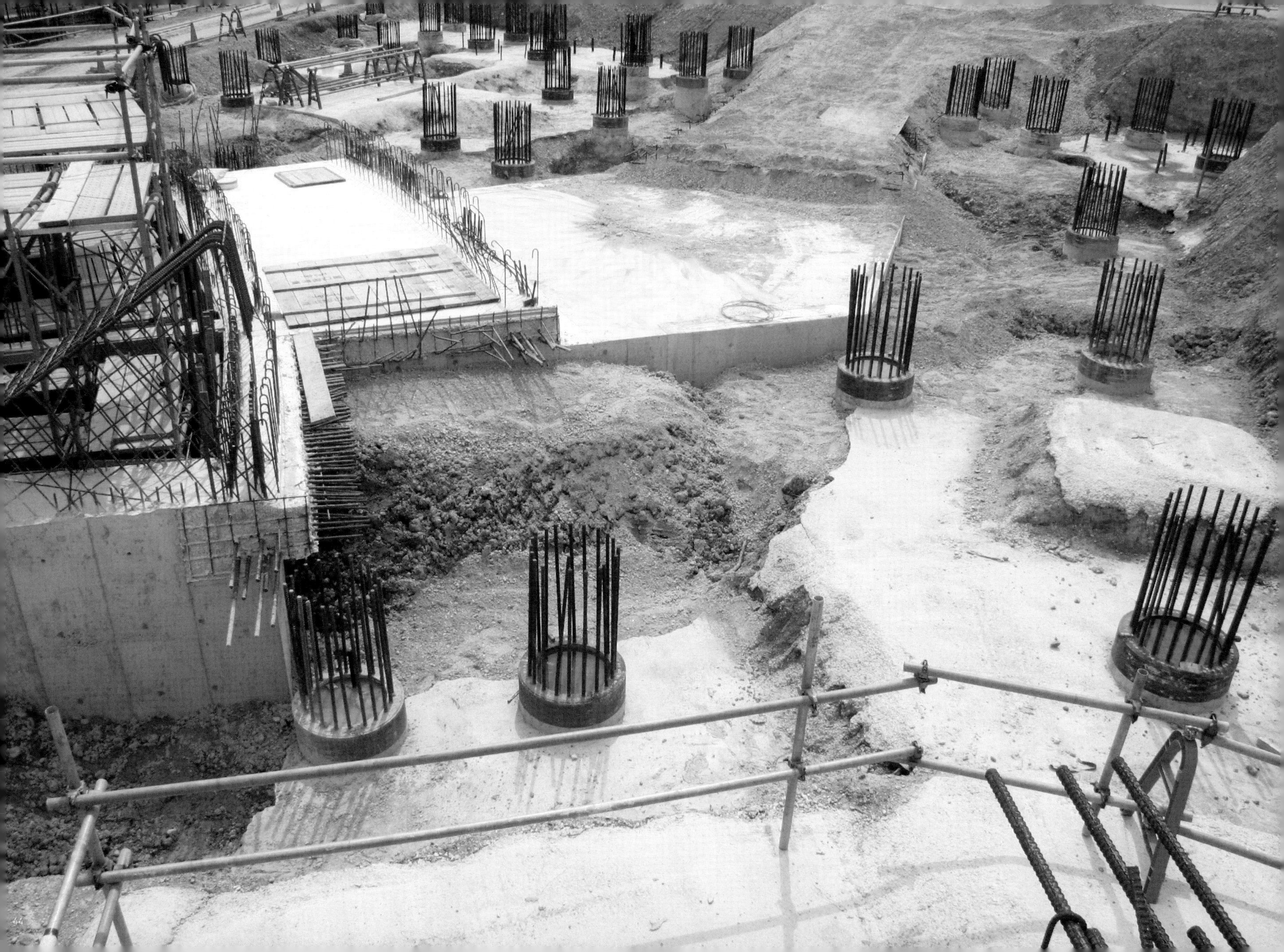

45

46

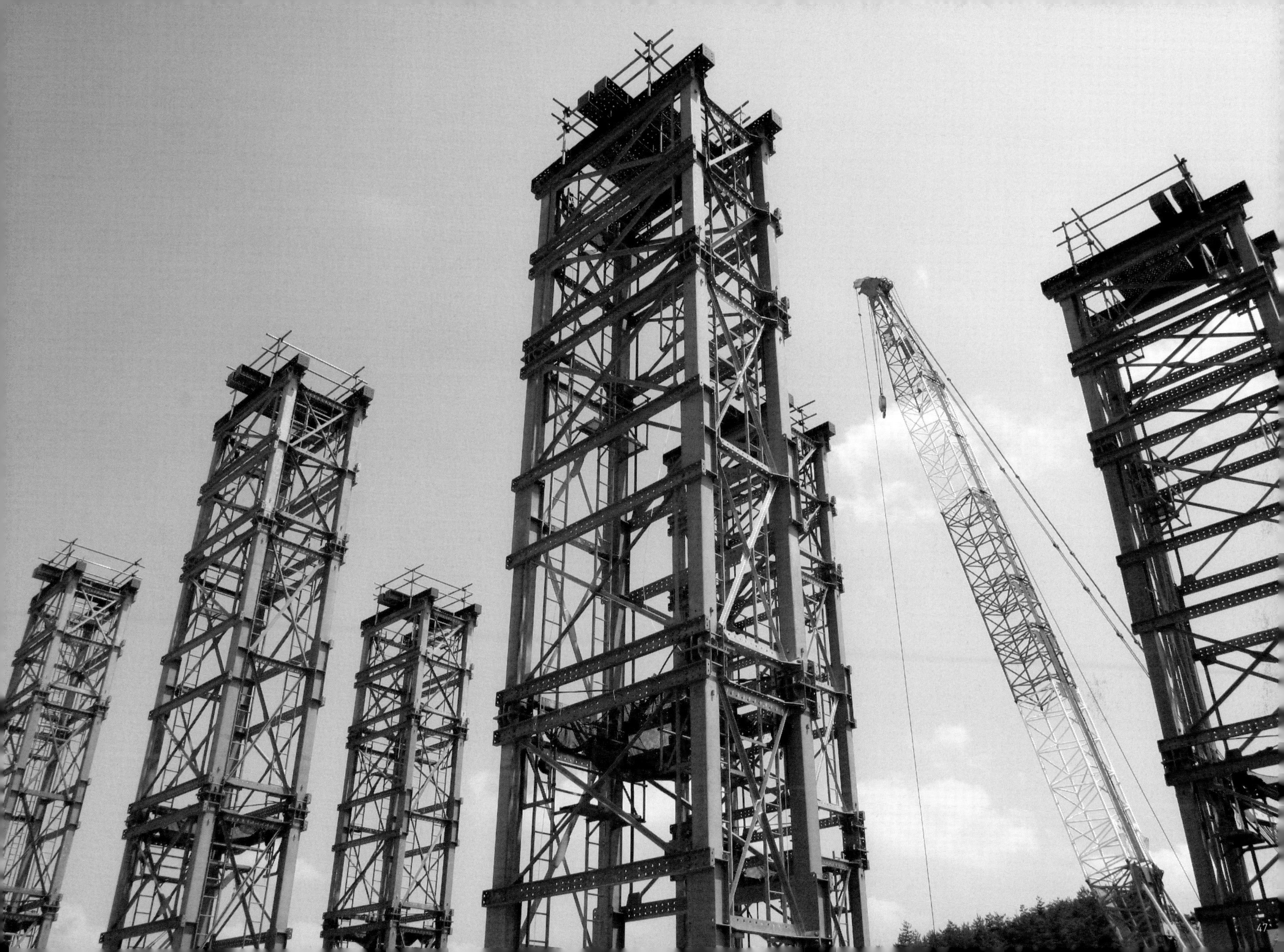

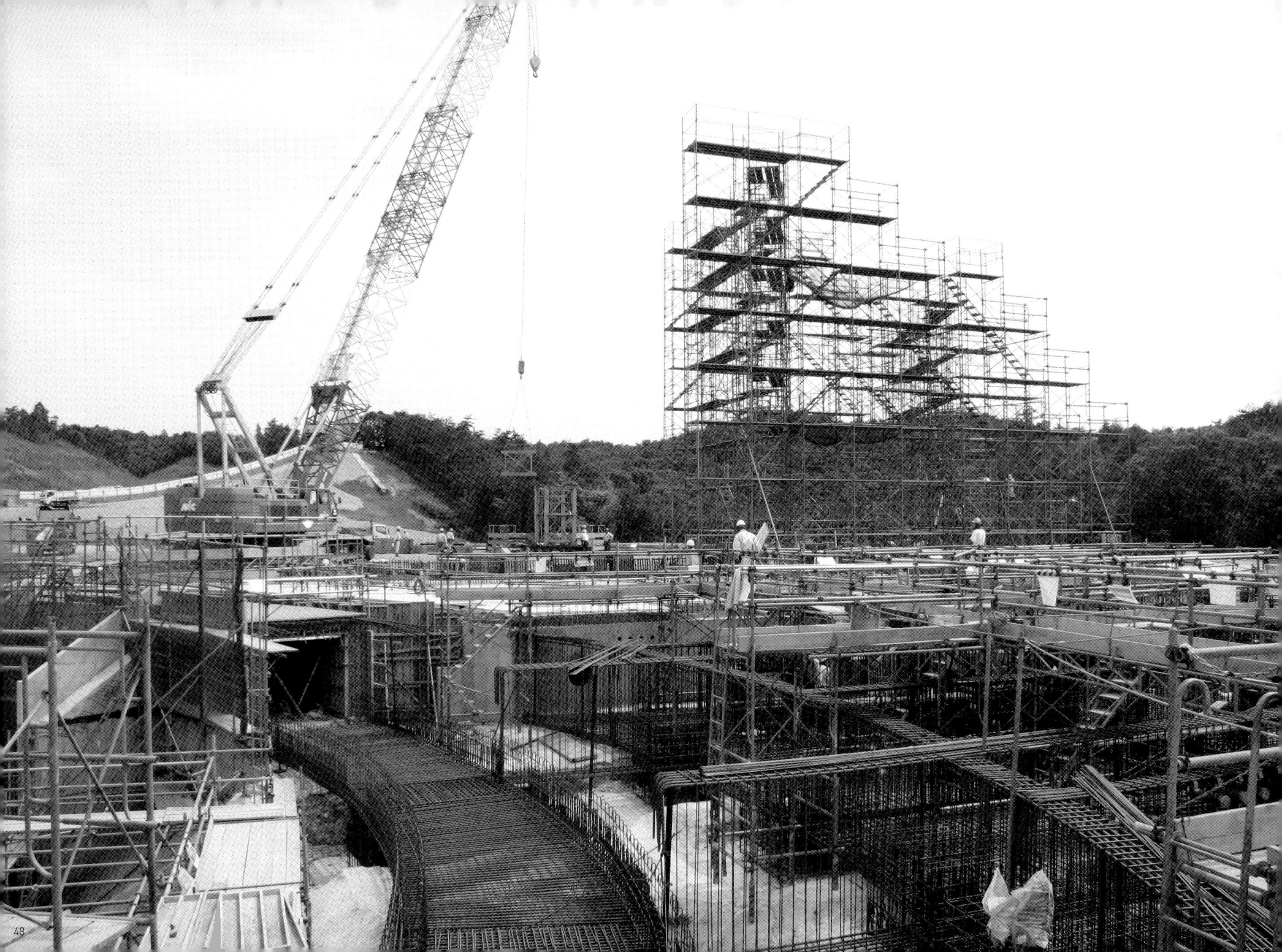

49

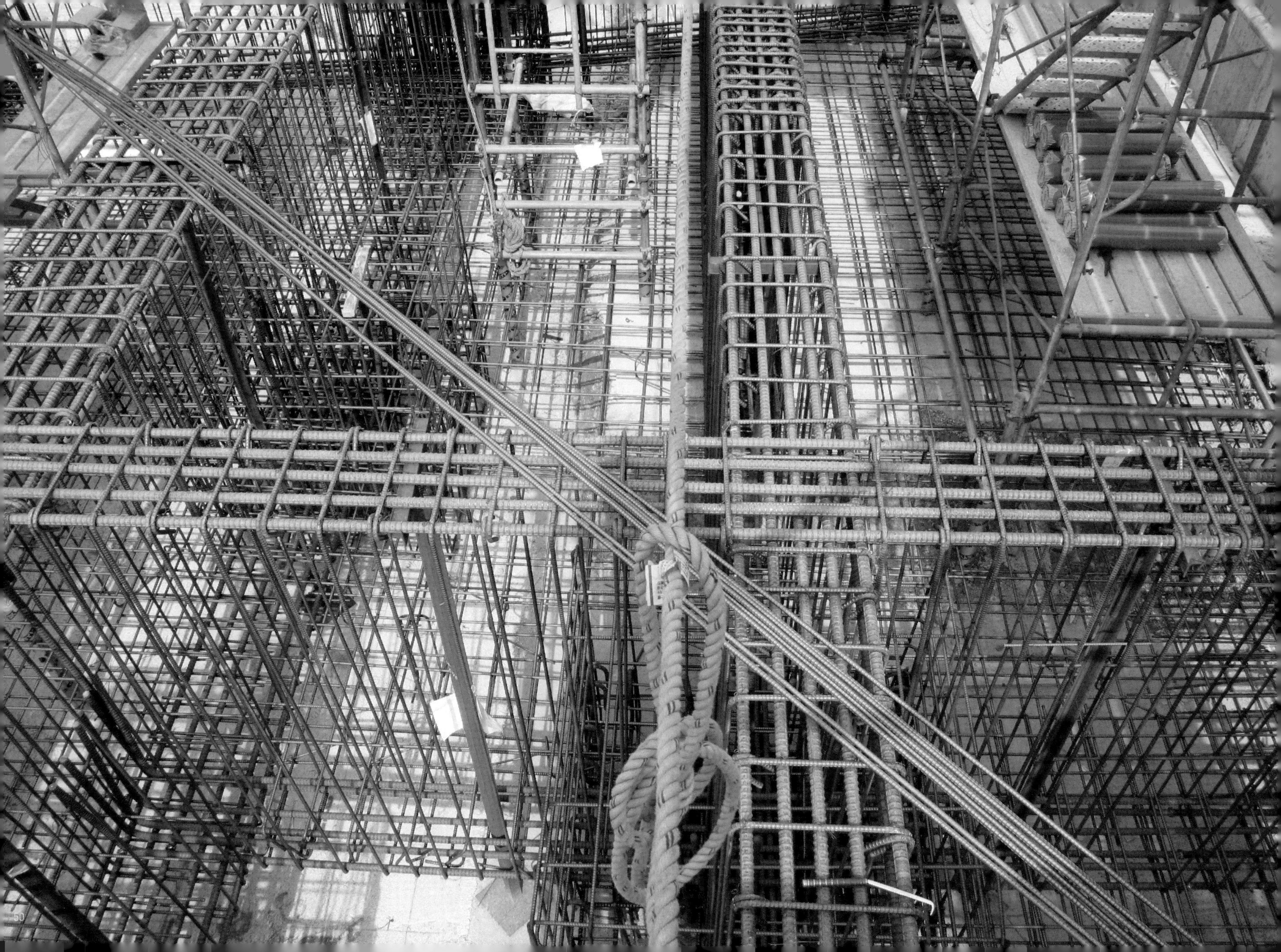

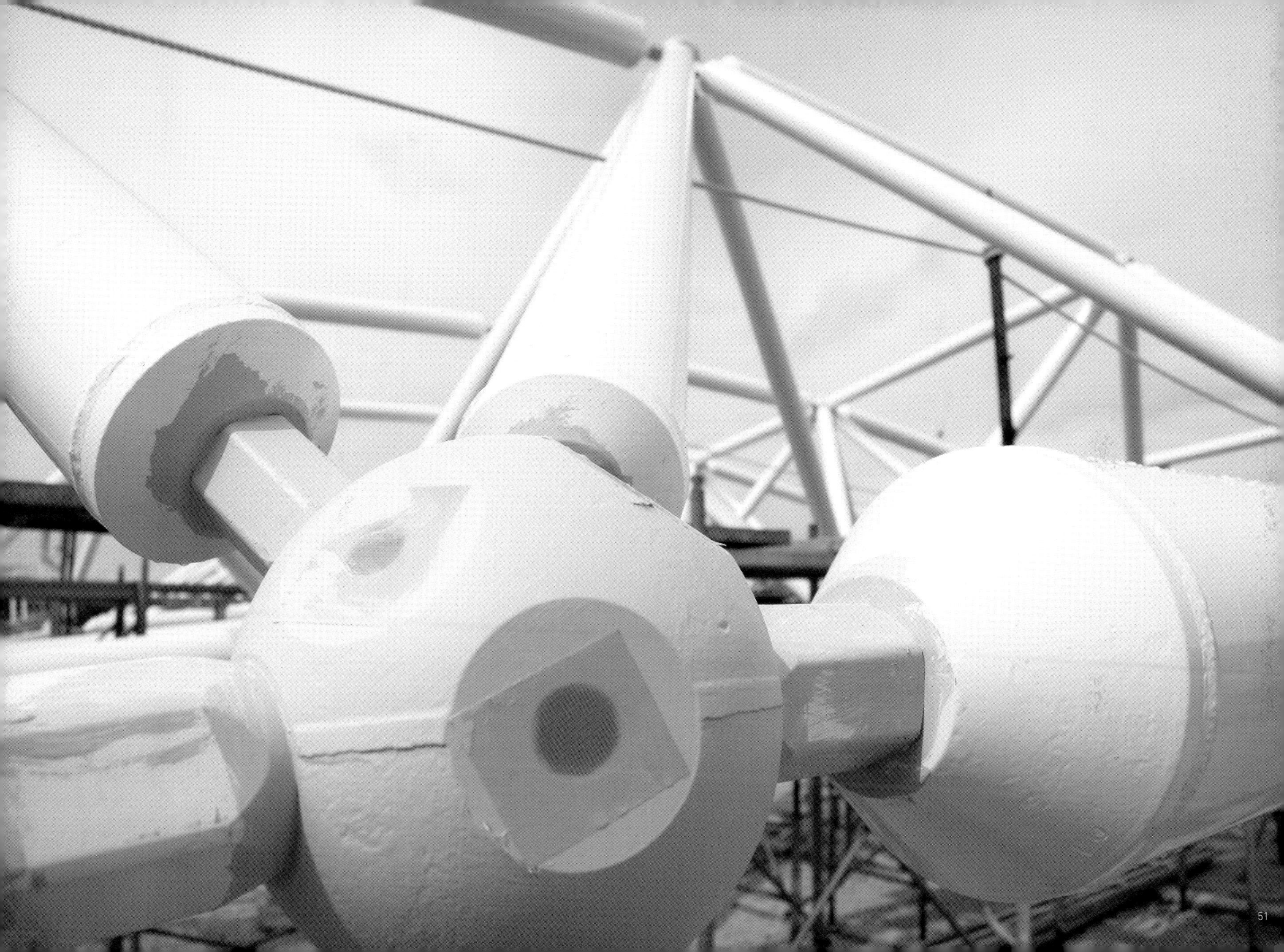

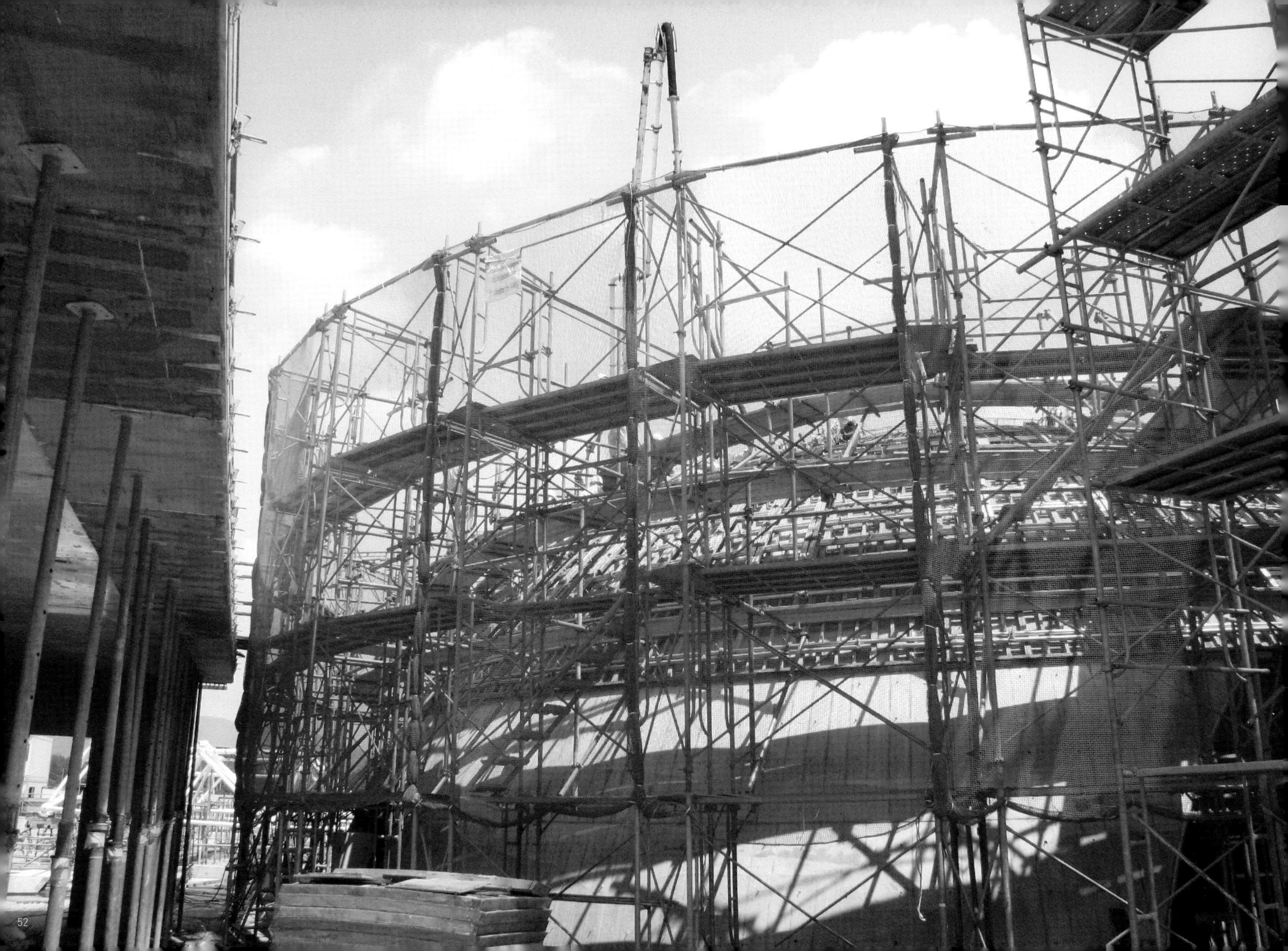

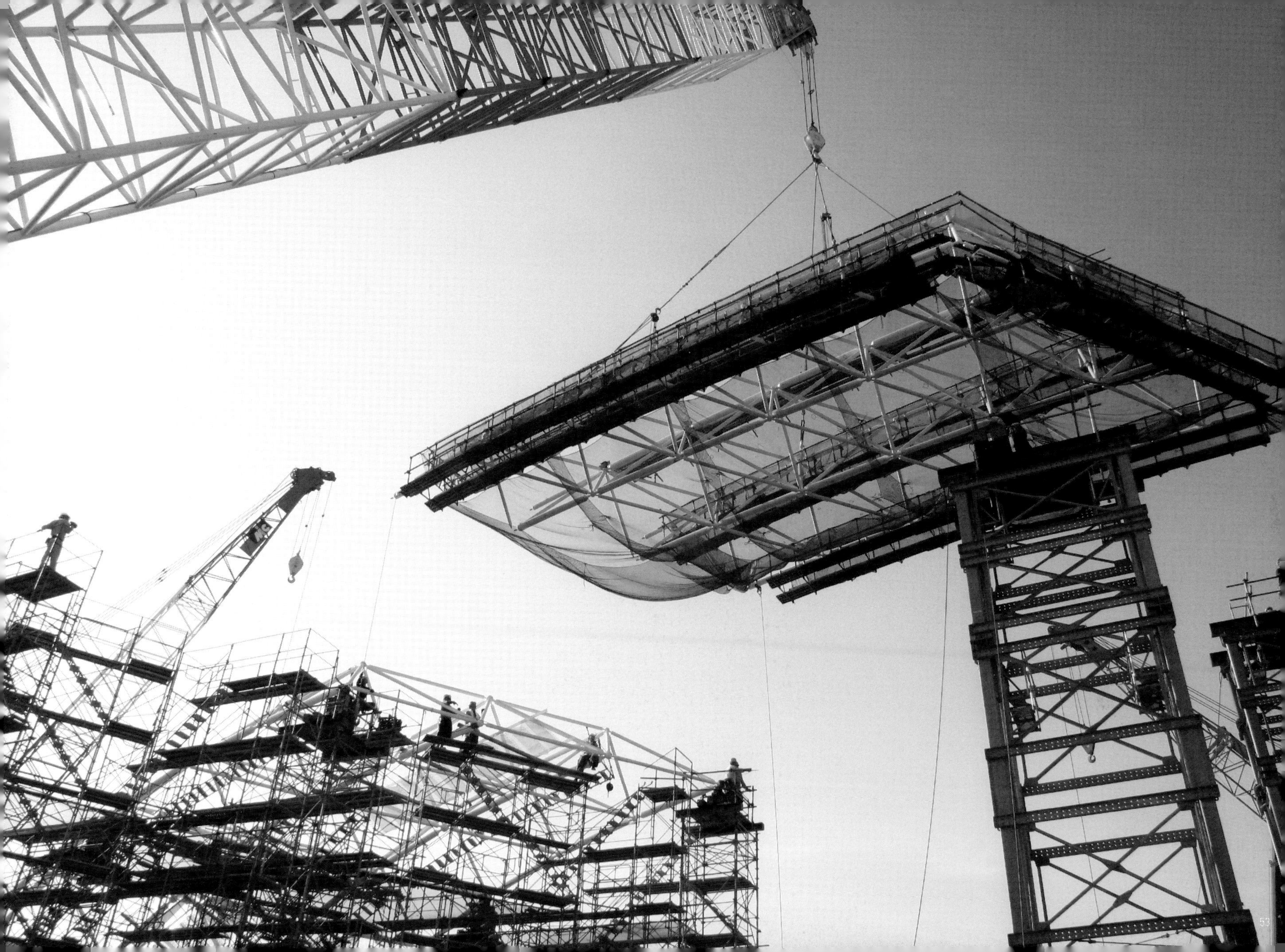

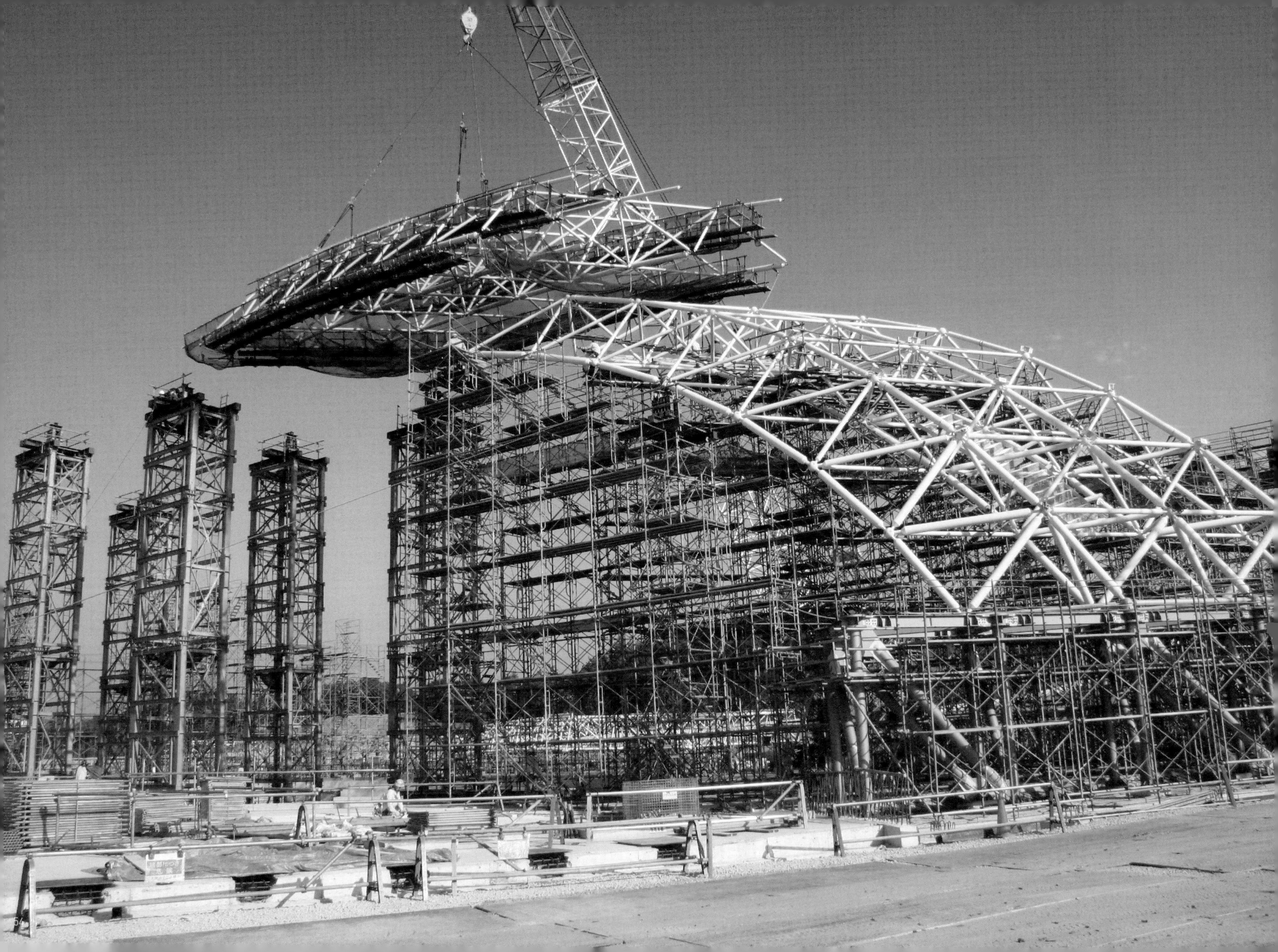

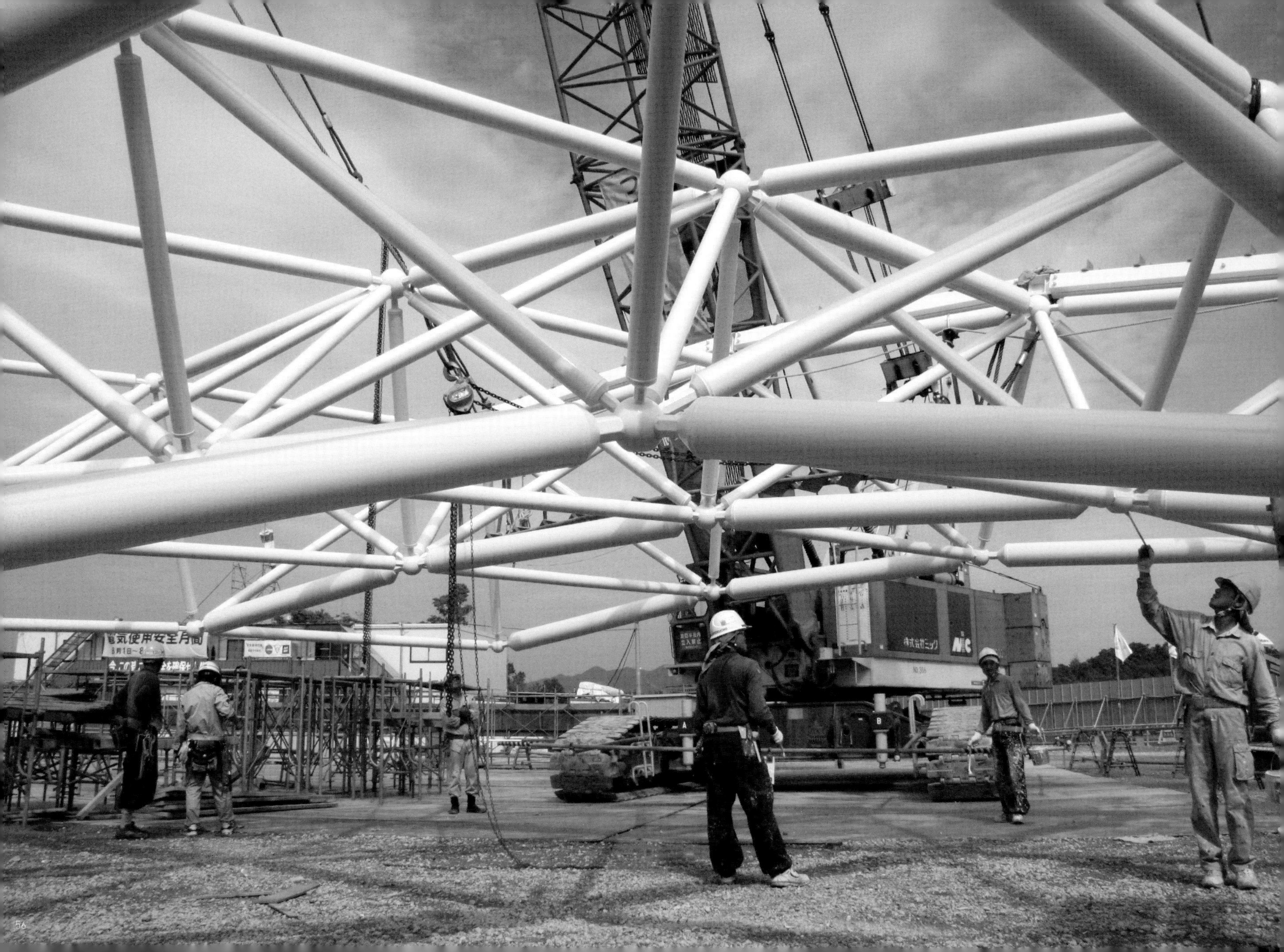
気使用安全月間

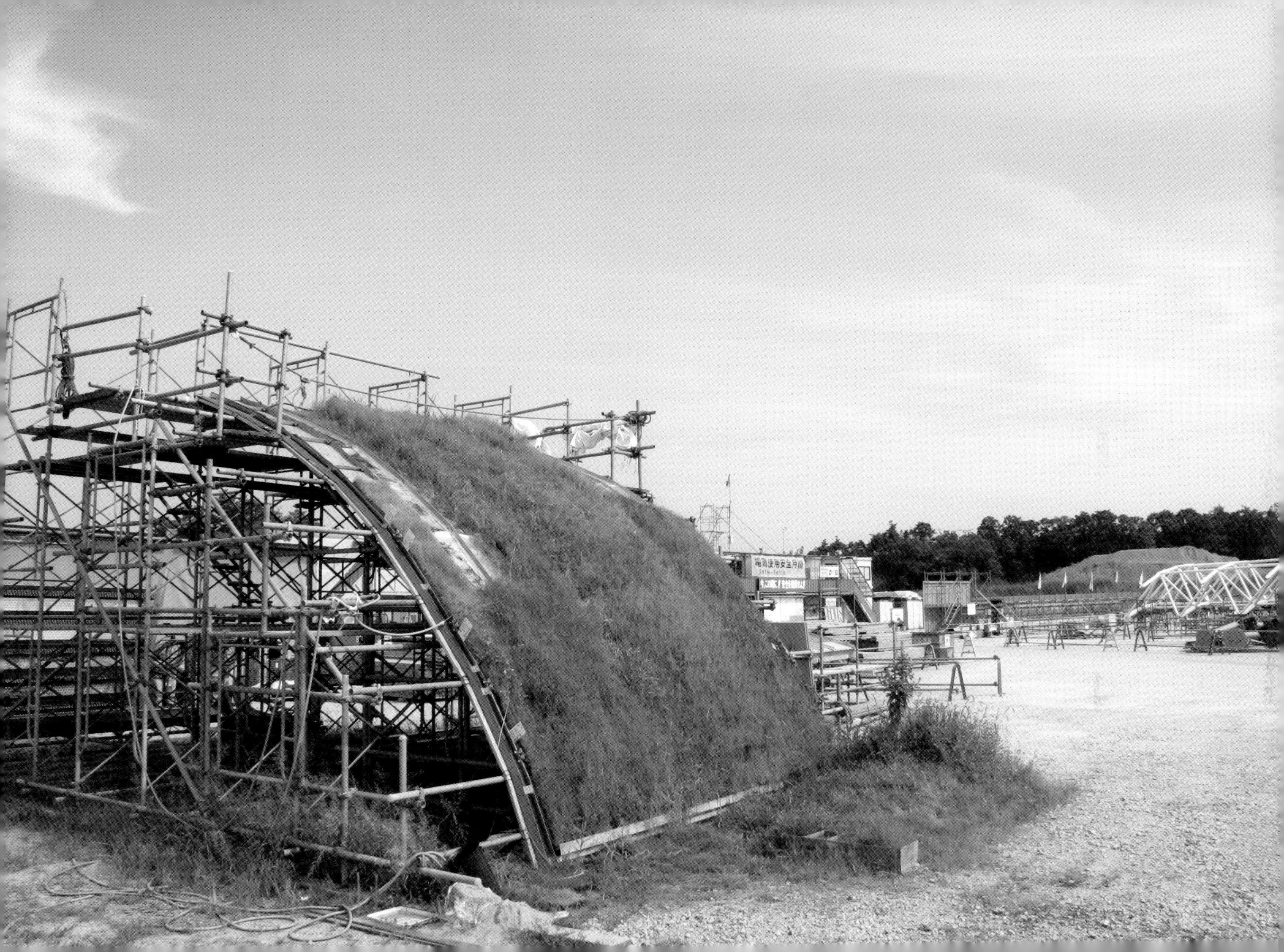

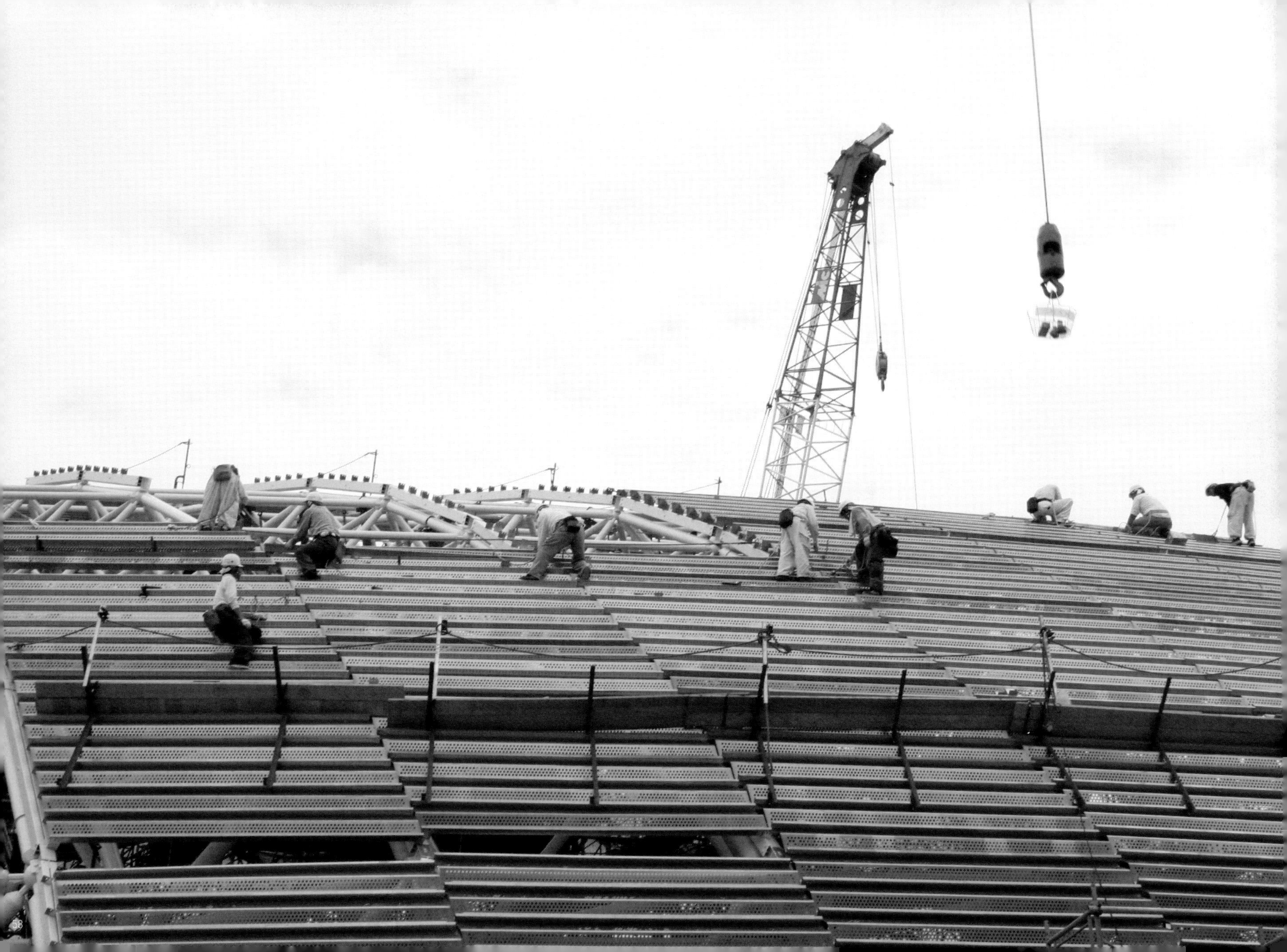

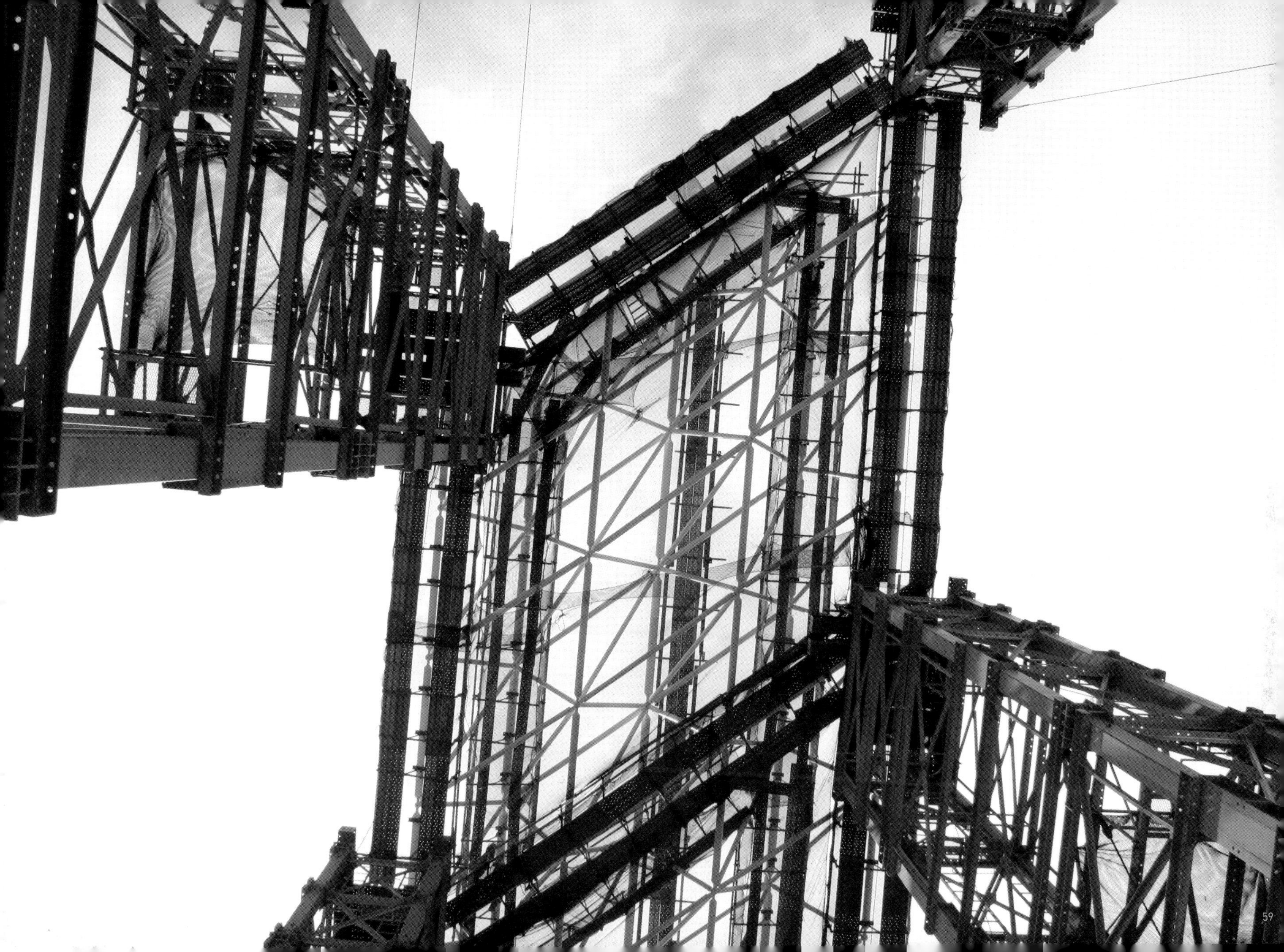

60

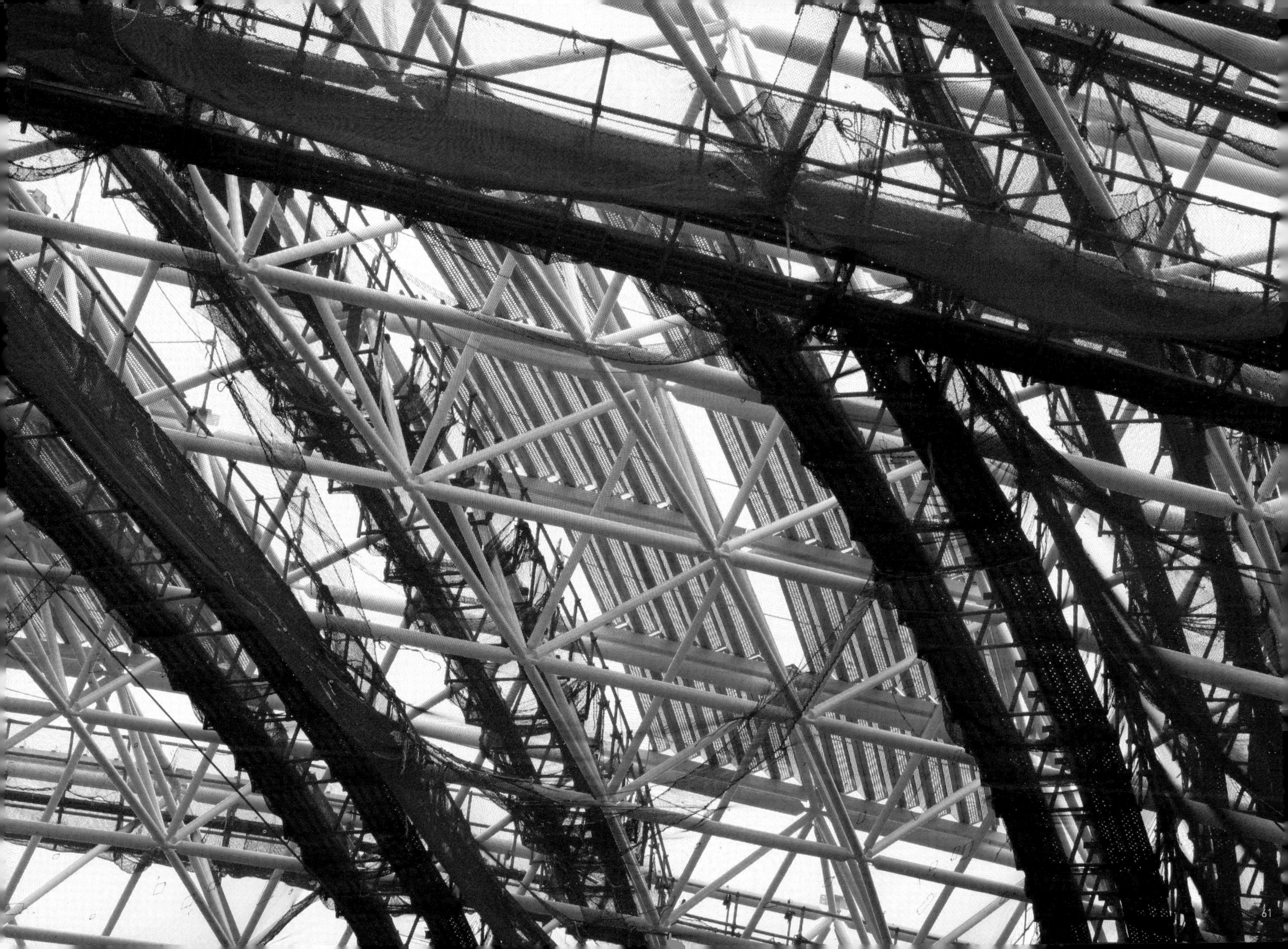

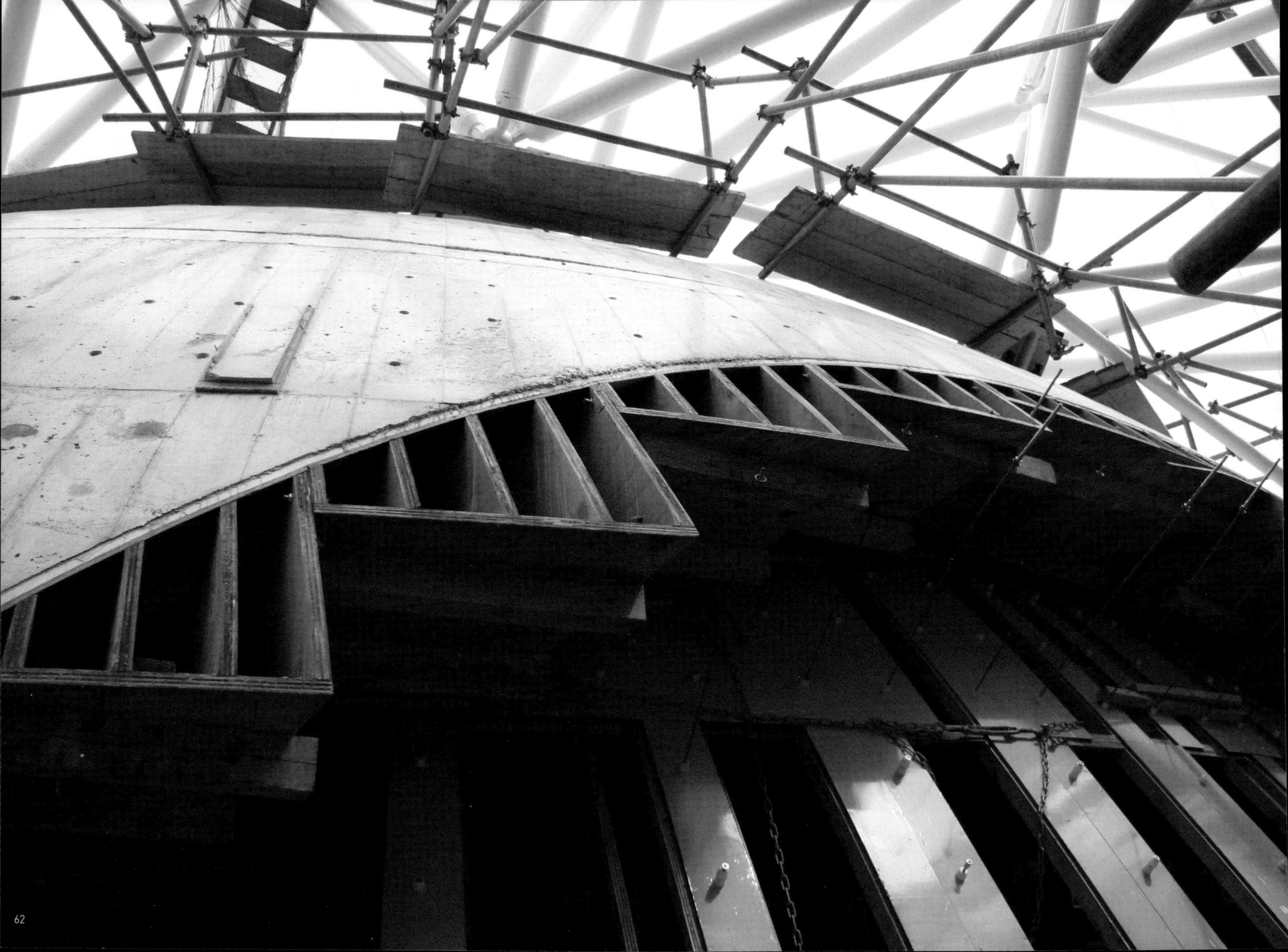

作業通路

東15

足場

東8

東14

開口B

立入禁止

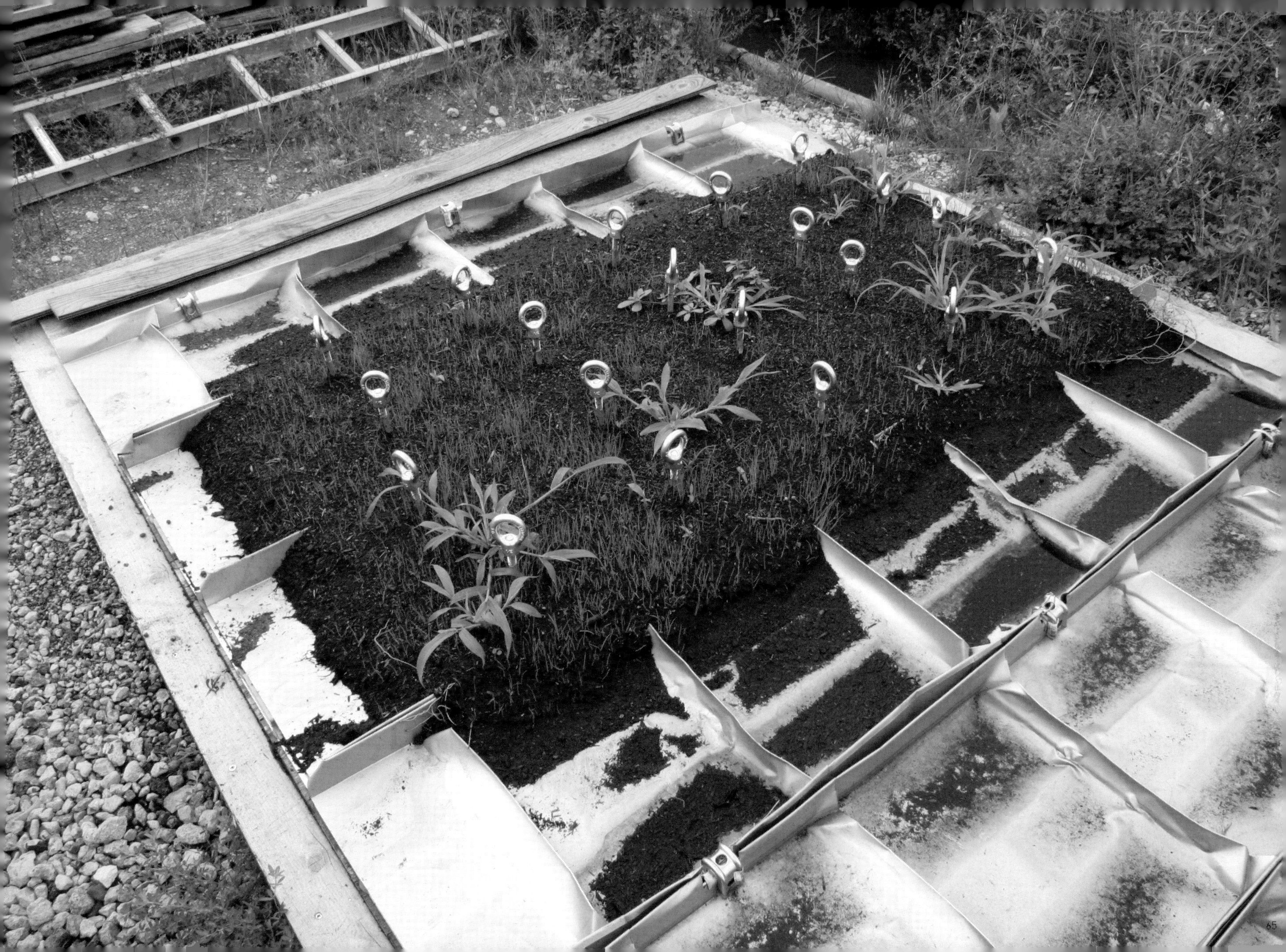

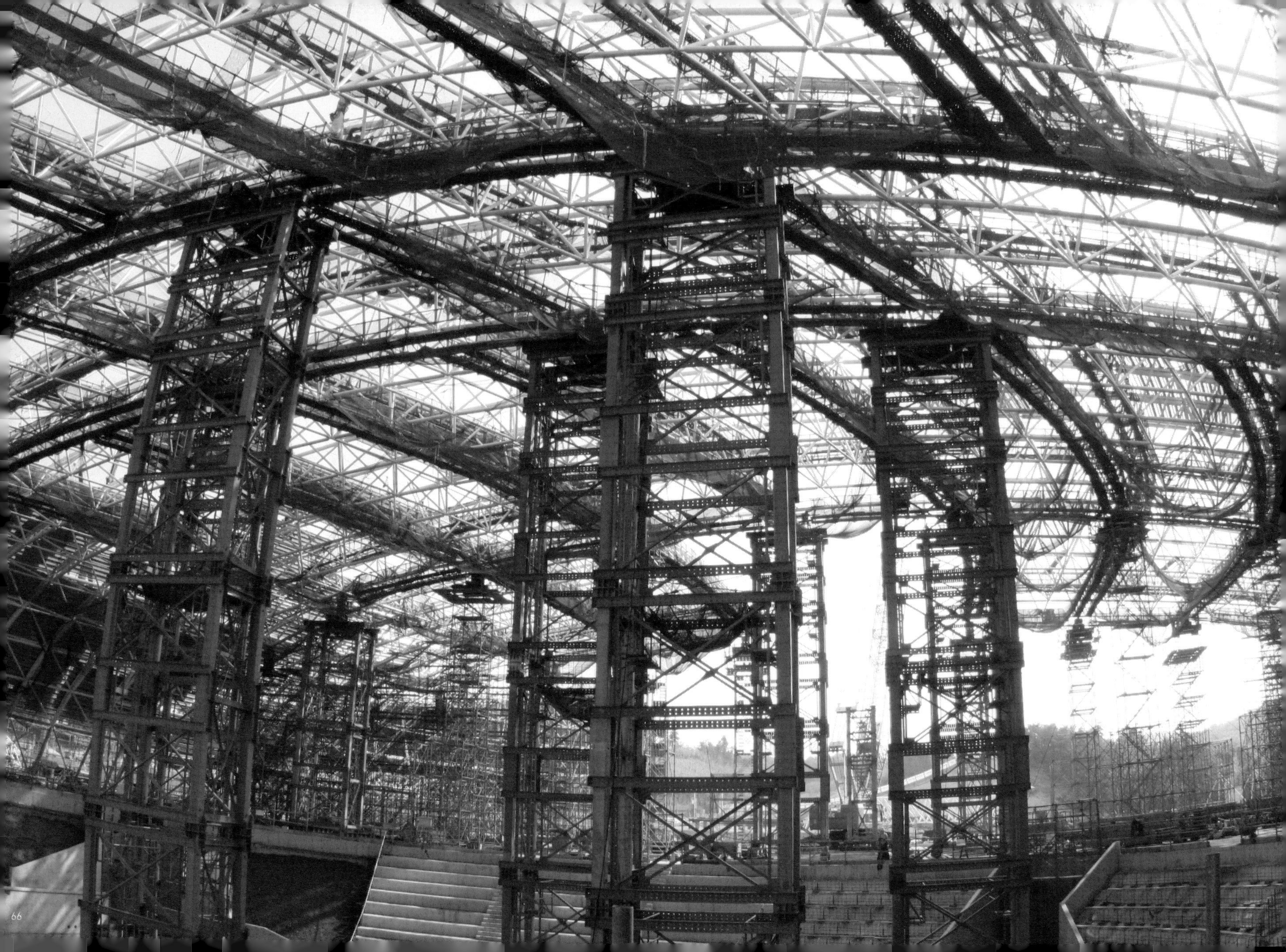

67

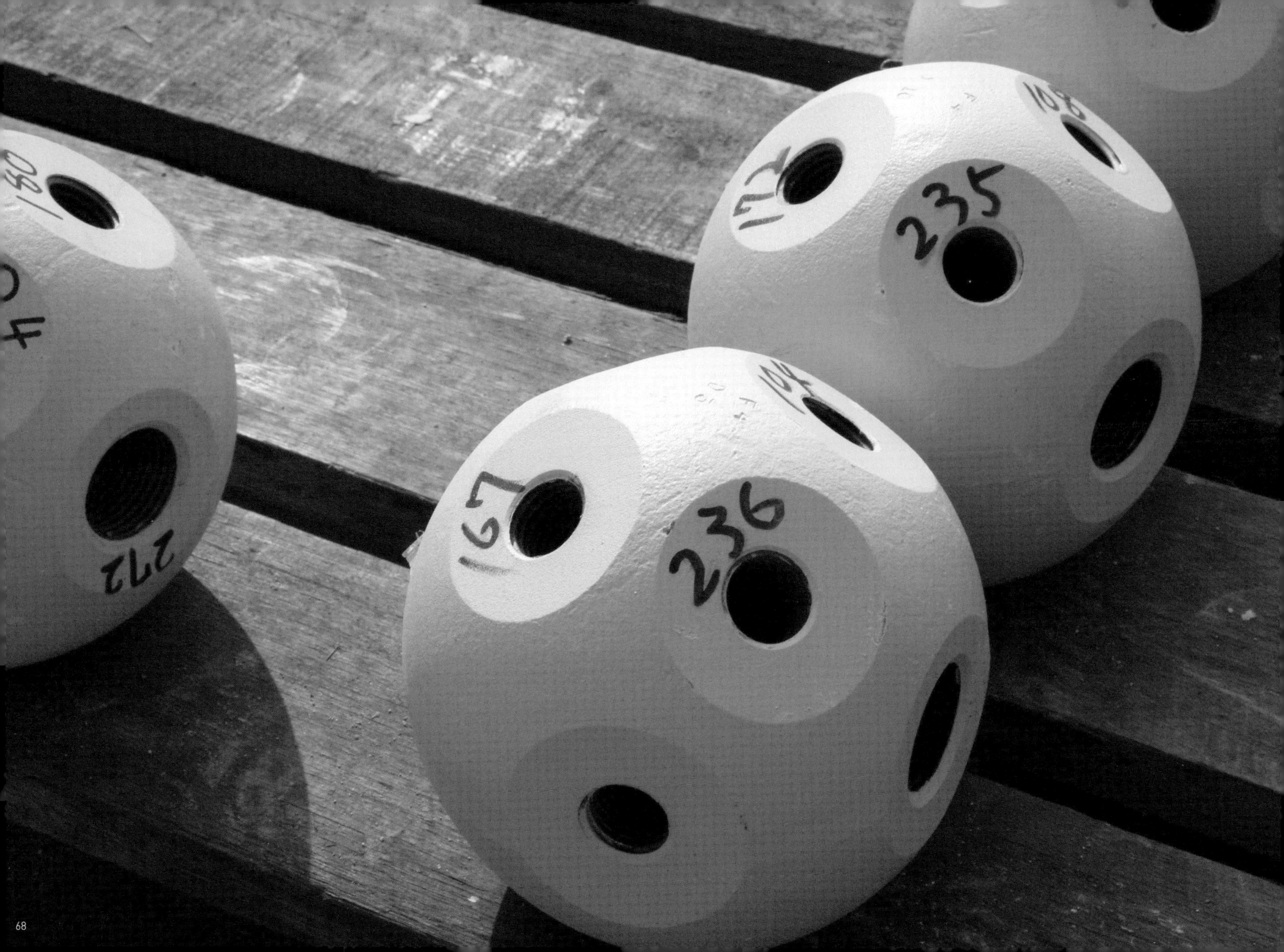
235
236
272

69

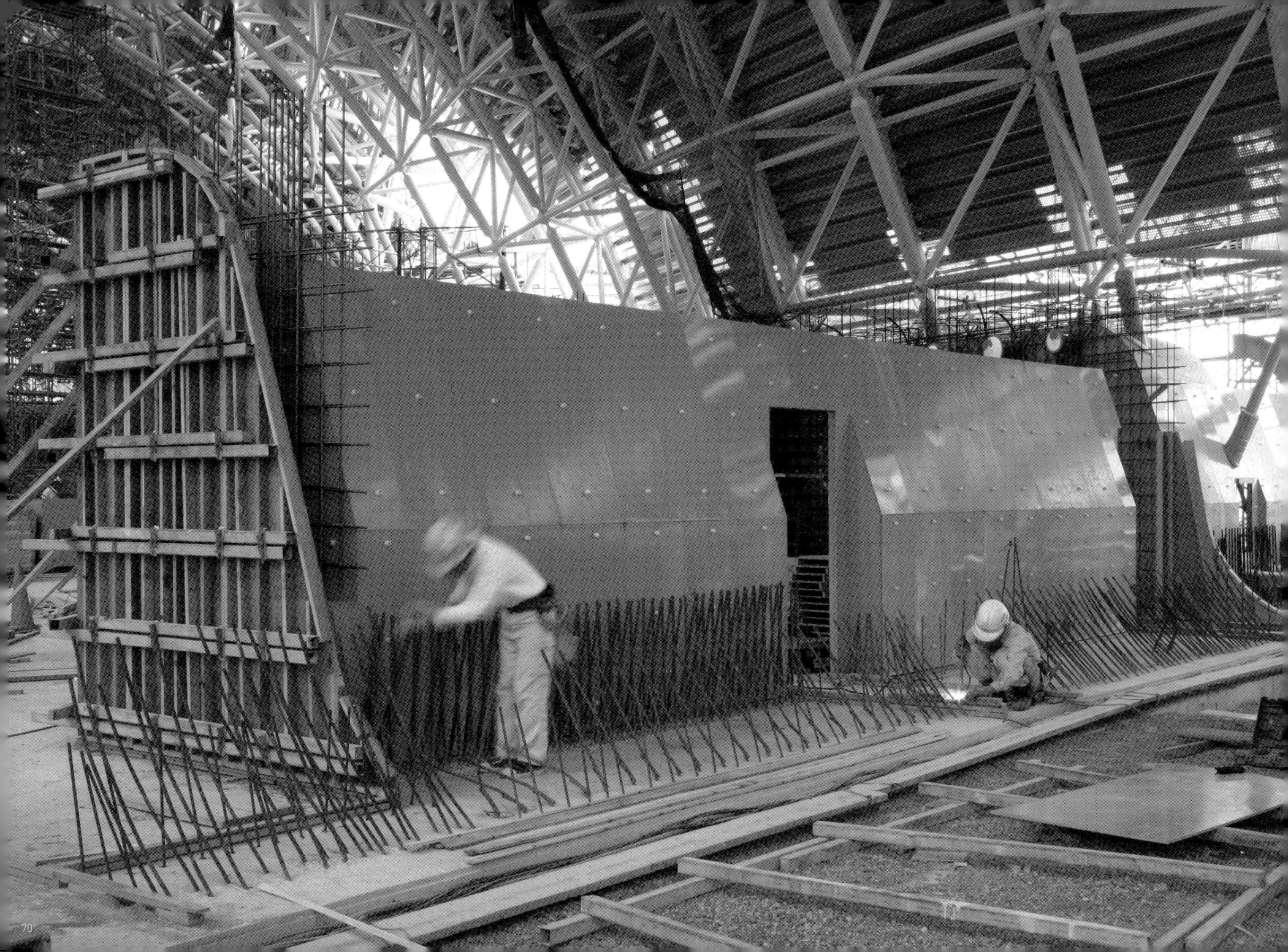

建築
一般　書店(帳合)印

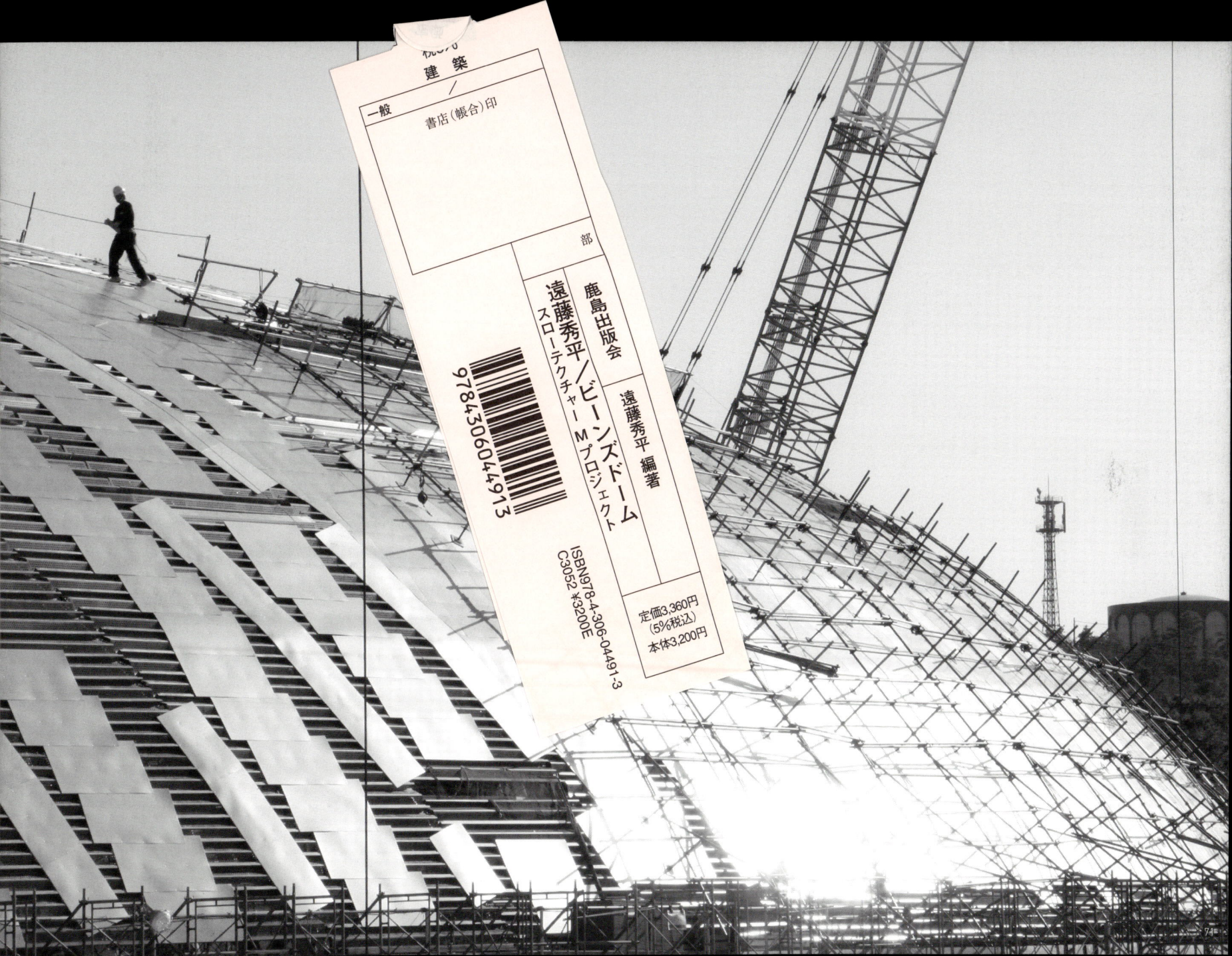

部

鹿島出版会
遠藤秀平／ビーンズドーム
スローテクチャーMプロジェクト

遠藤秀平 編著

9784306044913

ISBN978-4-306-04491-3
C3052 ¥3200E

定価3,360円
(5%税込)
本体3,200円

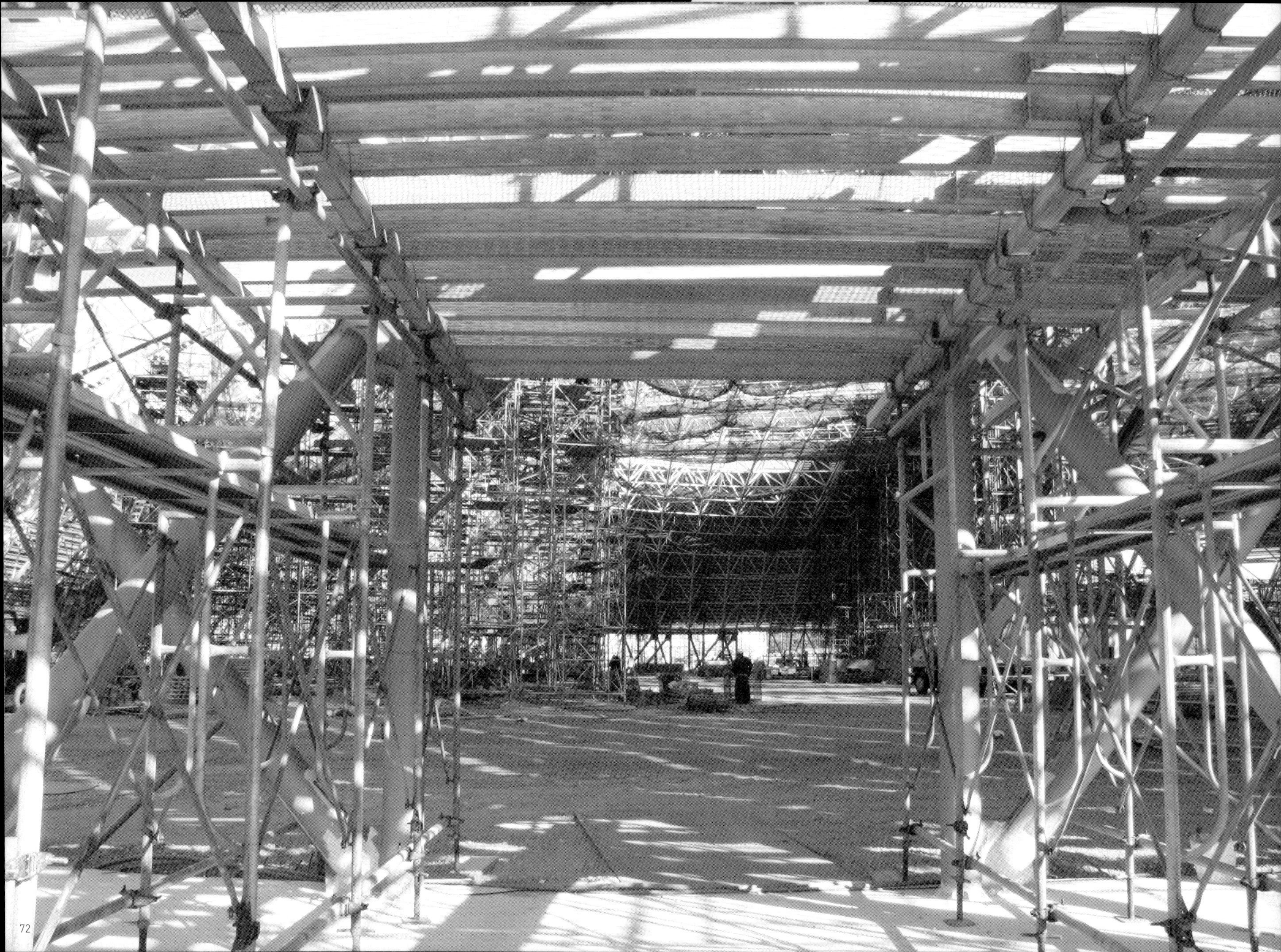

73

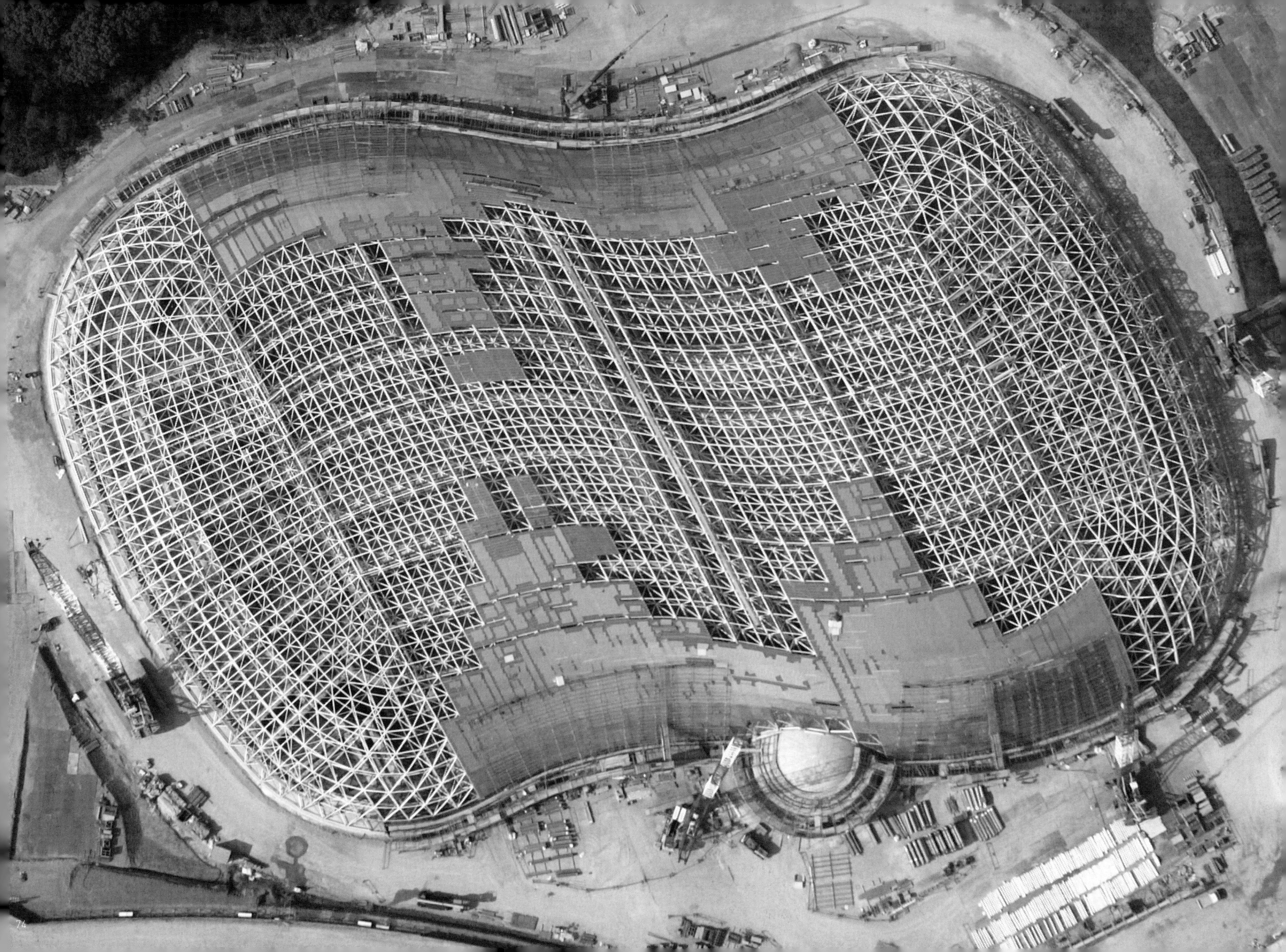

75

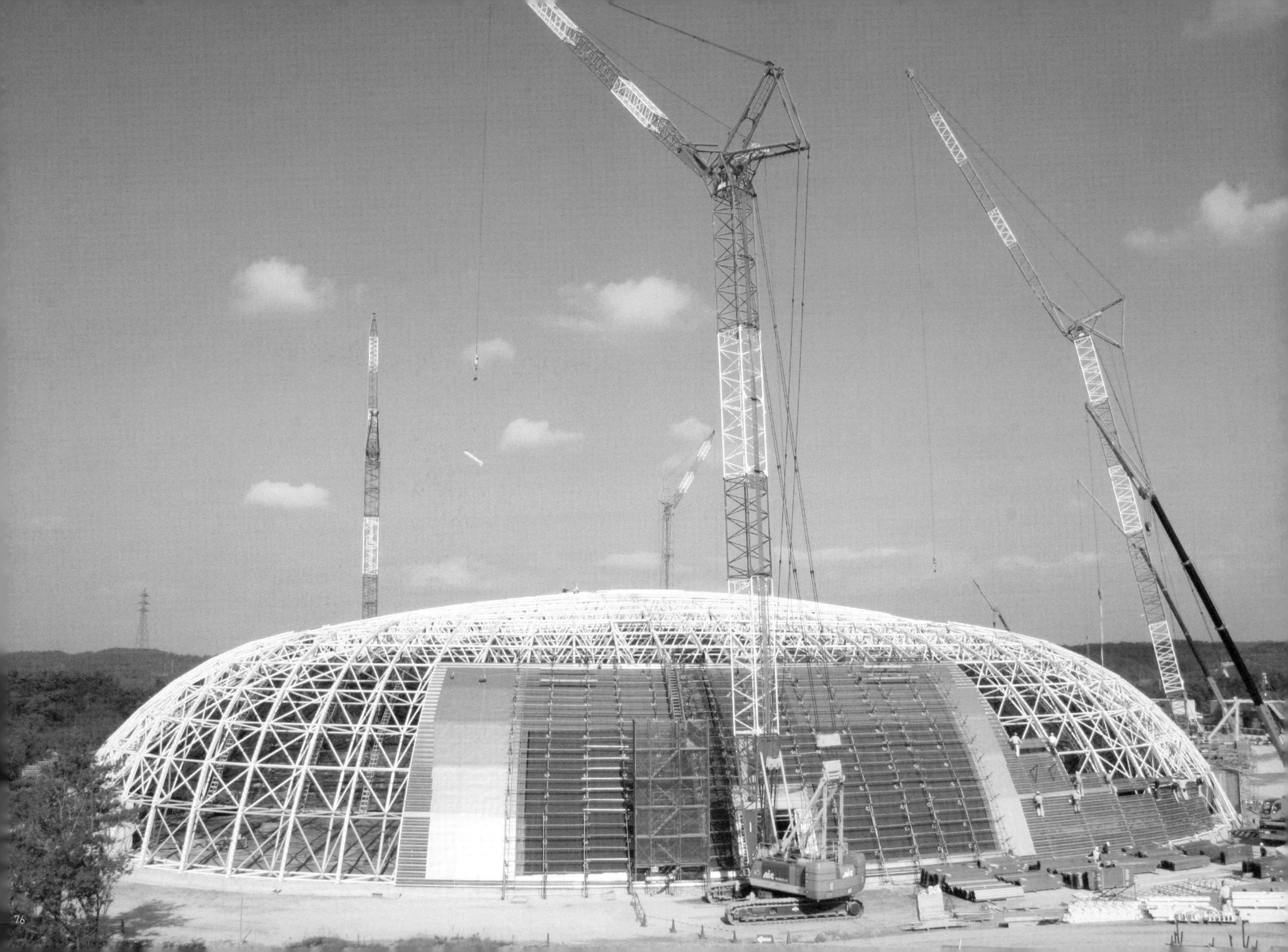

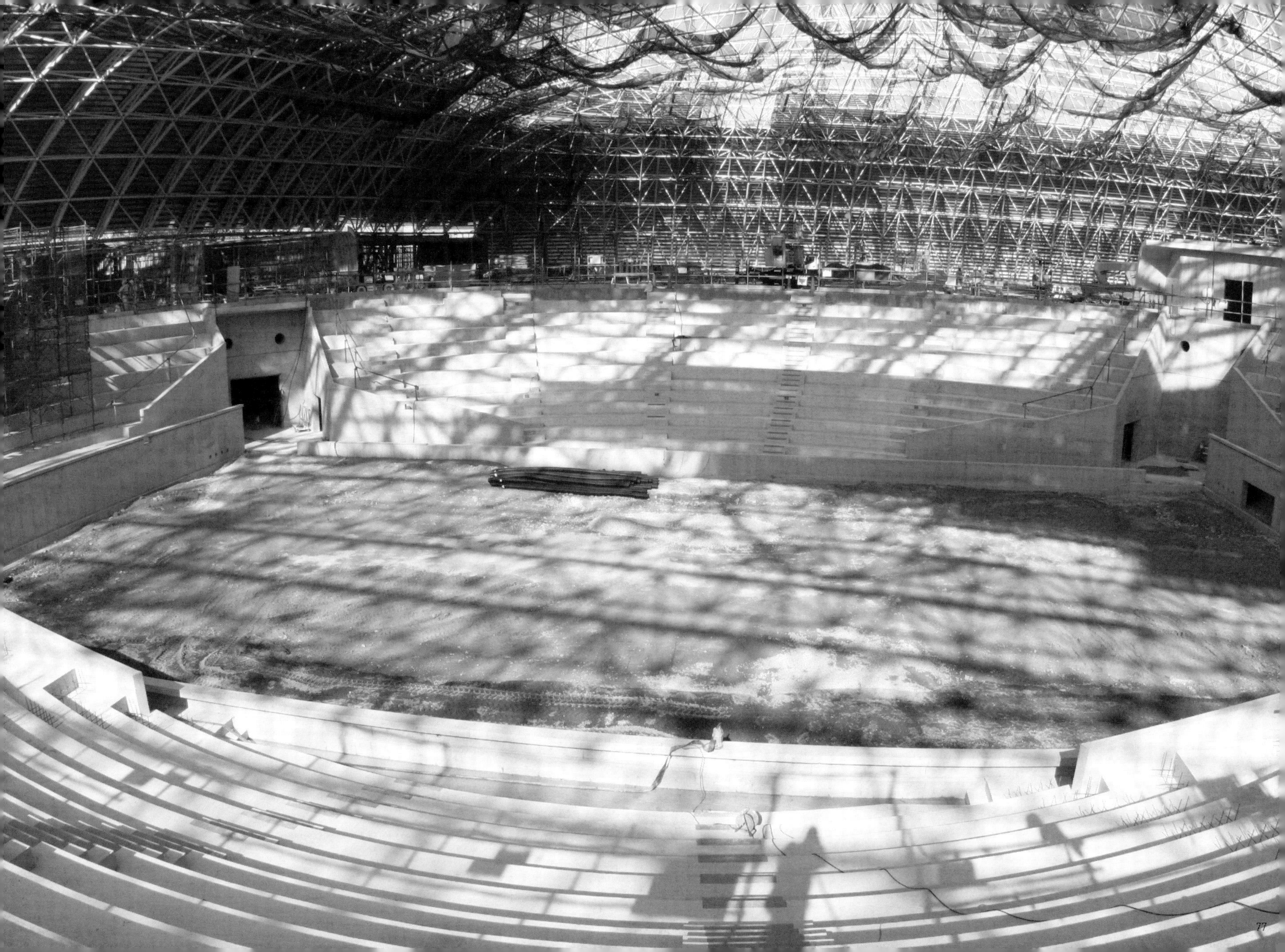

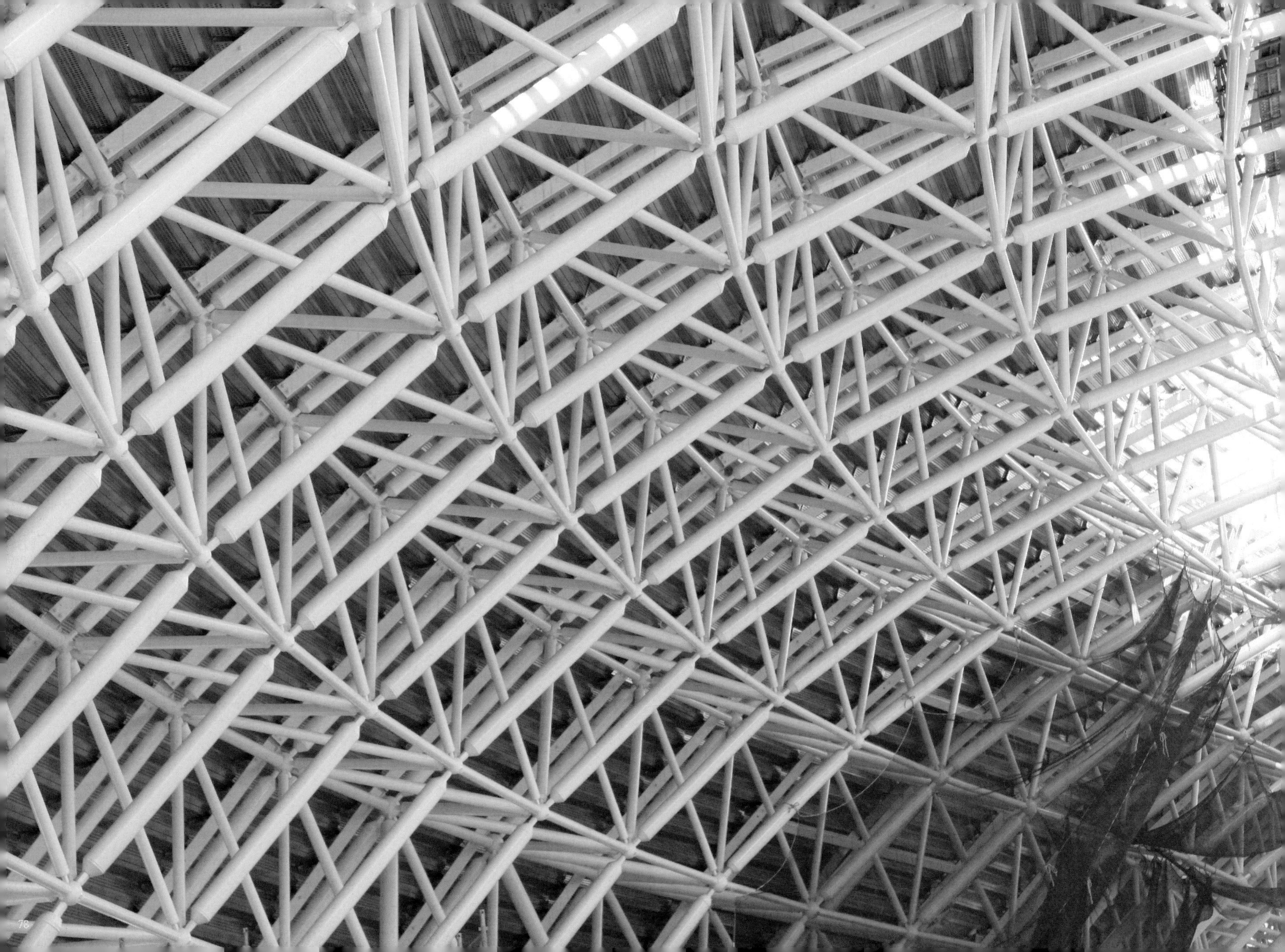

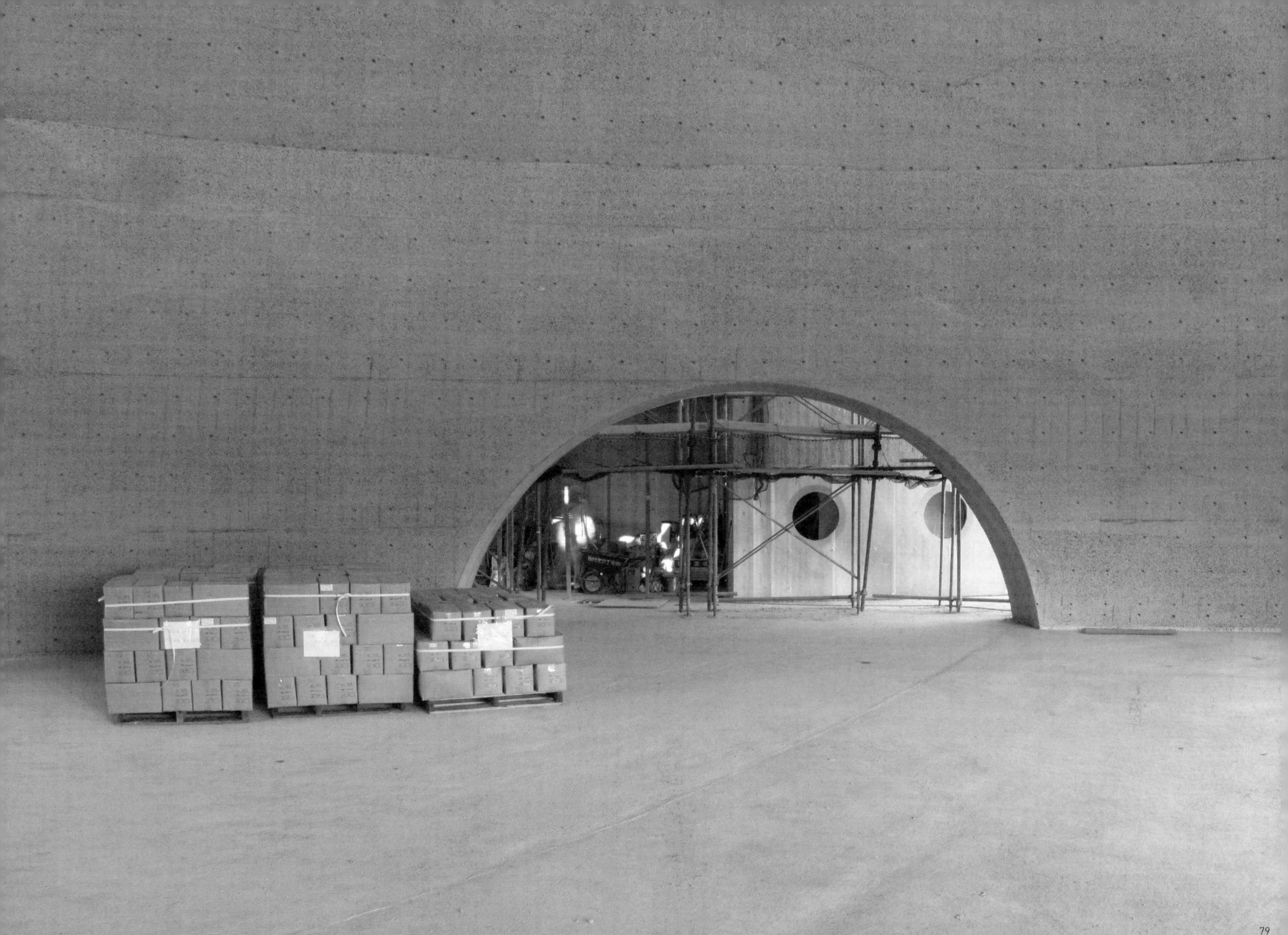

80

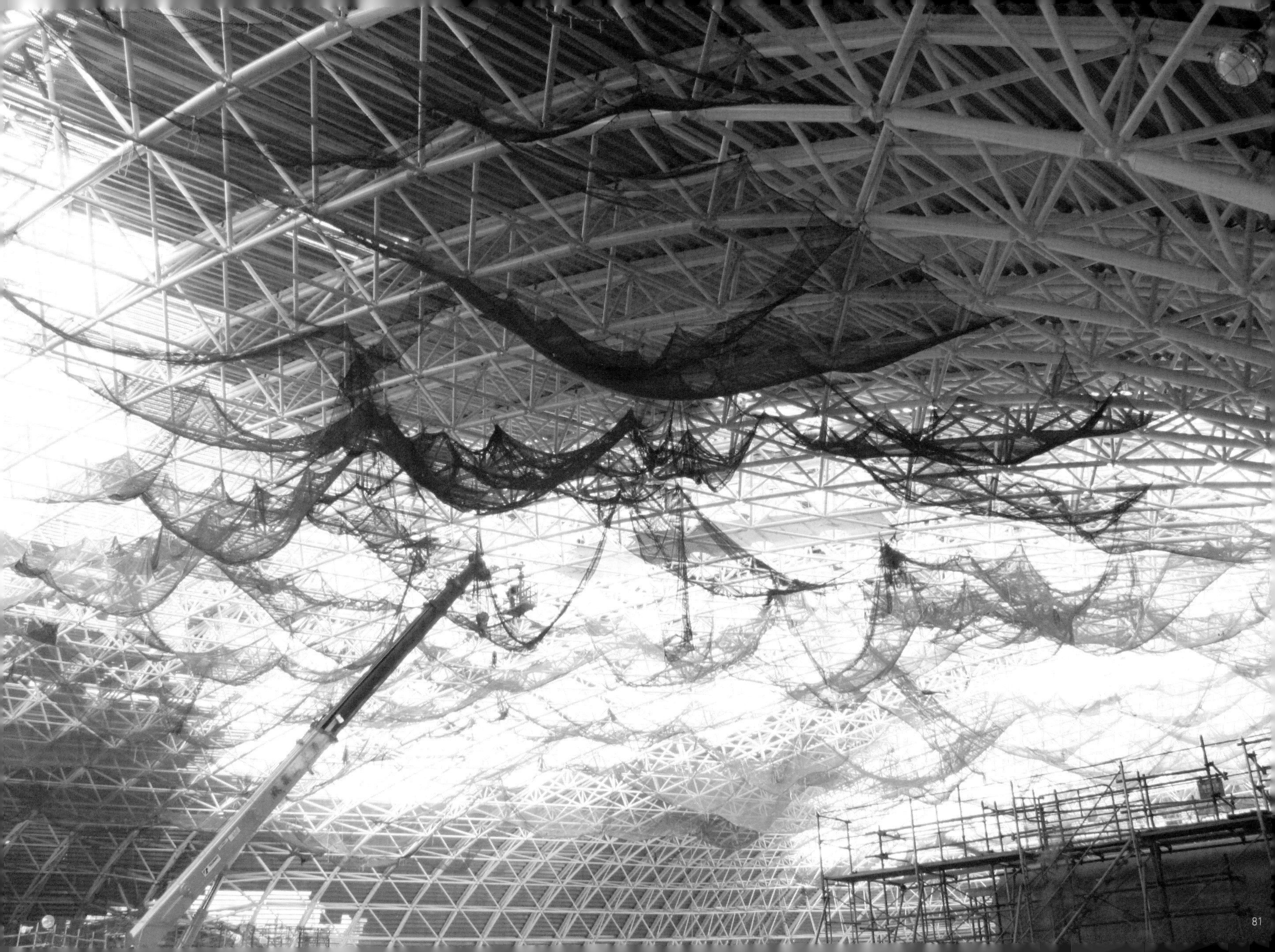

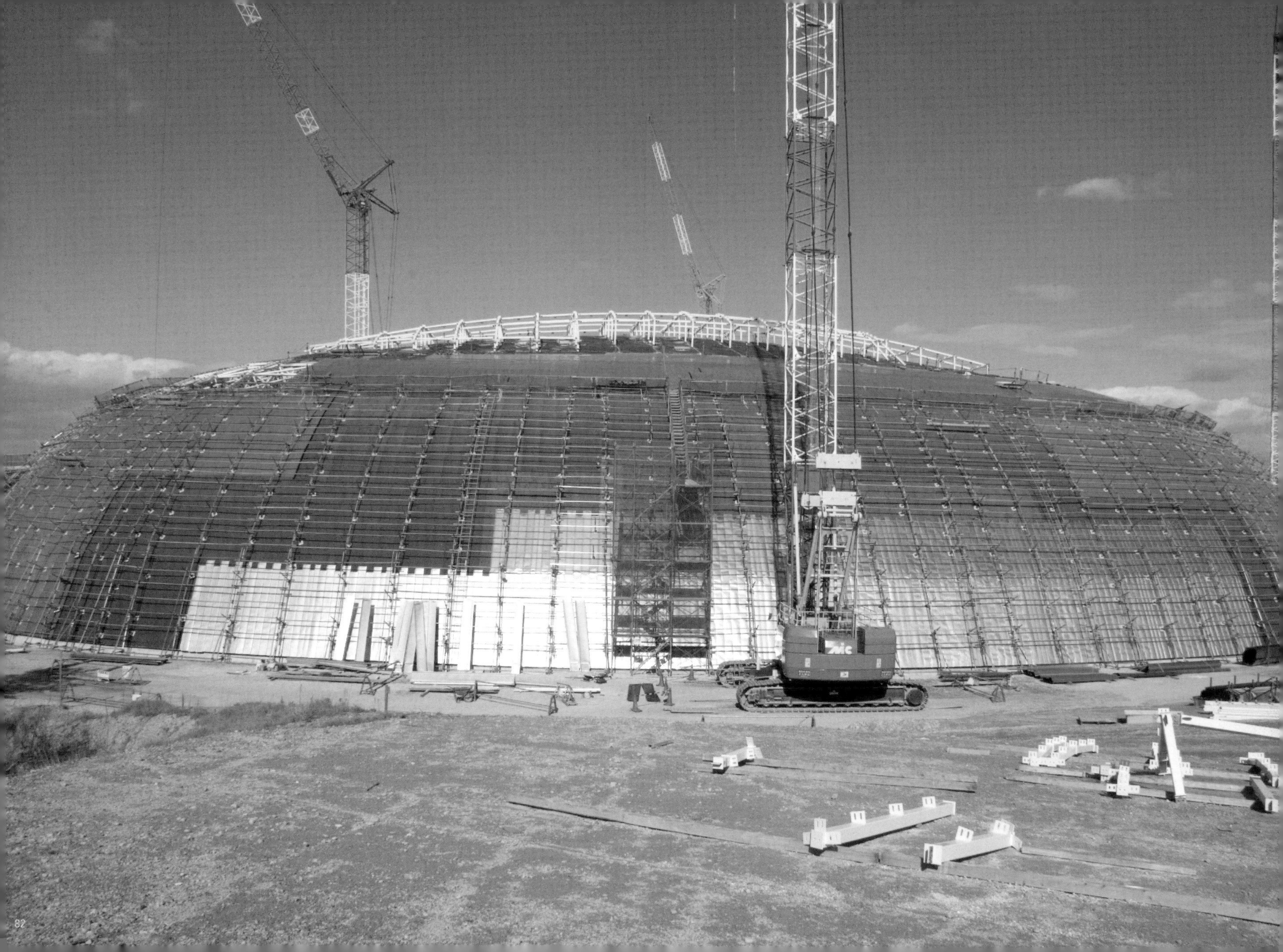

83

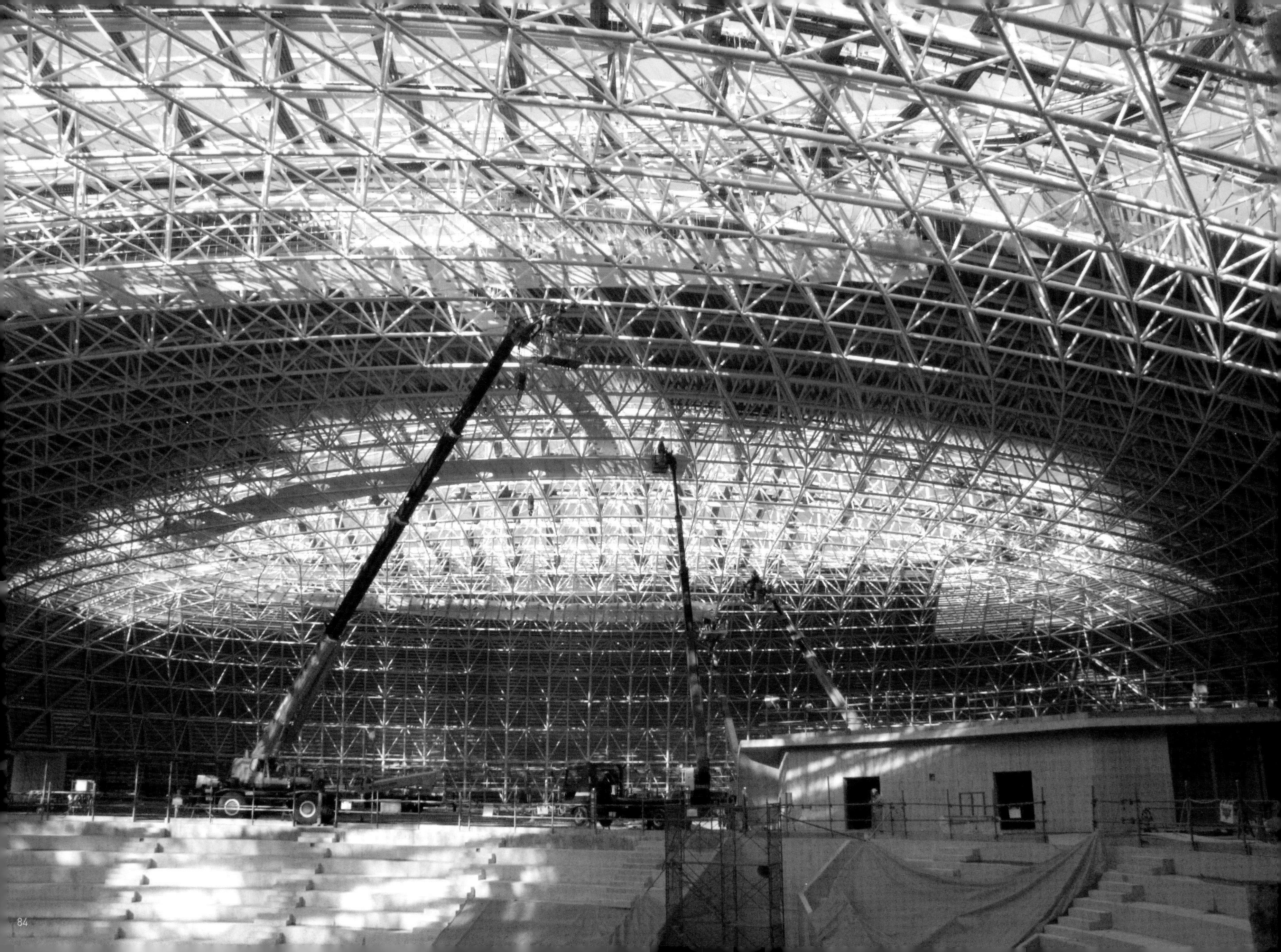

85

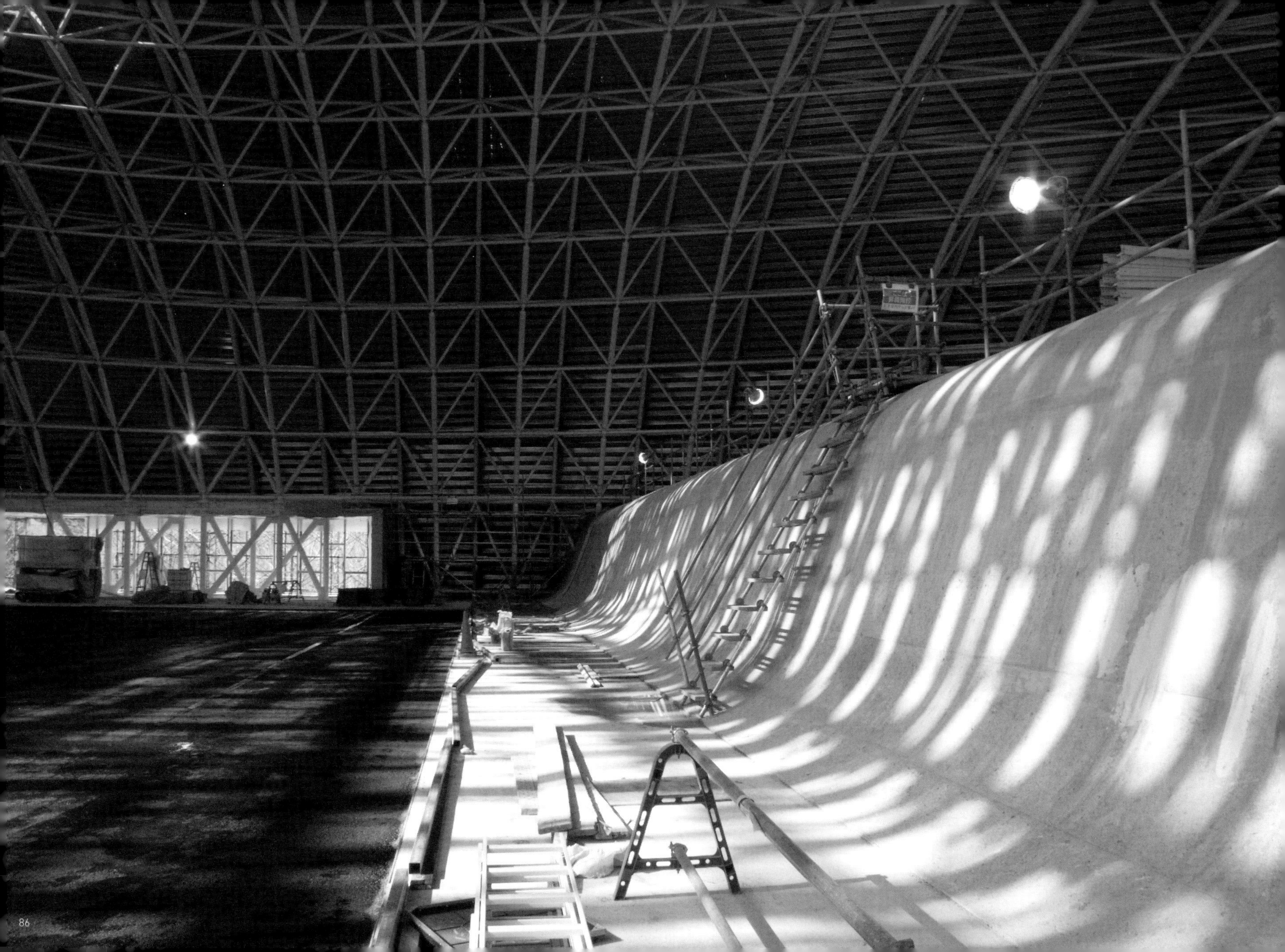

87

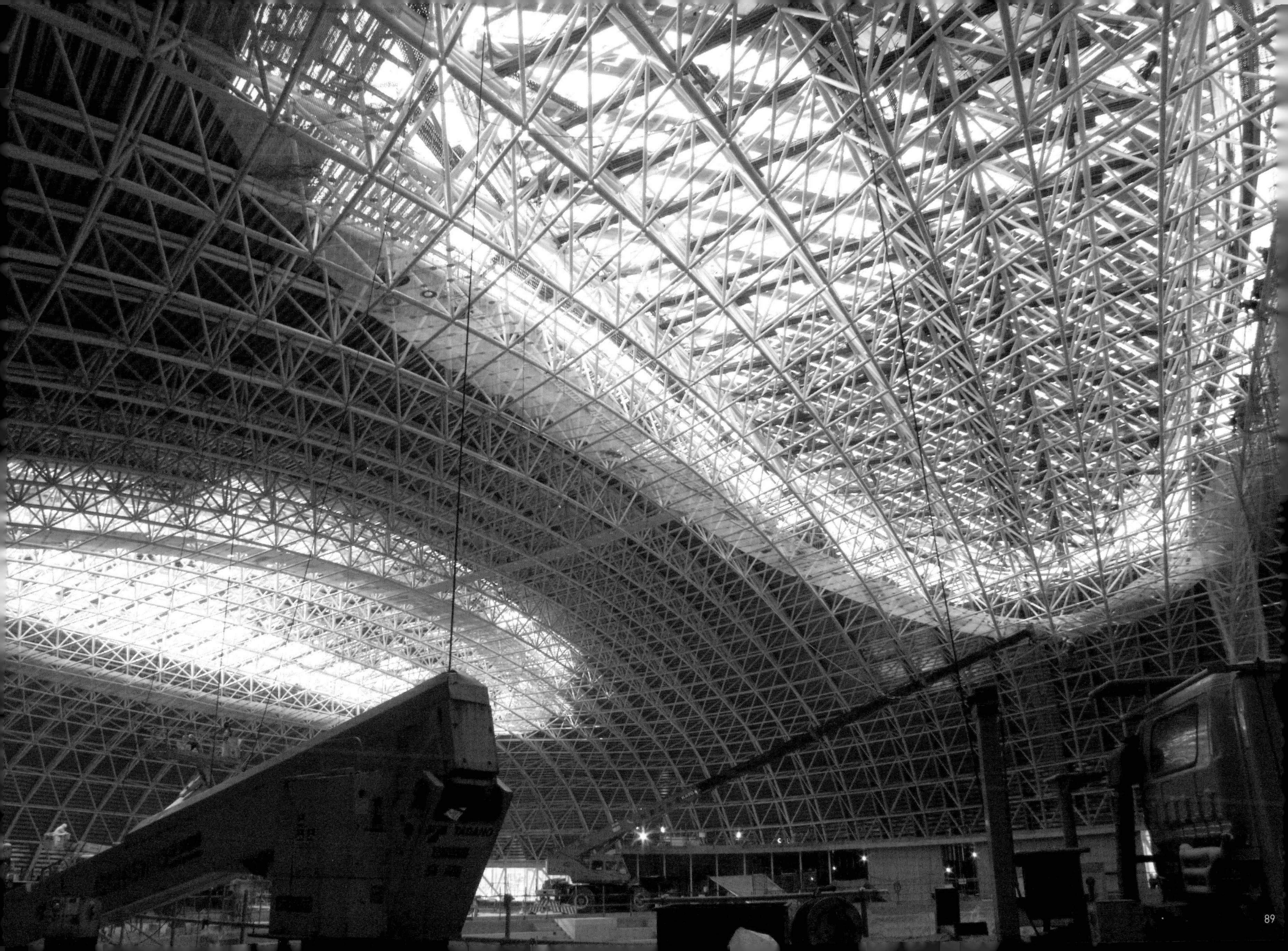

90

91

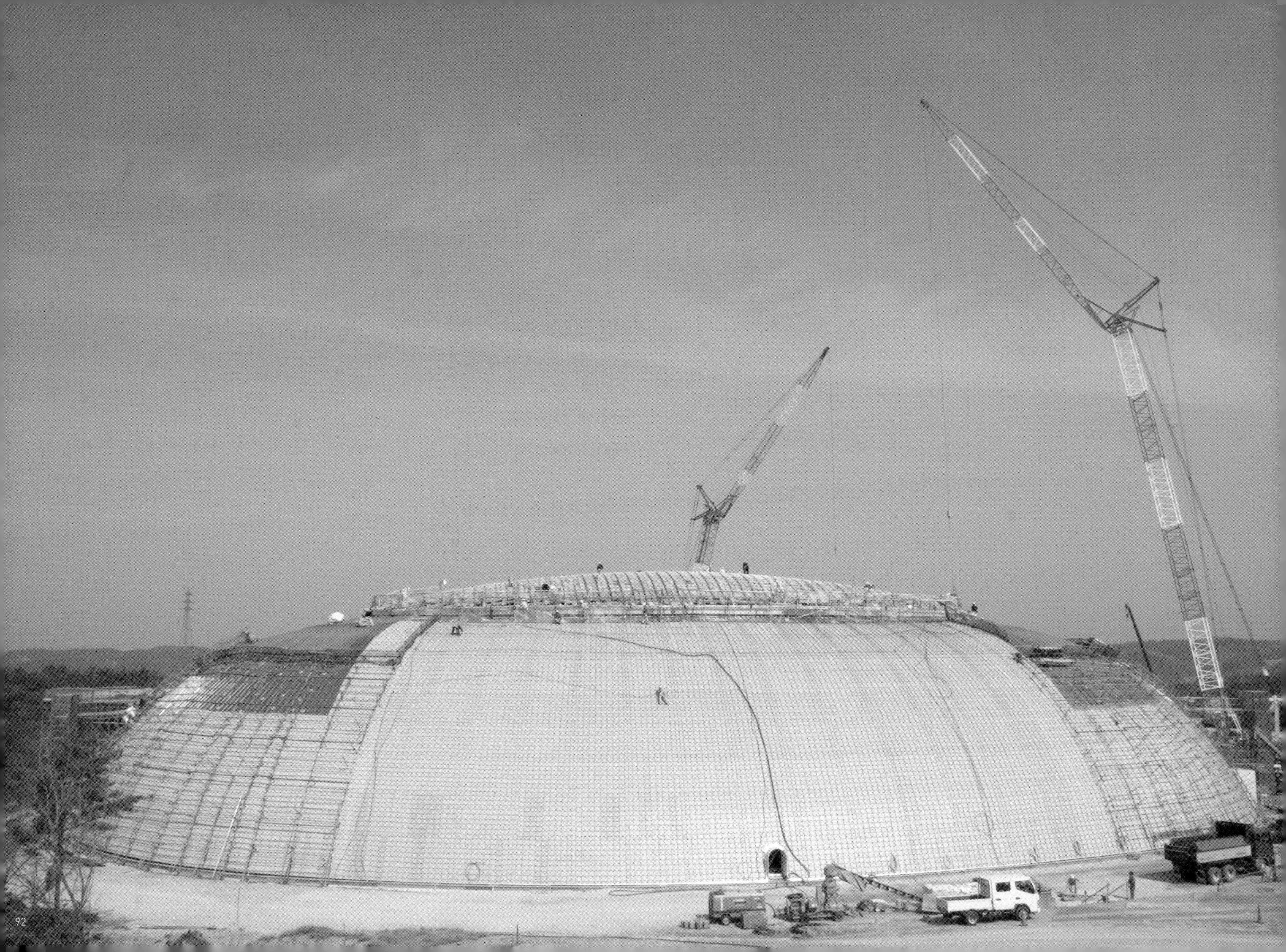

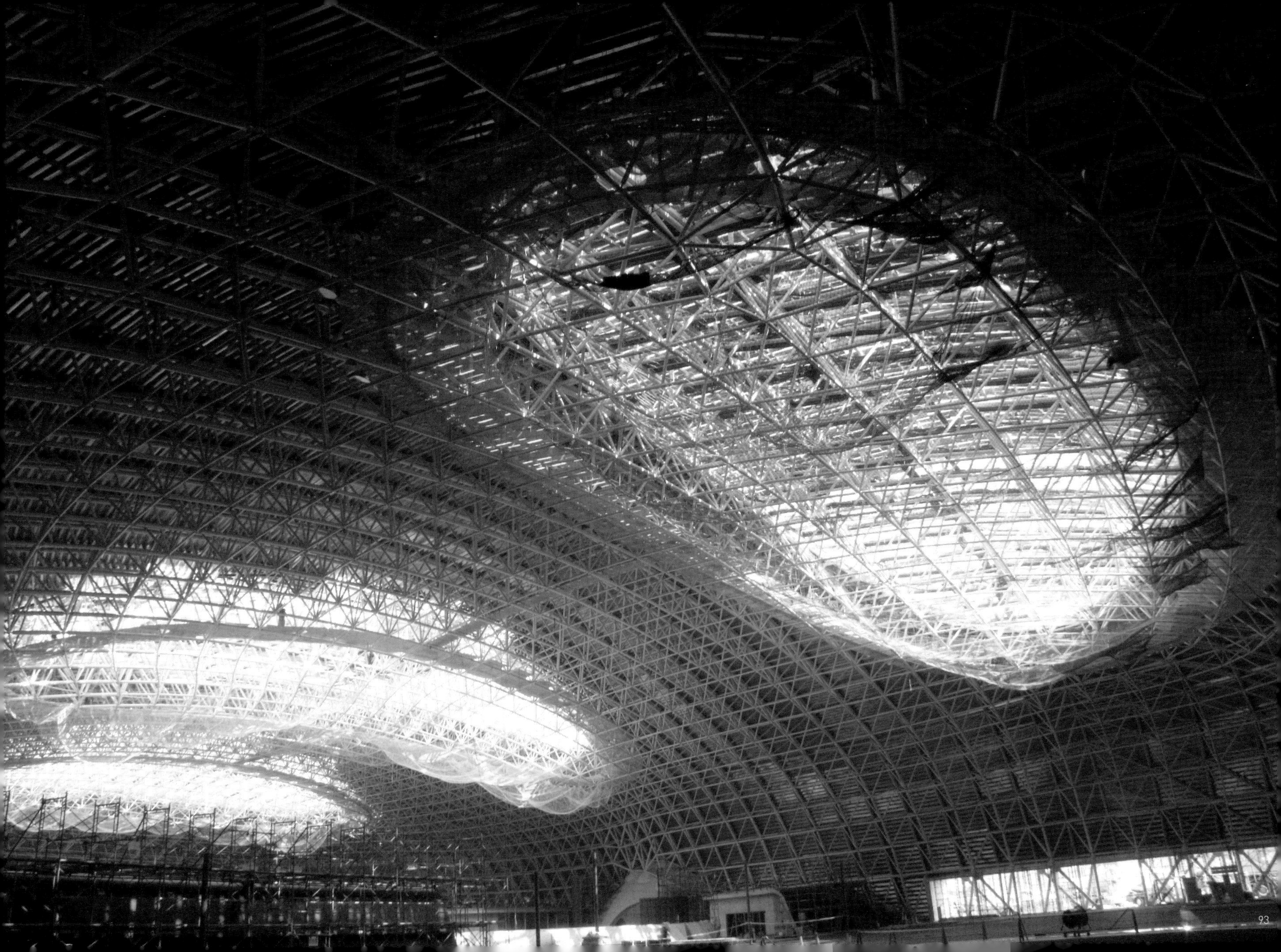

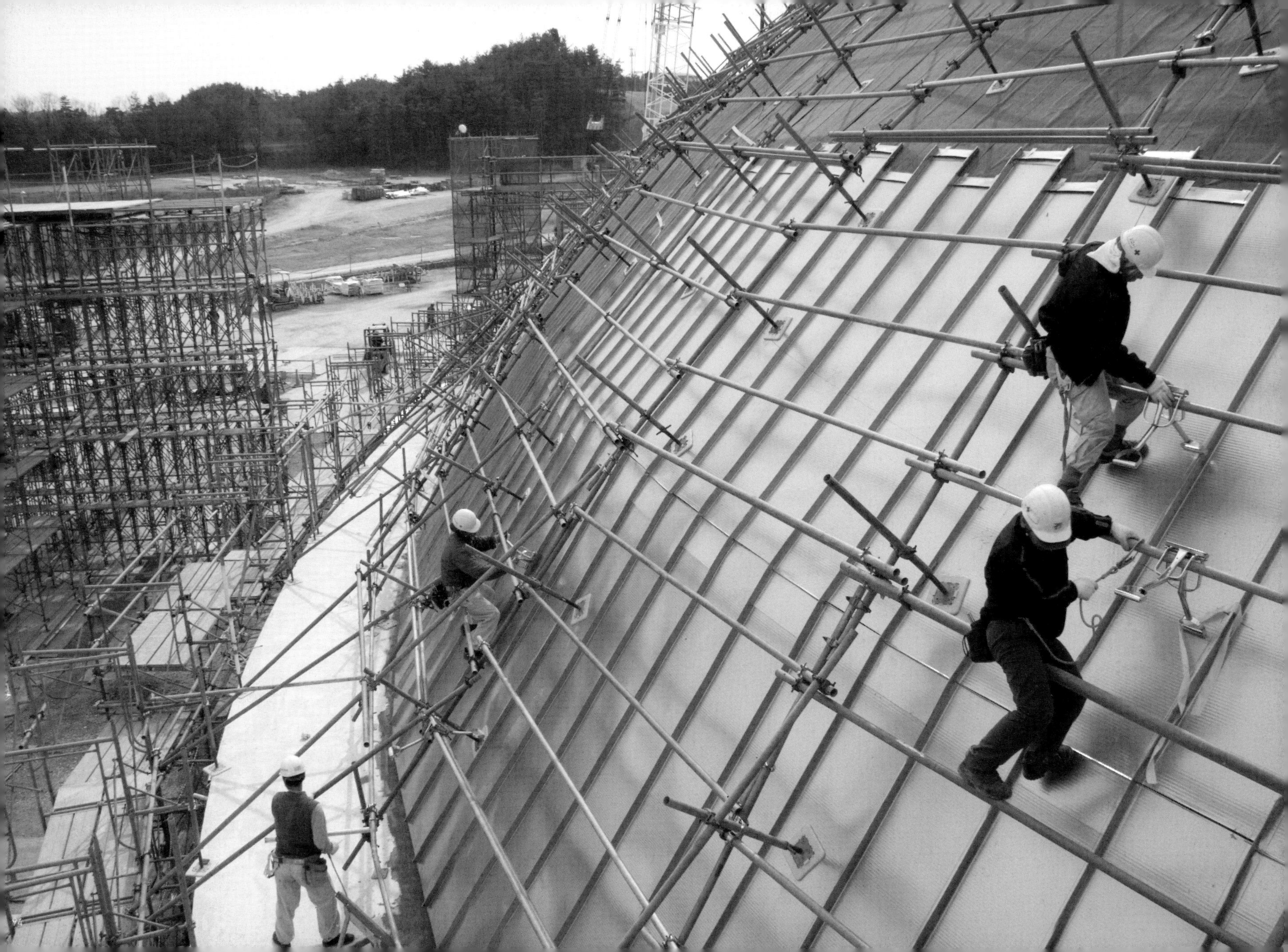

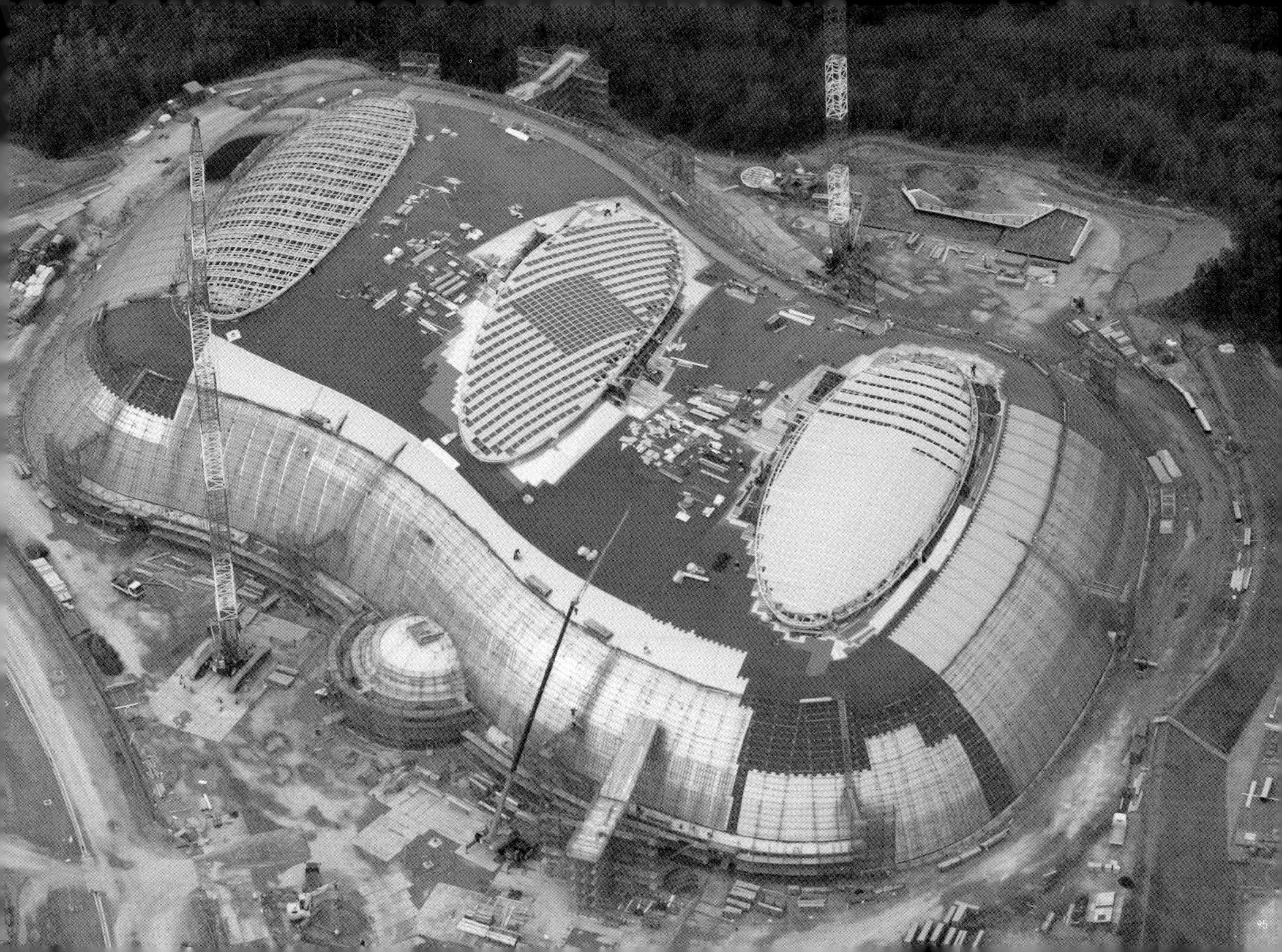

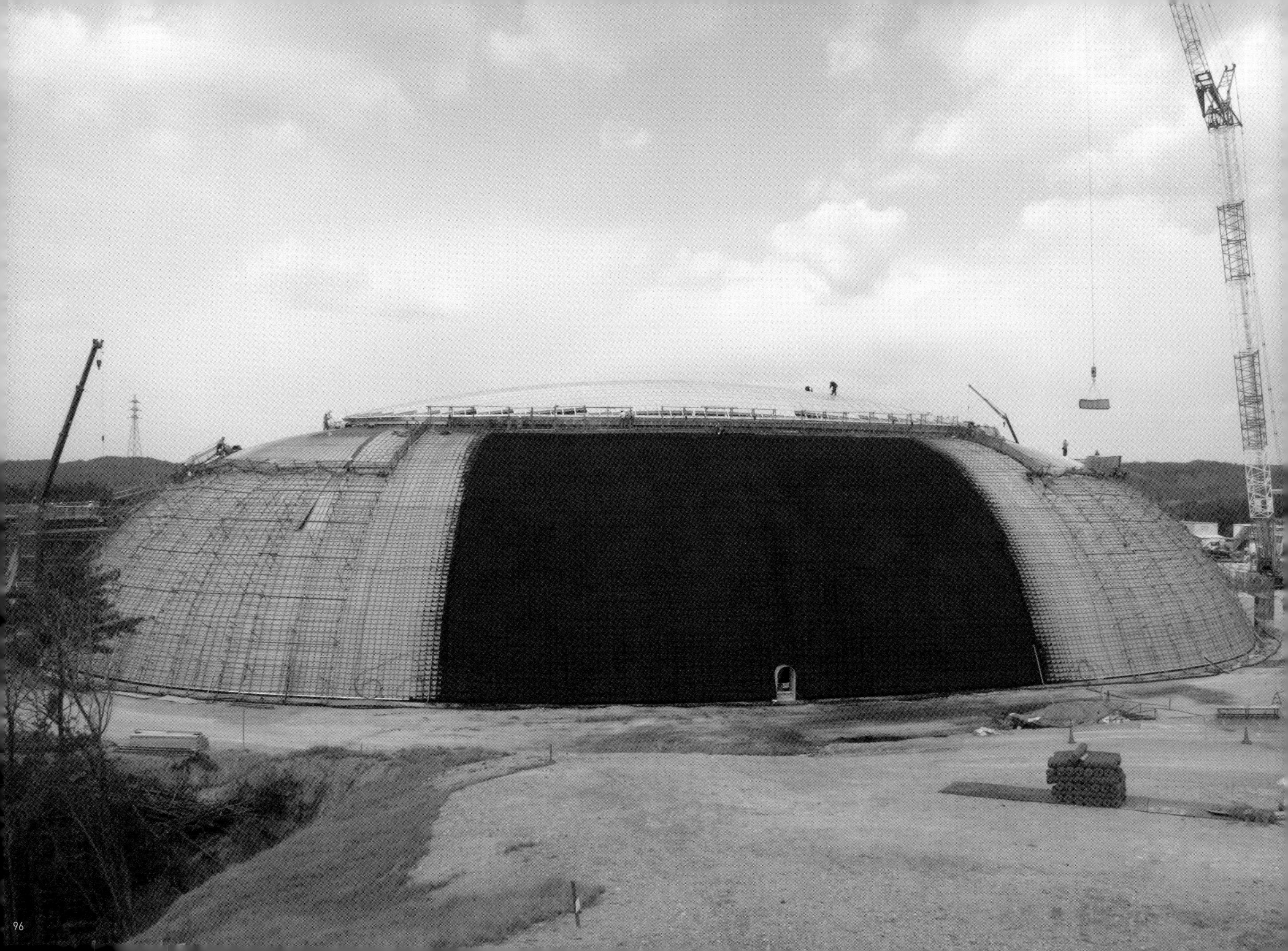

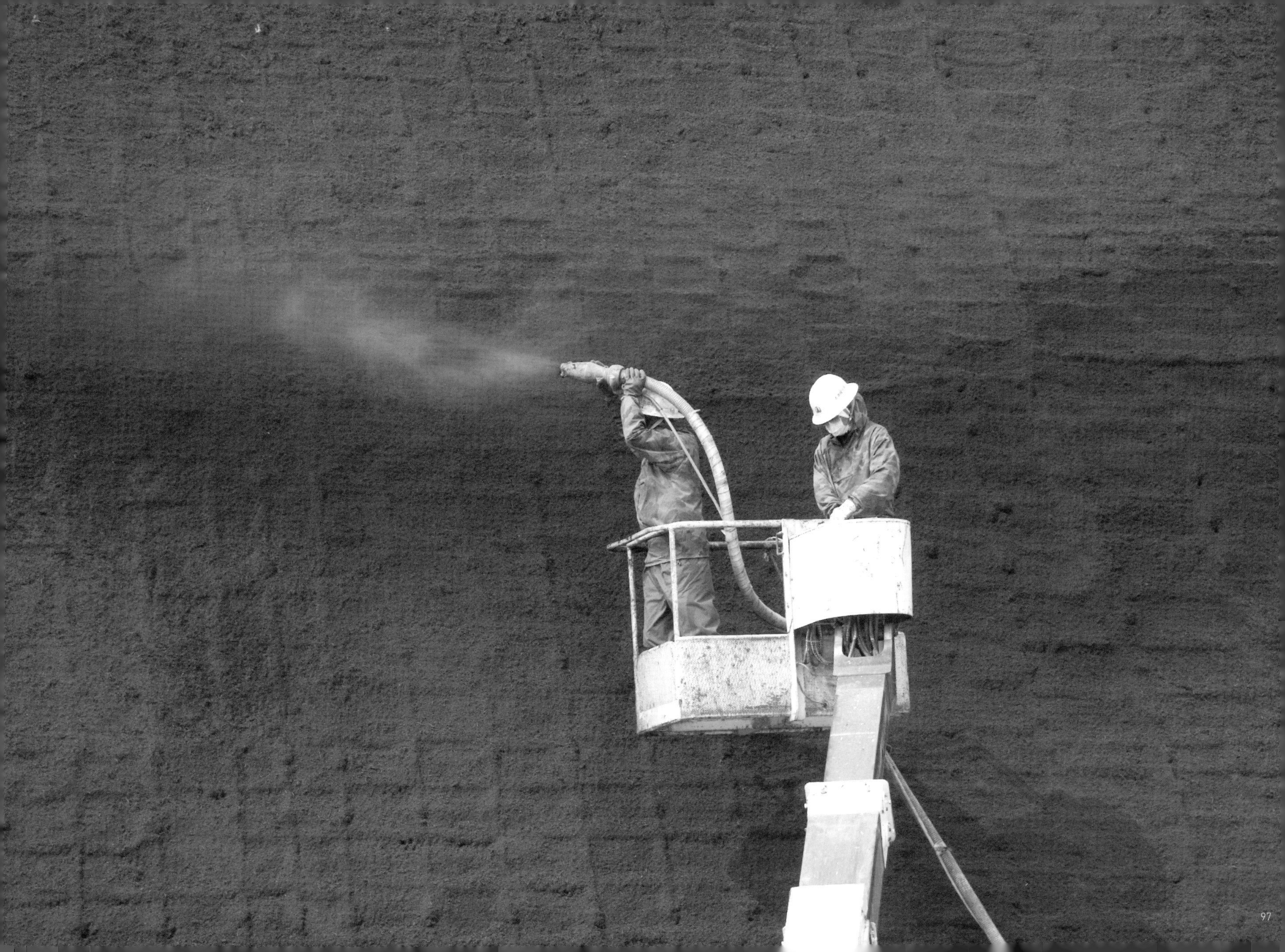

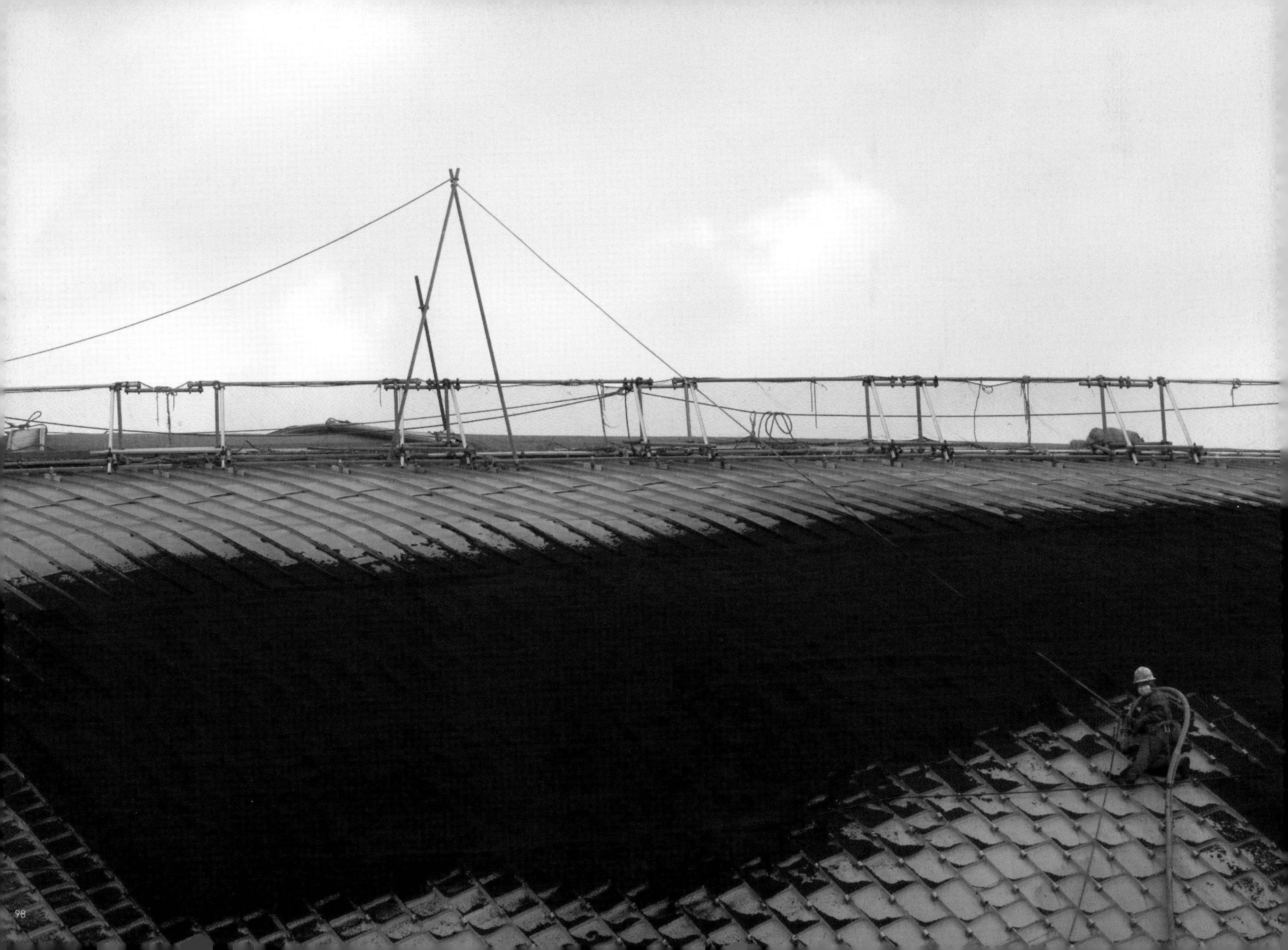

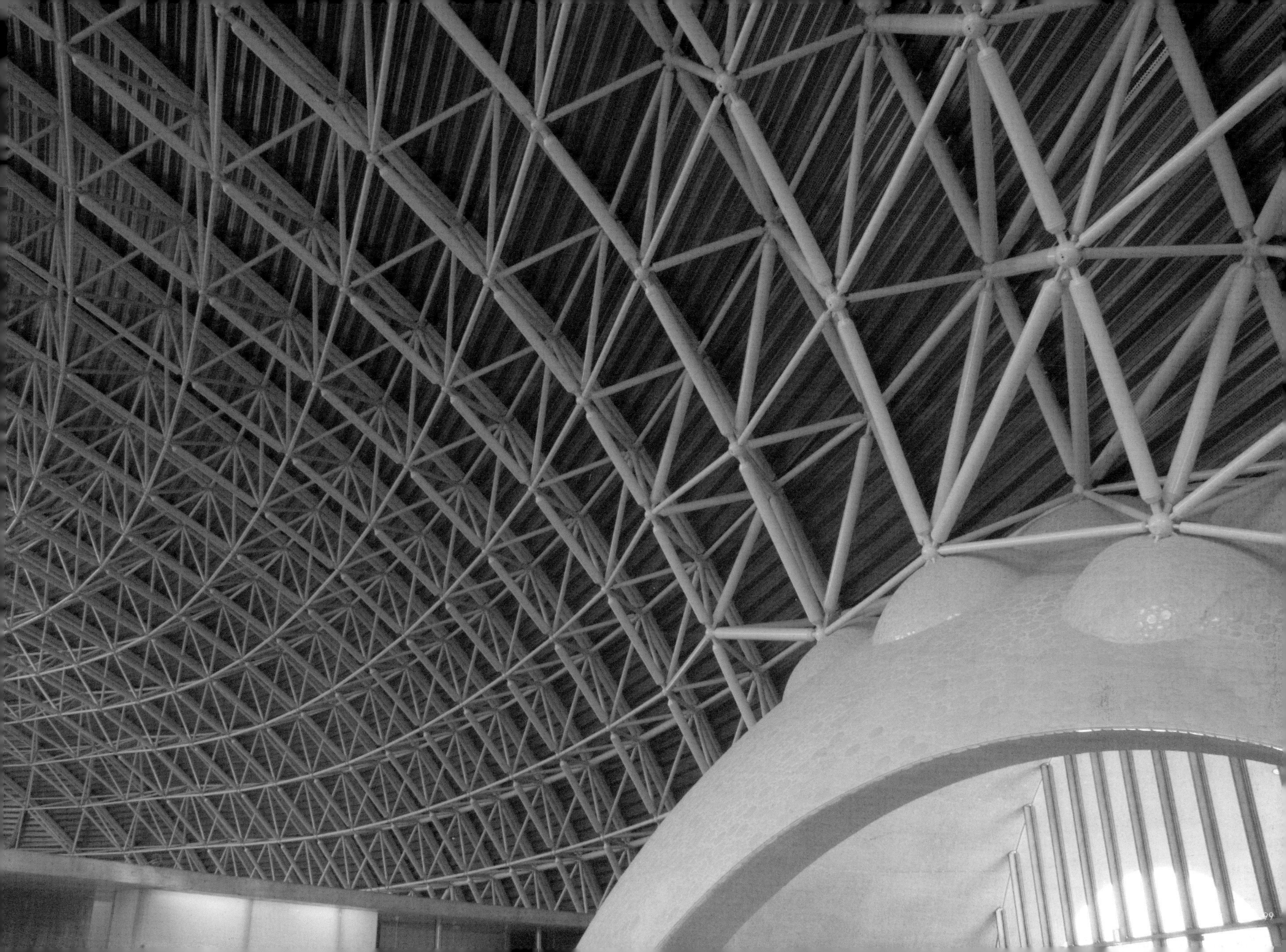

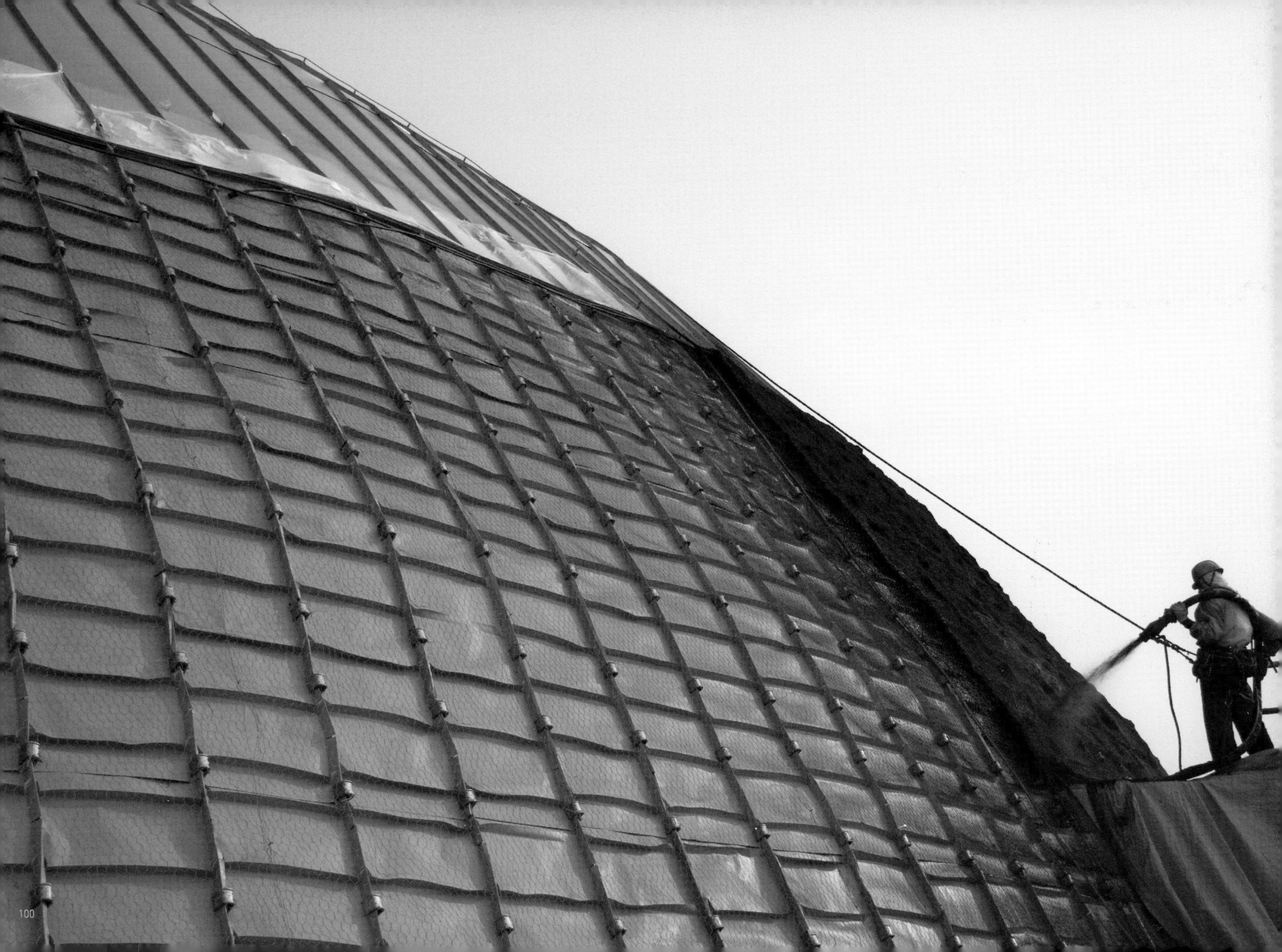

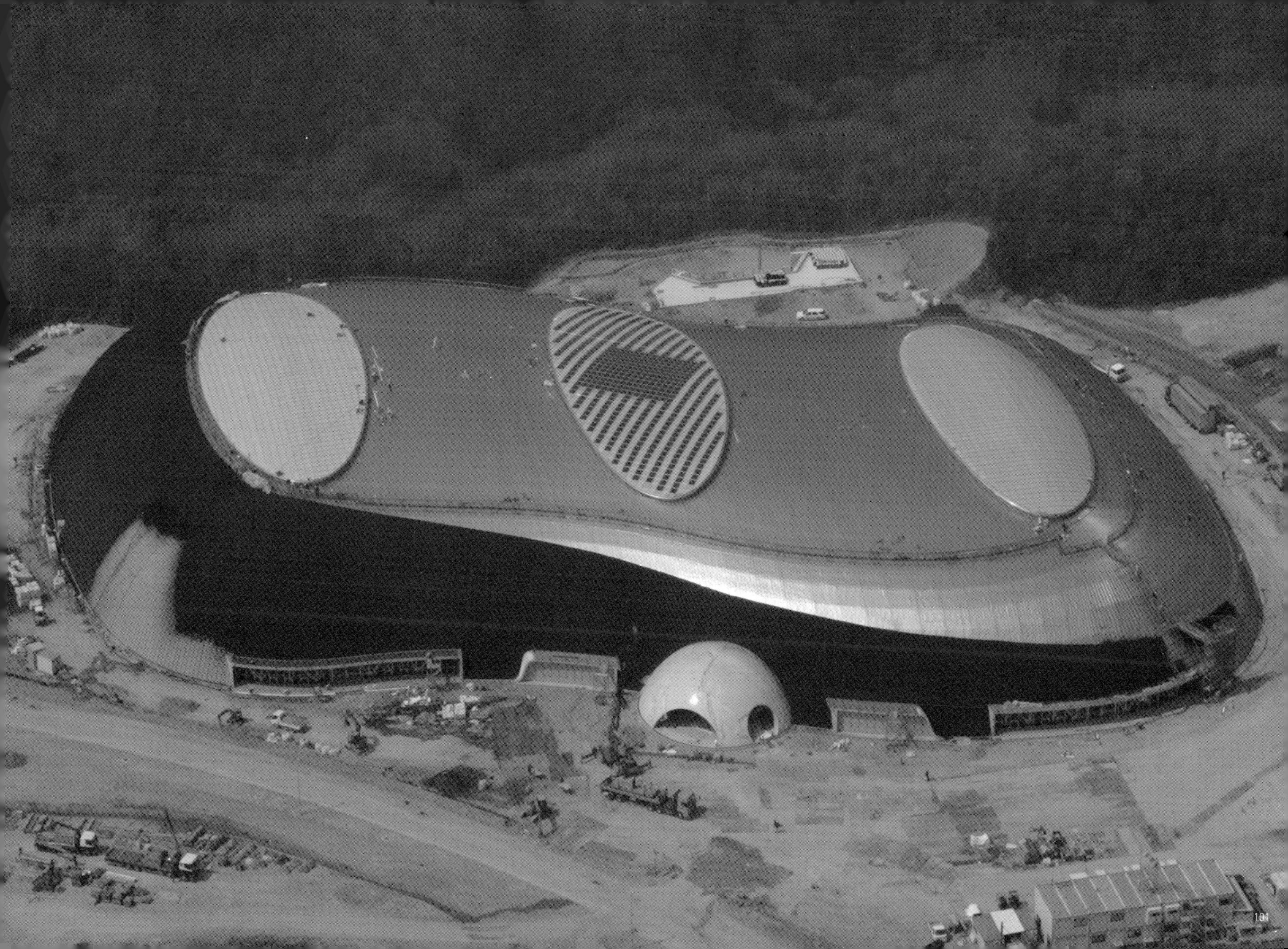

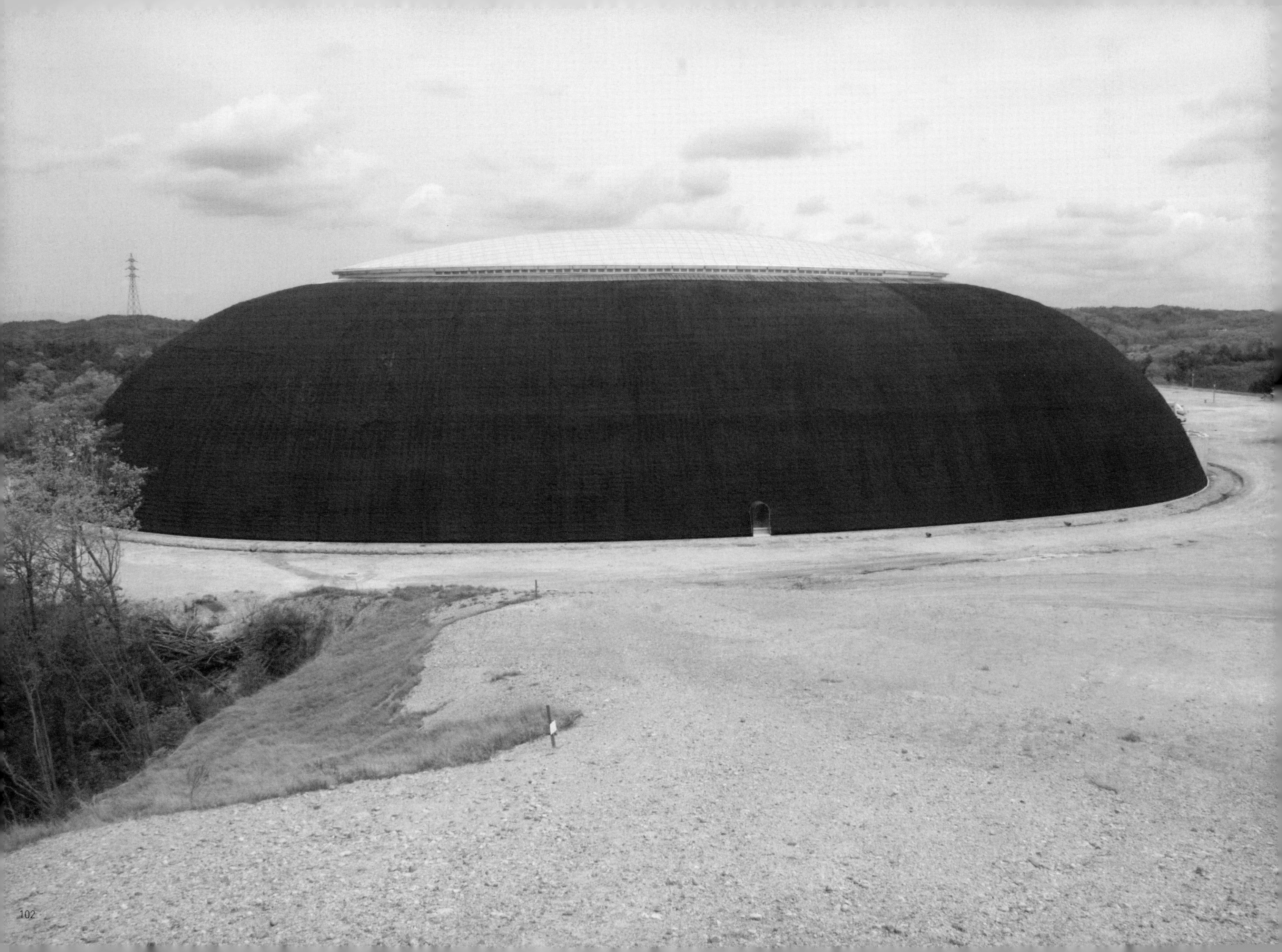

103

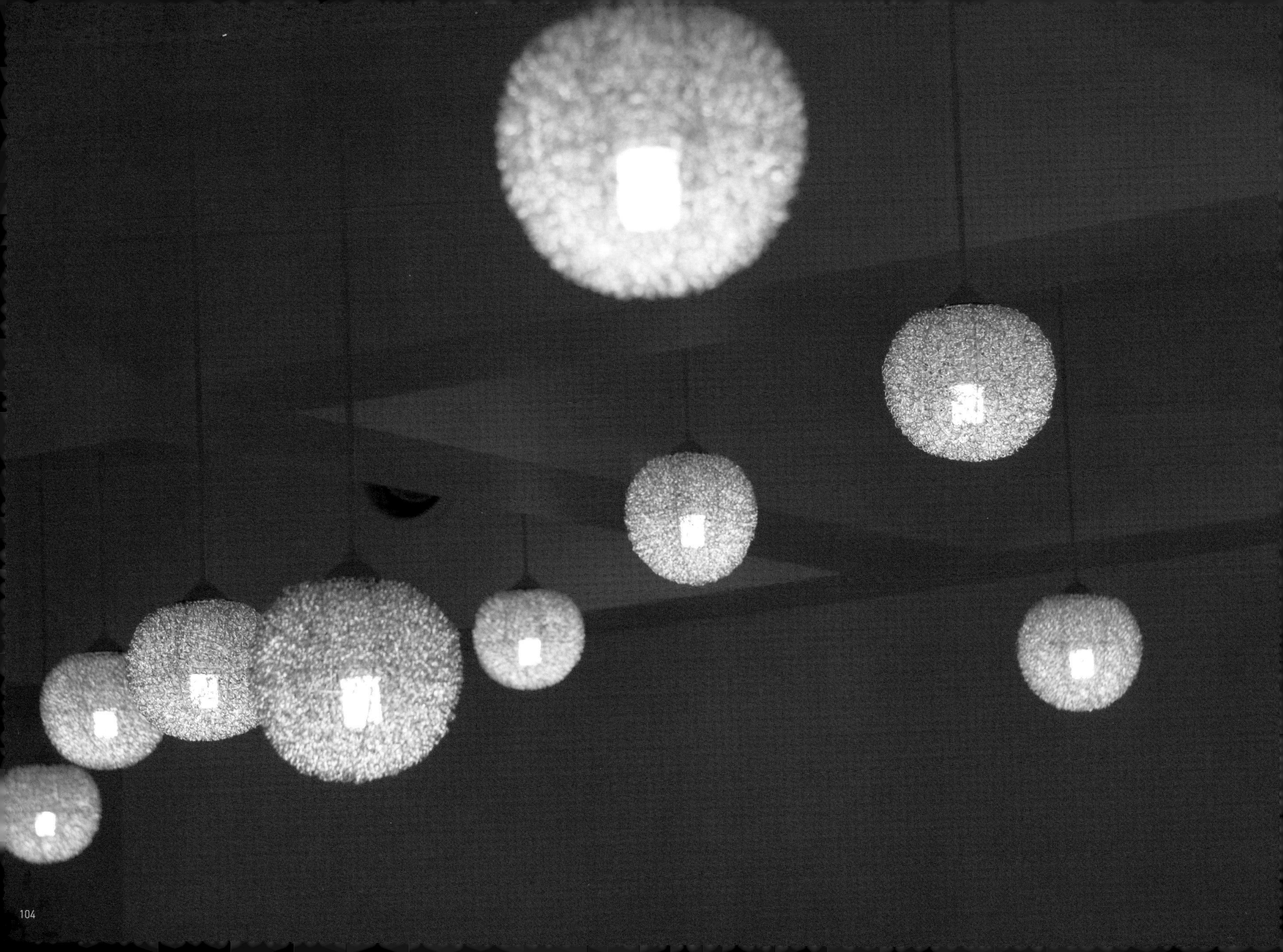

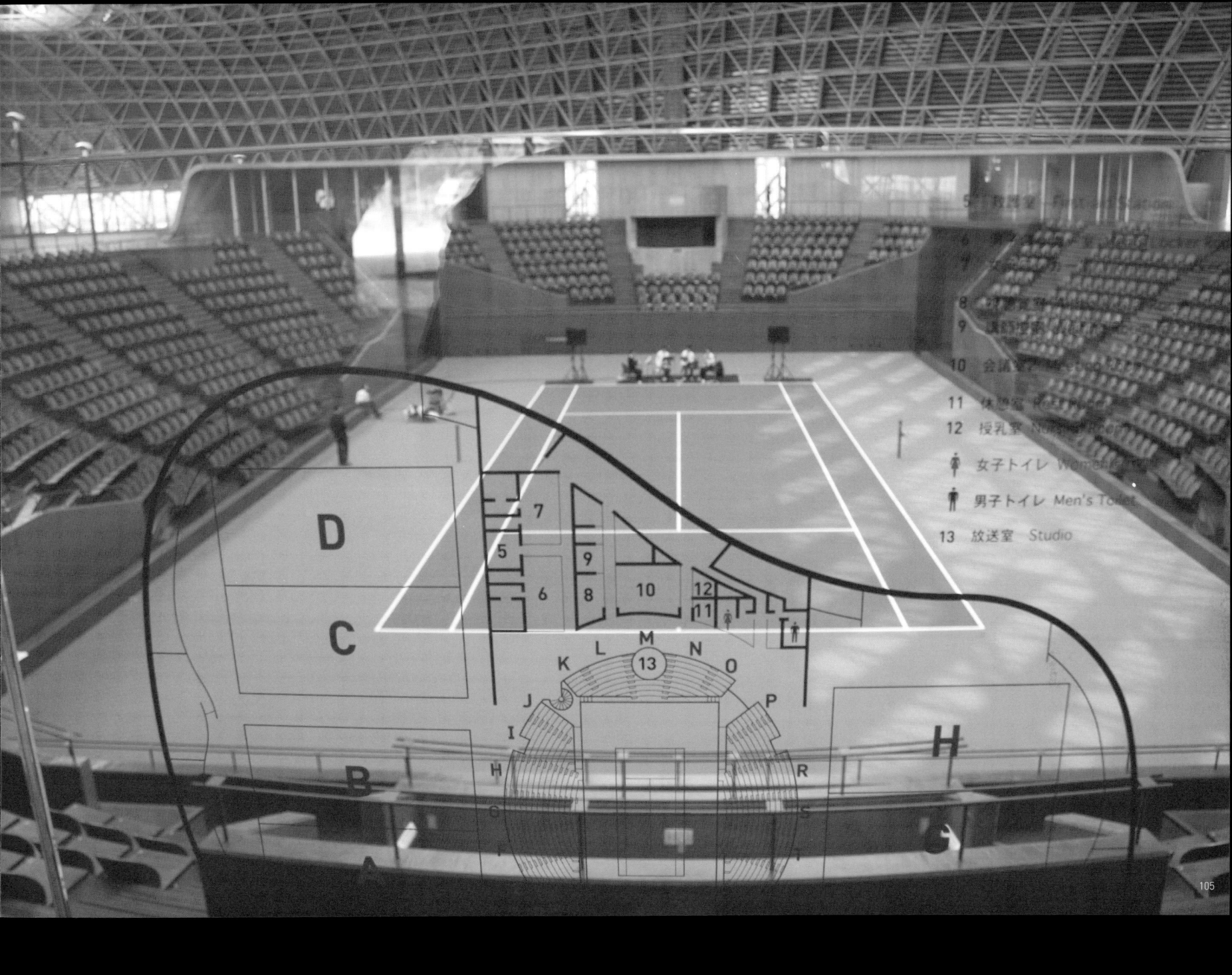

5	教師室
8	
9	
10	会議
11	休憩室
12	授乳室
	女子トイレ Women's
	男子トイレ Men's Toilet
13	放送室 Studio

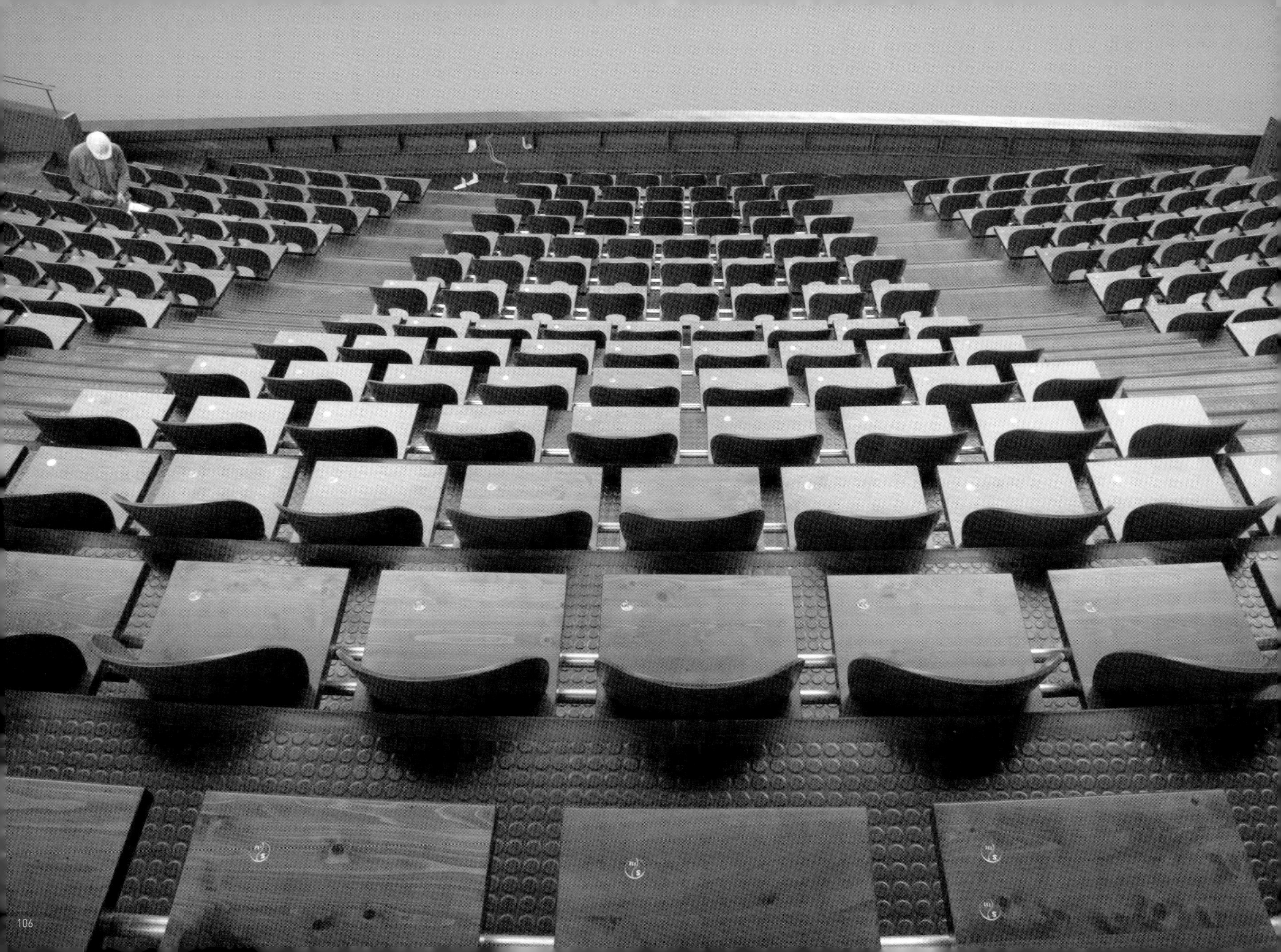

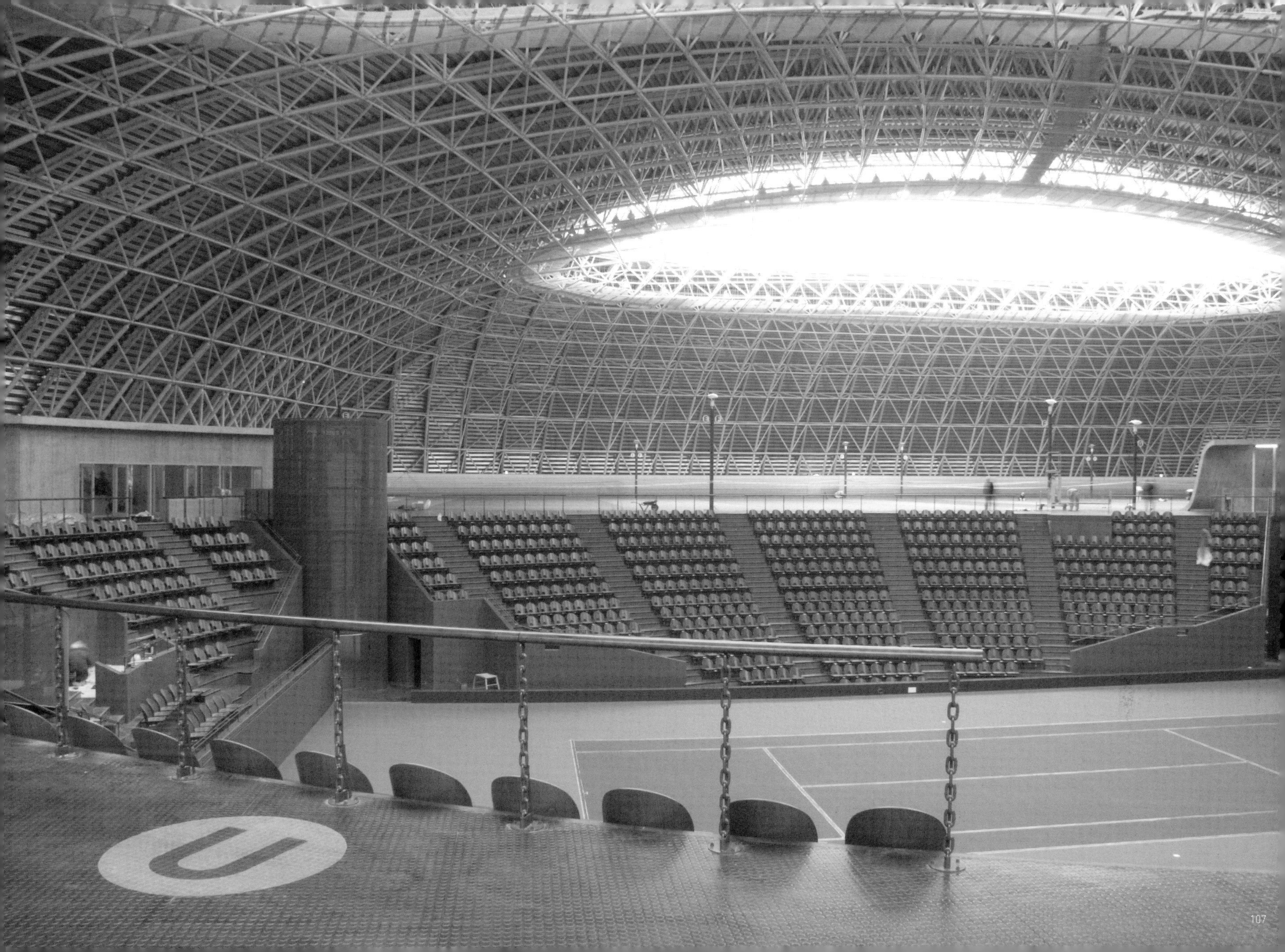

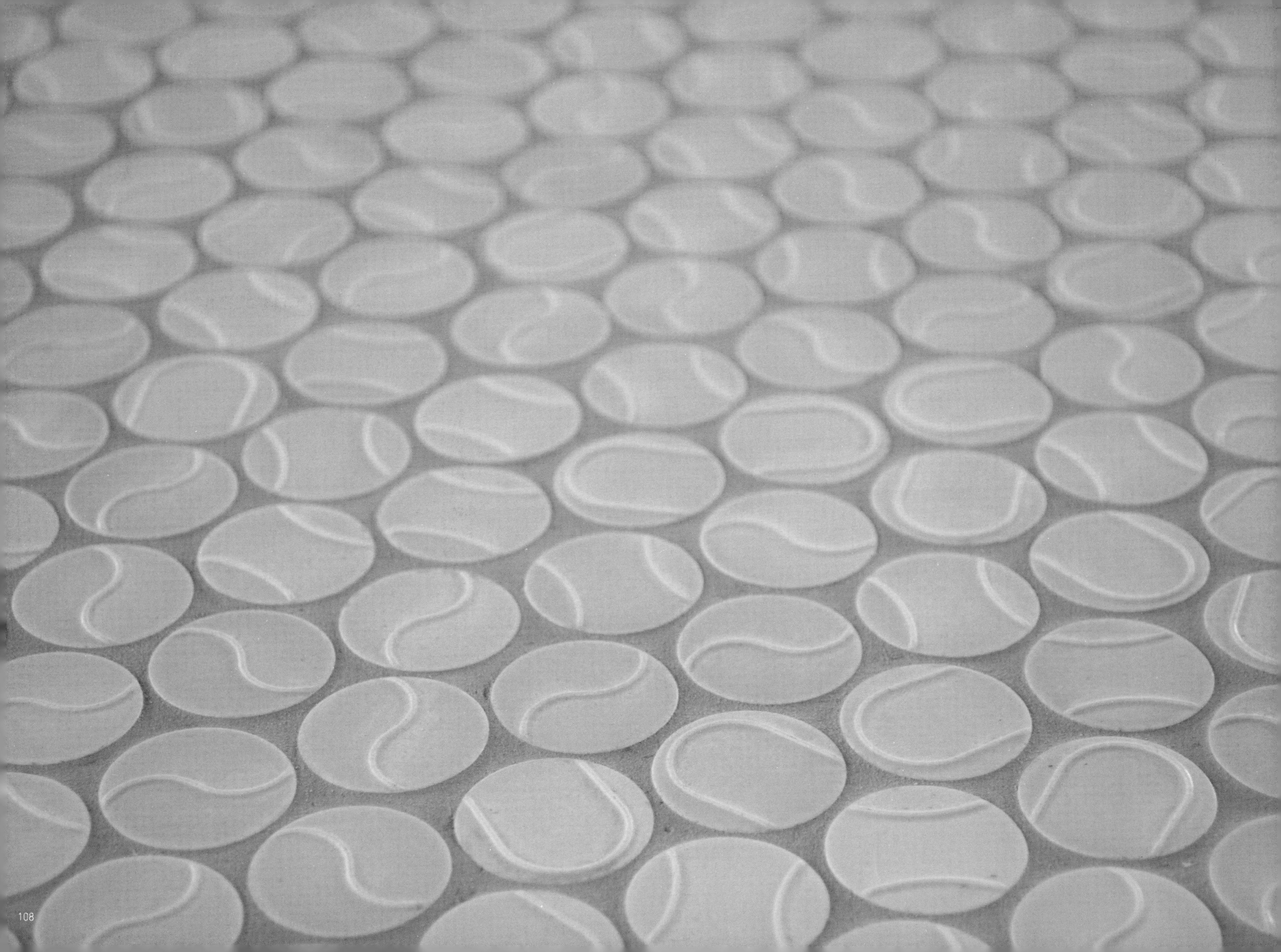

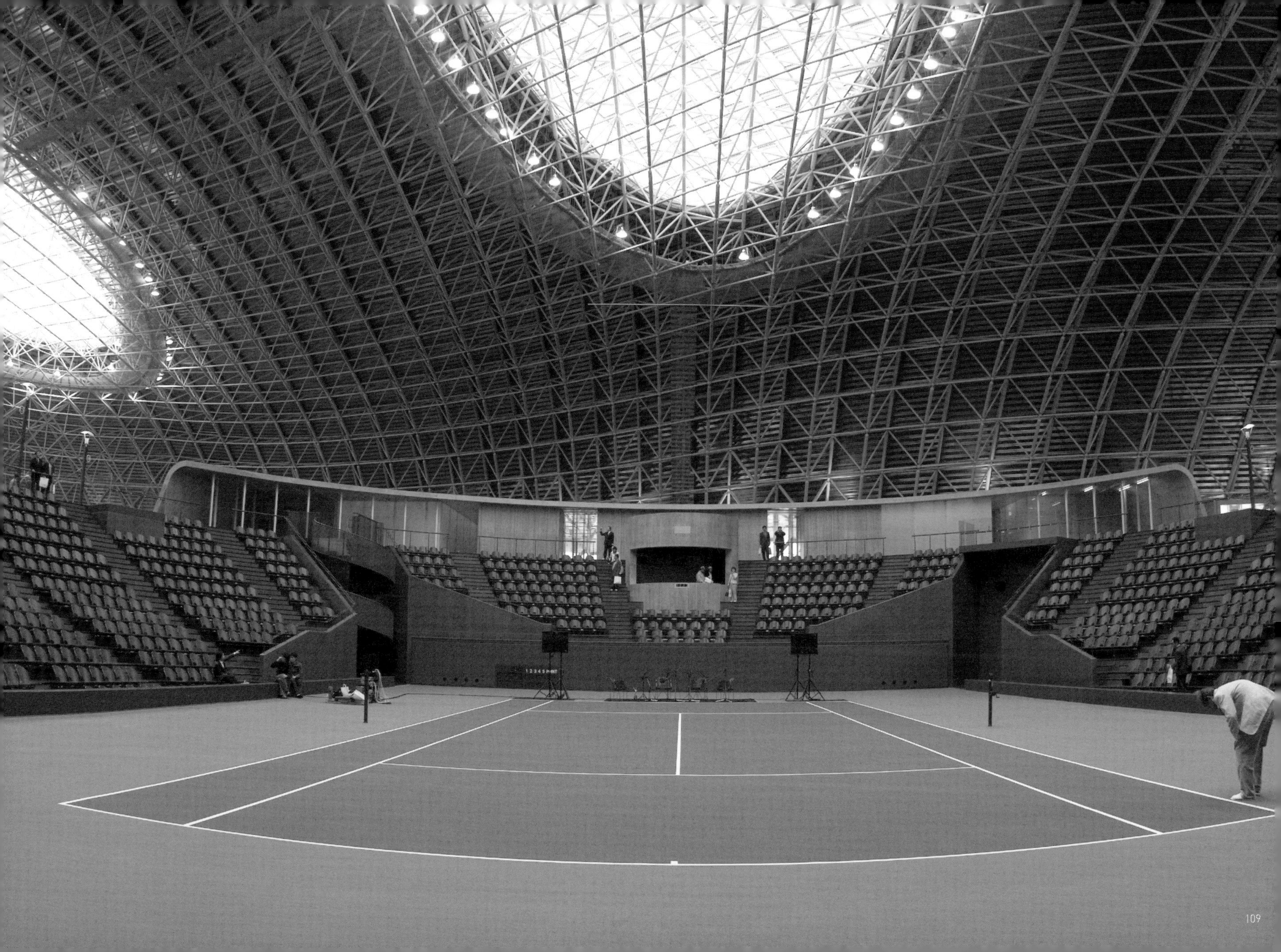

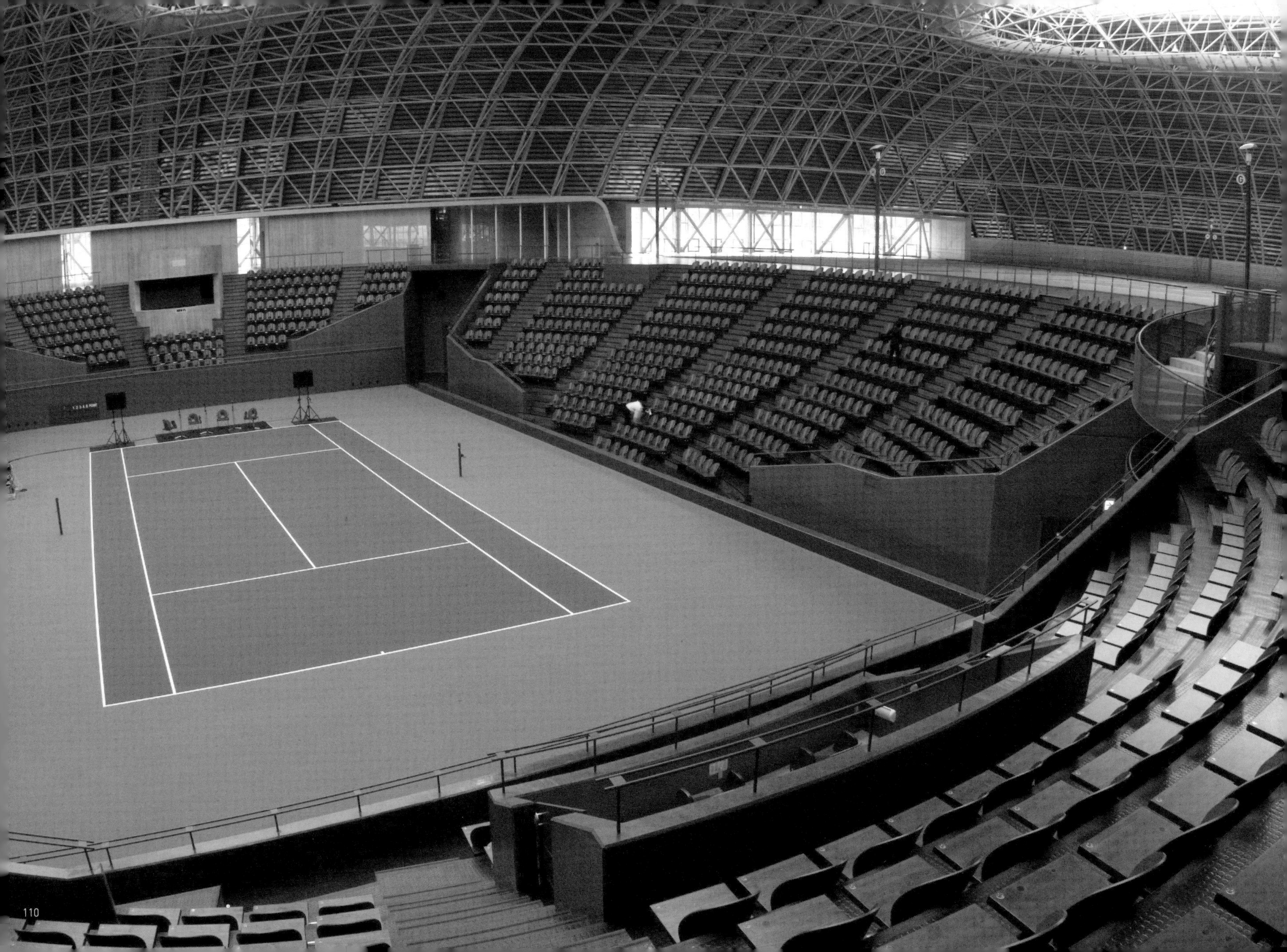

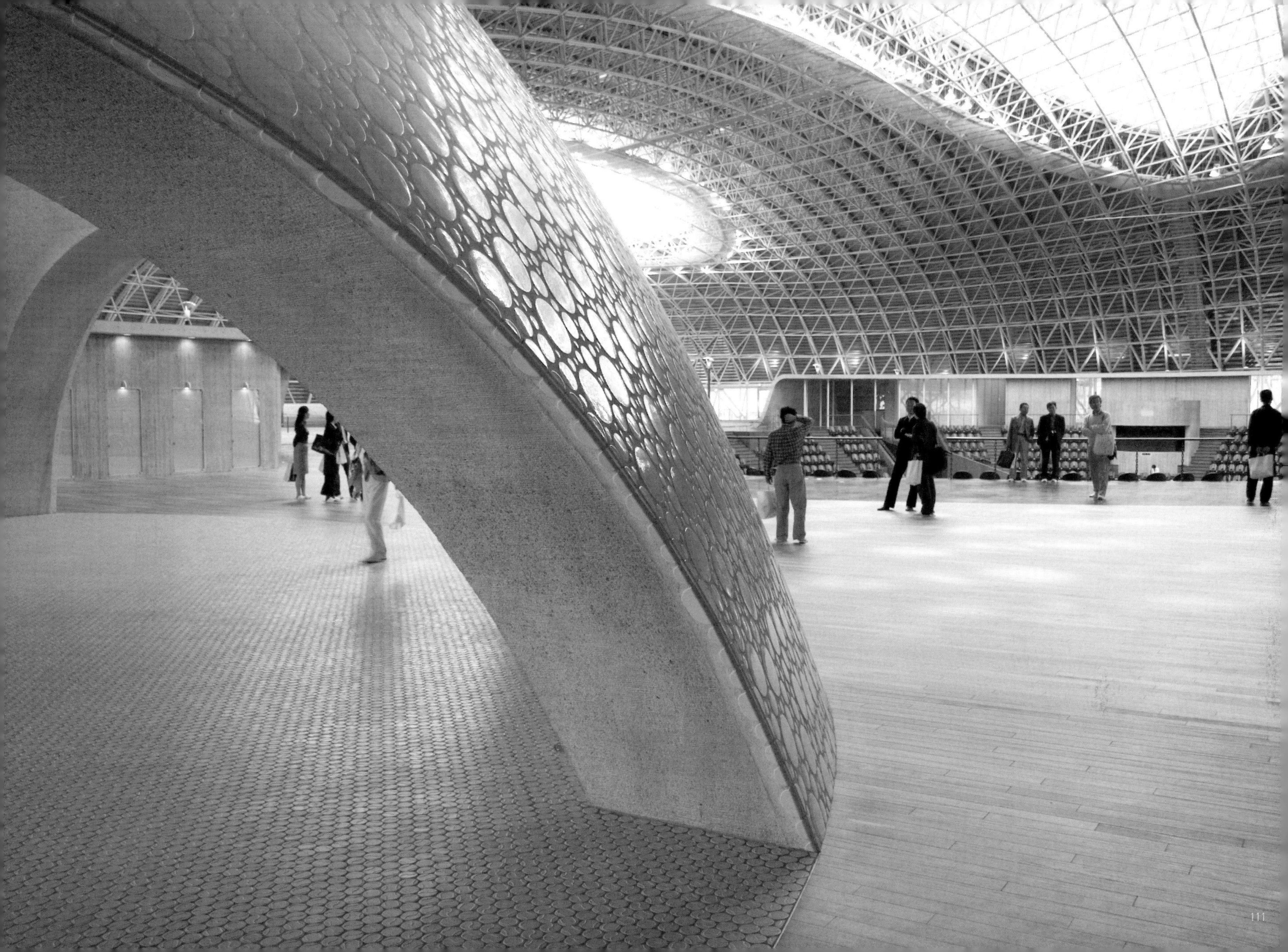

112

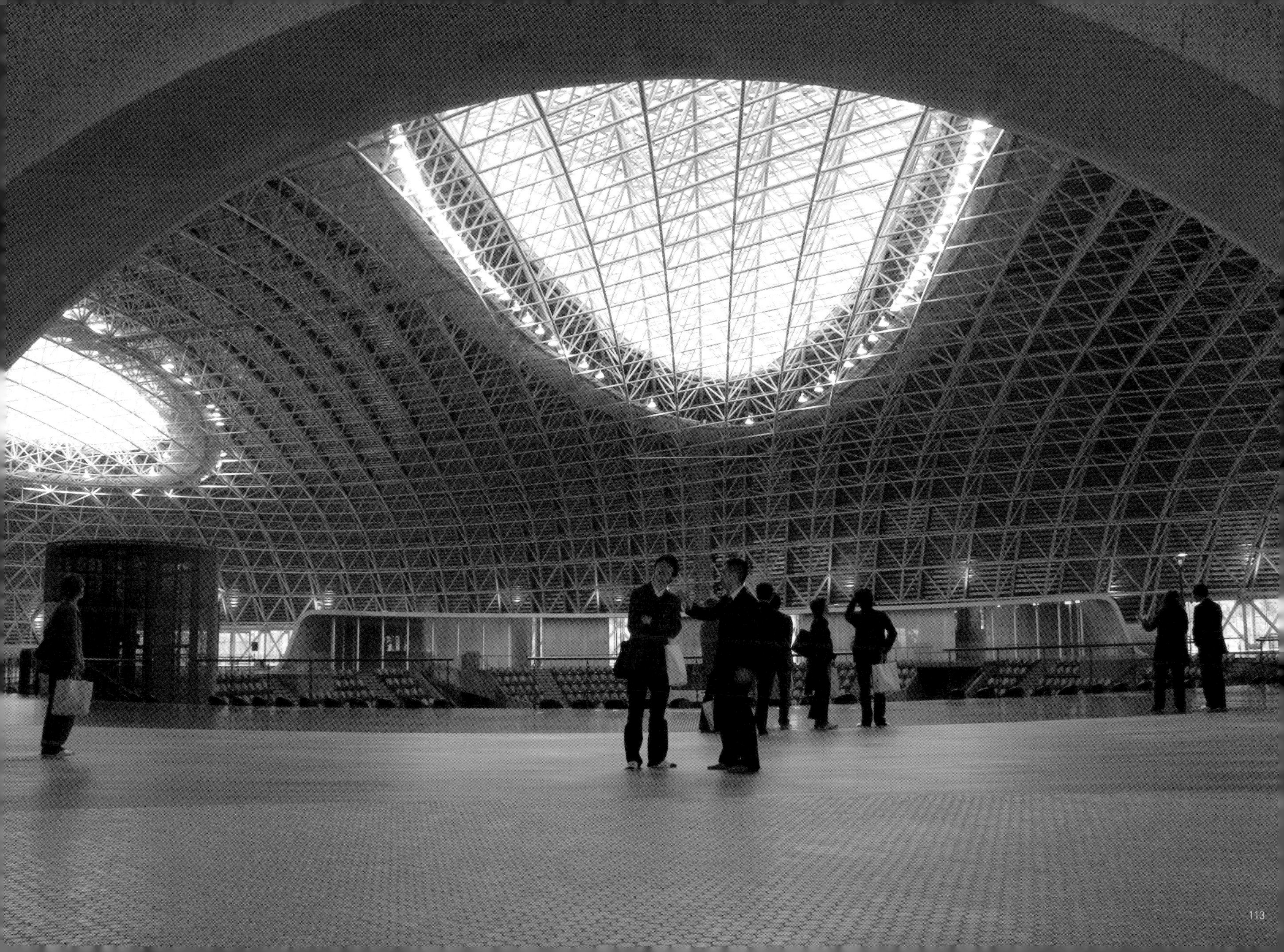

114

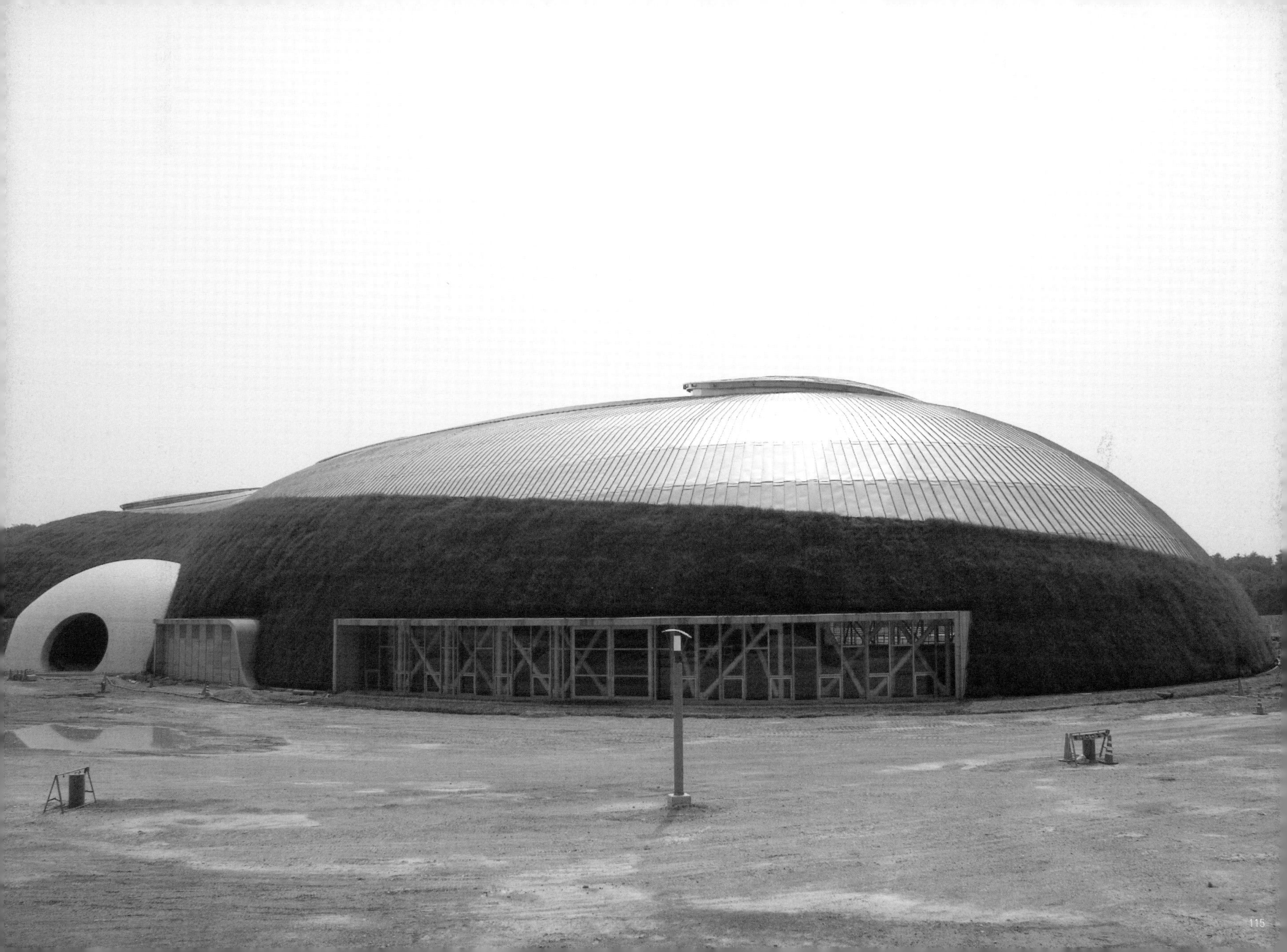

117

118

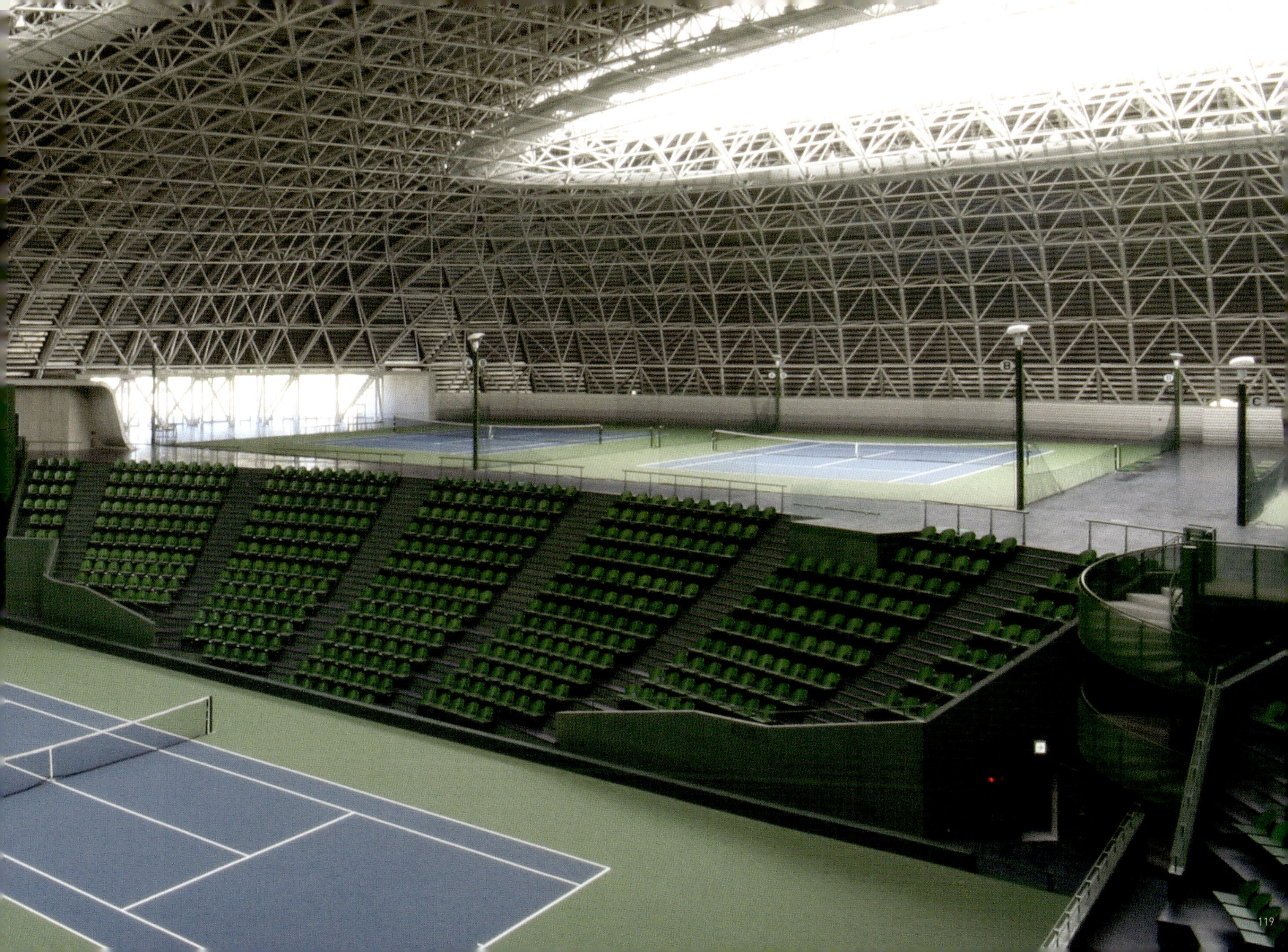

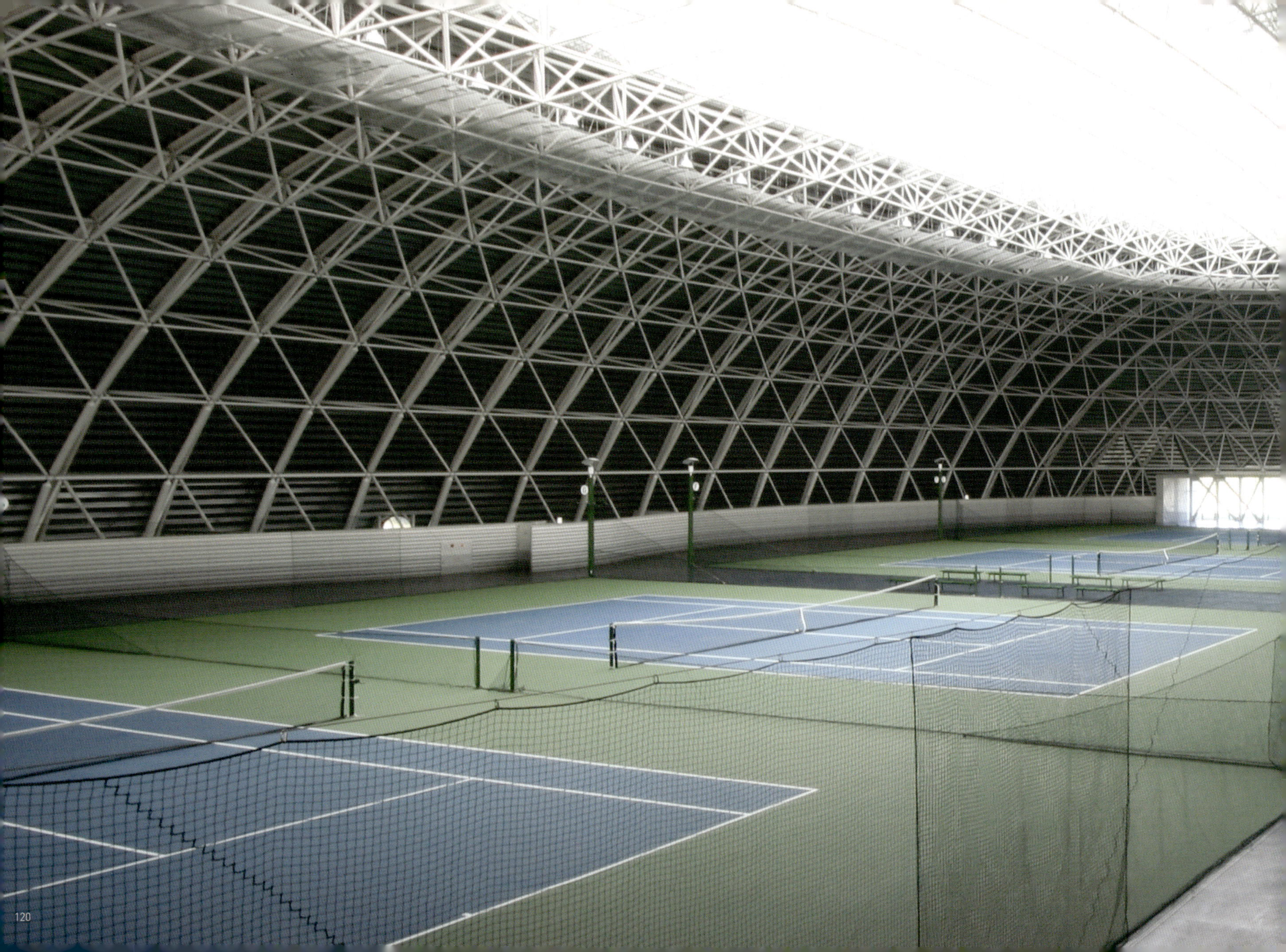

121

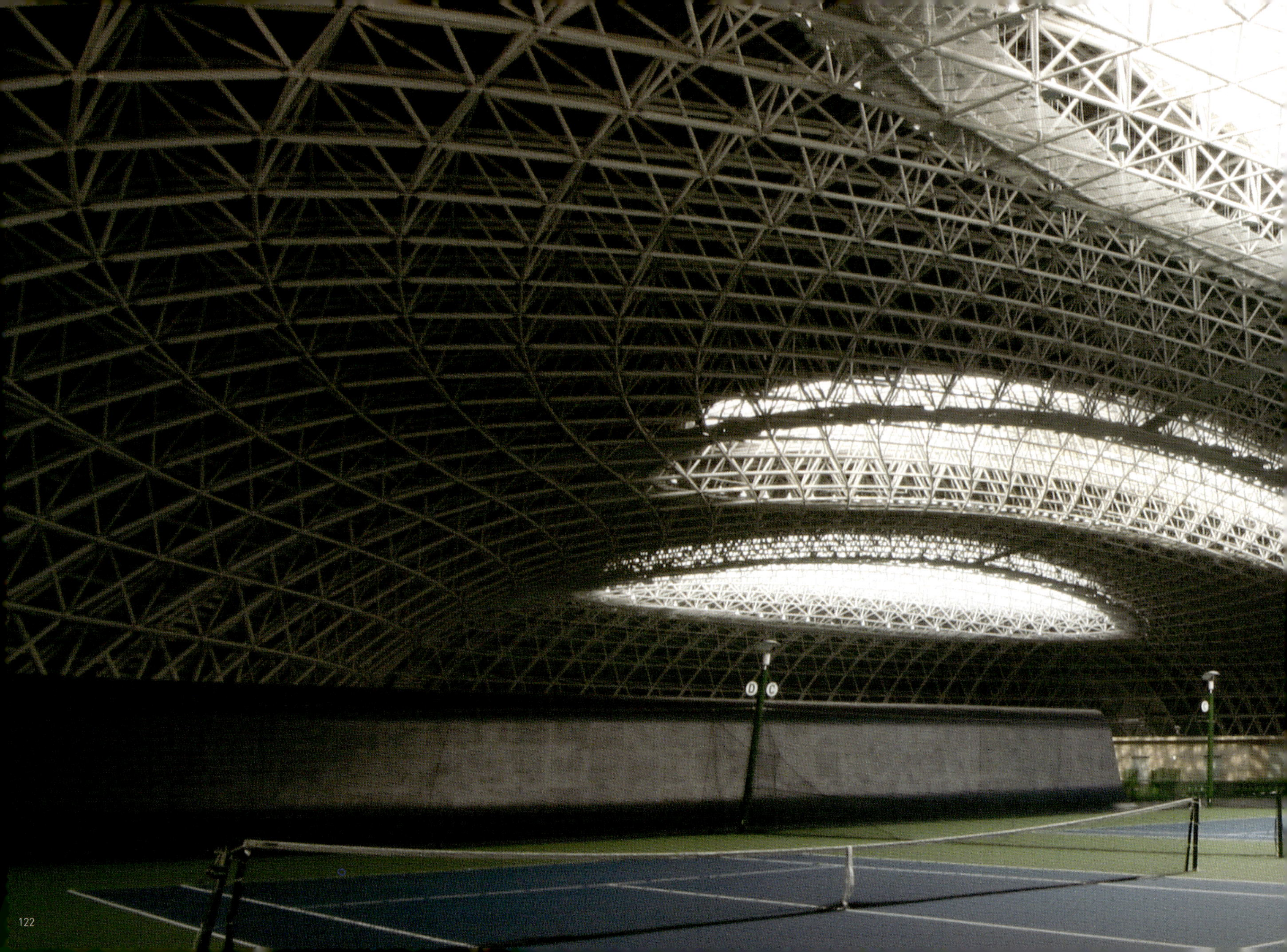

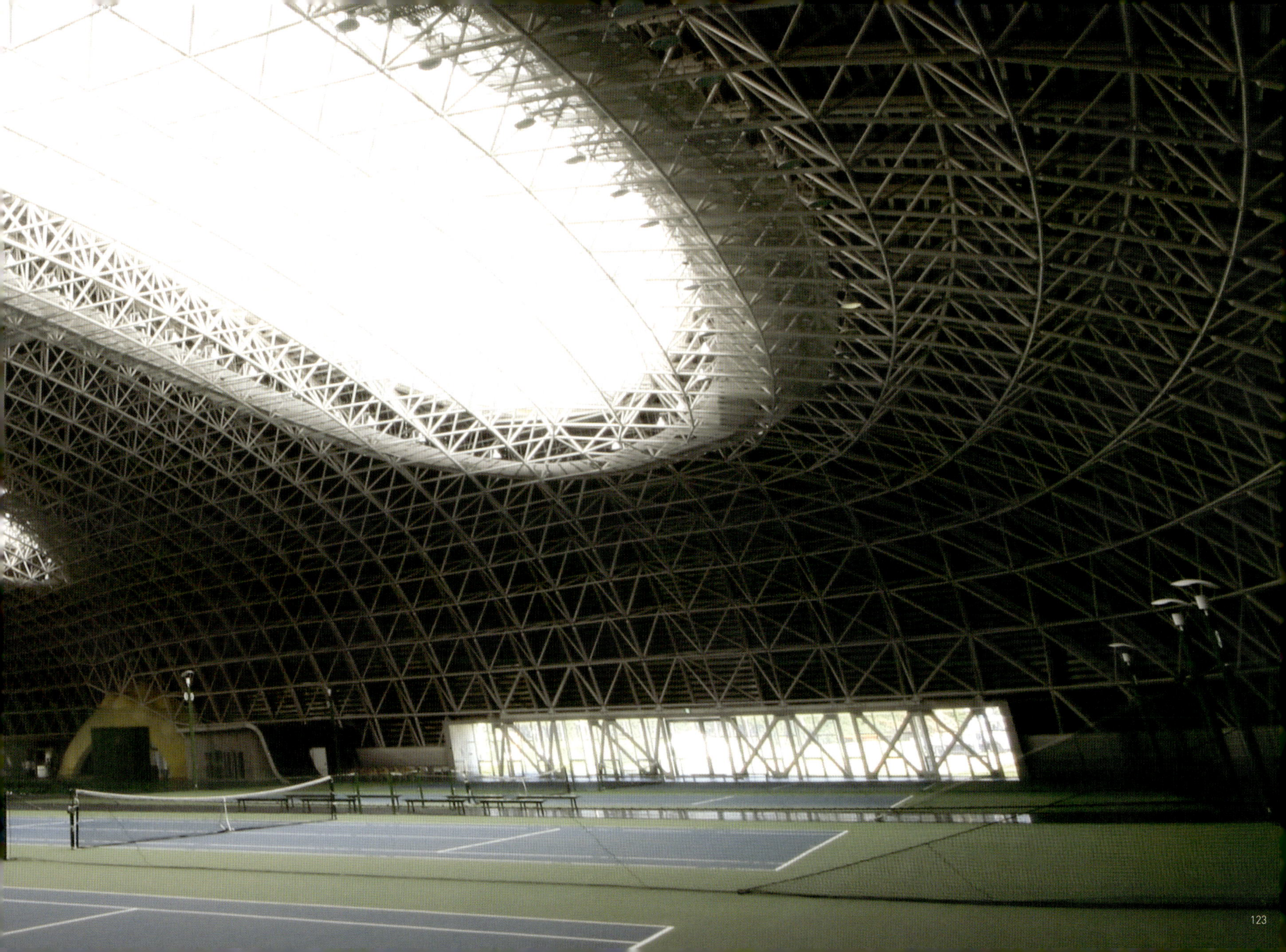

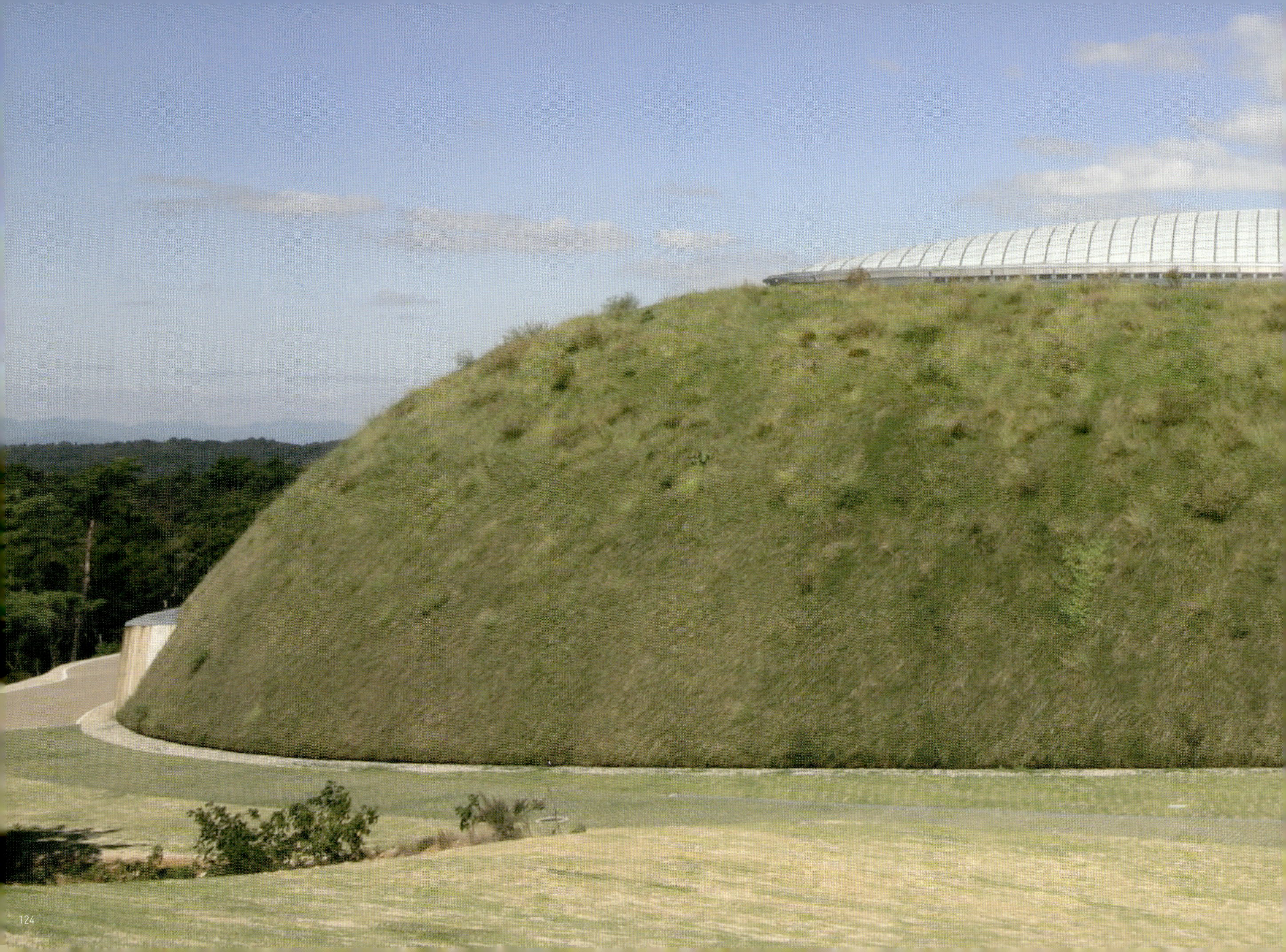

125

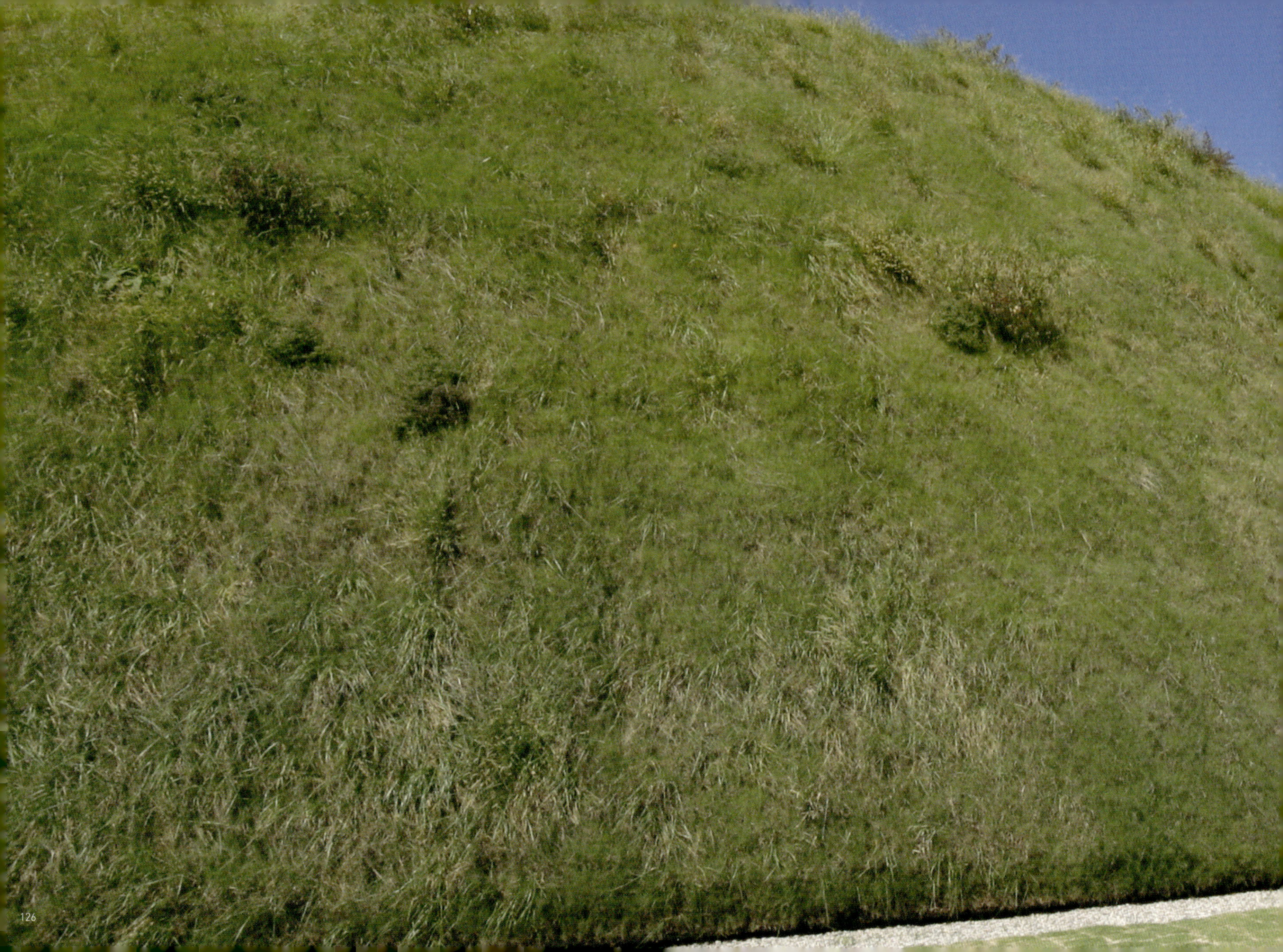

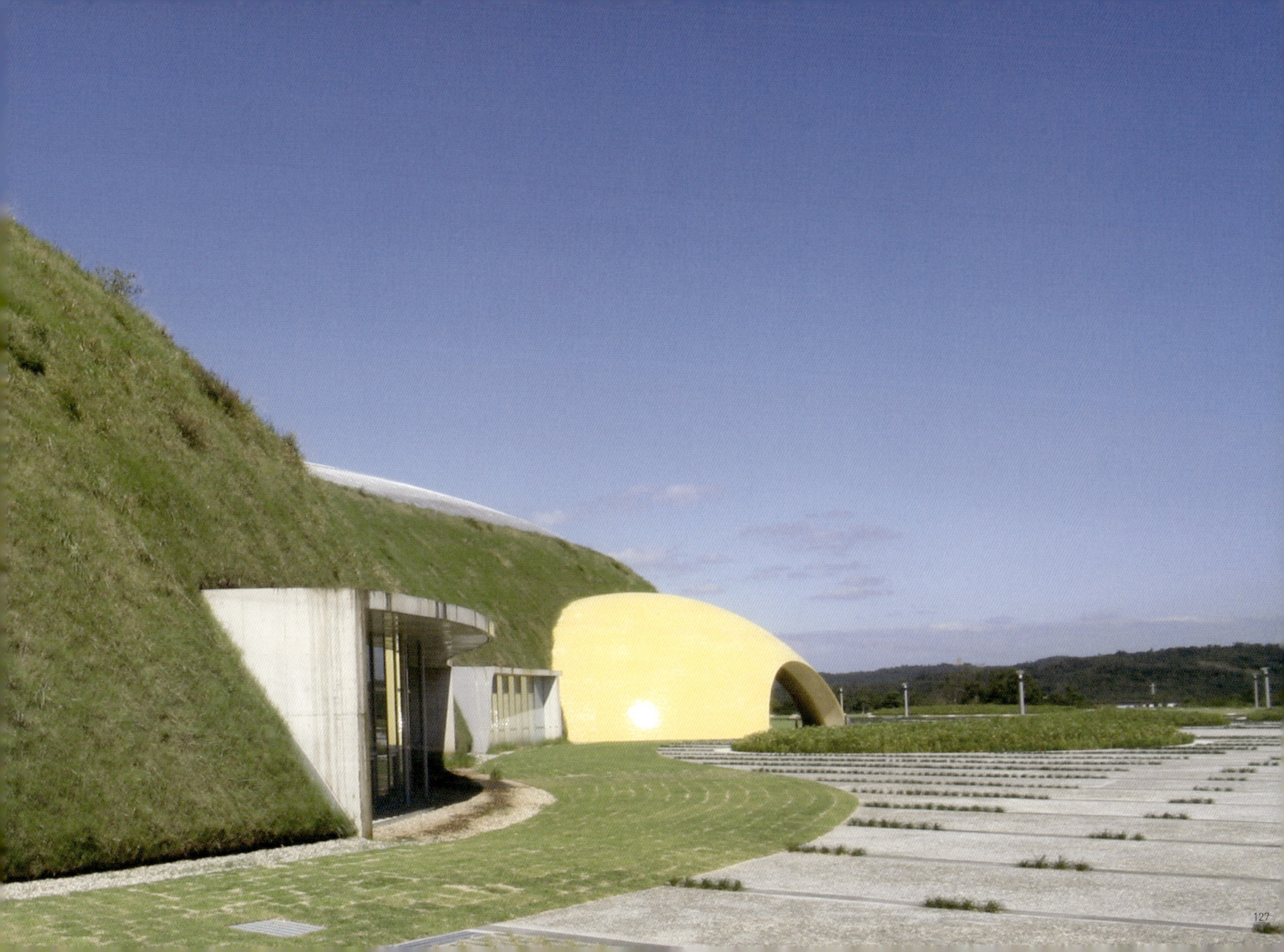

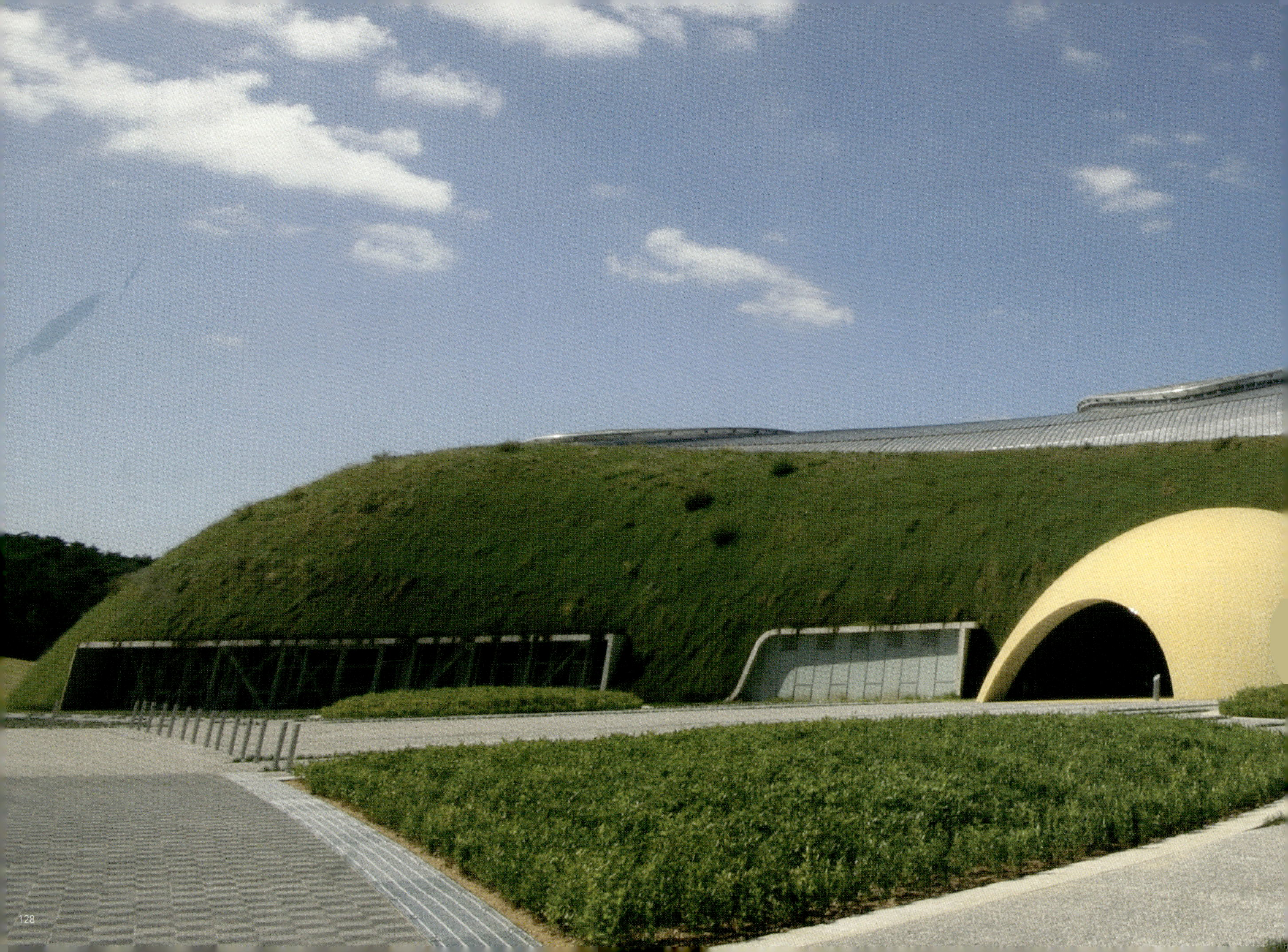

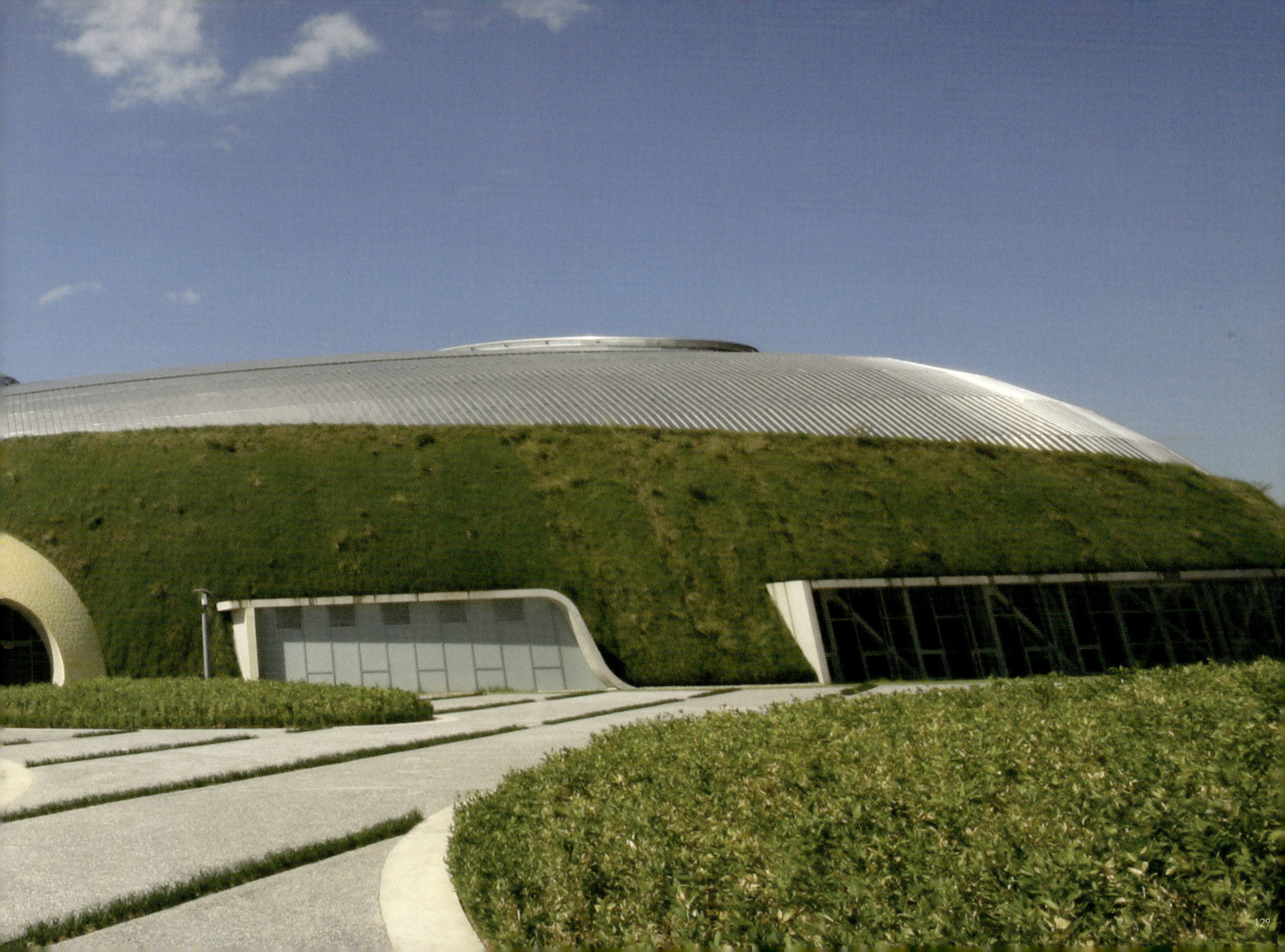

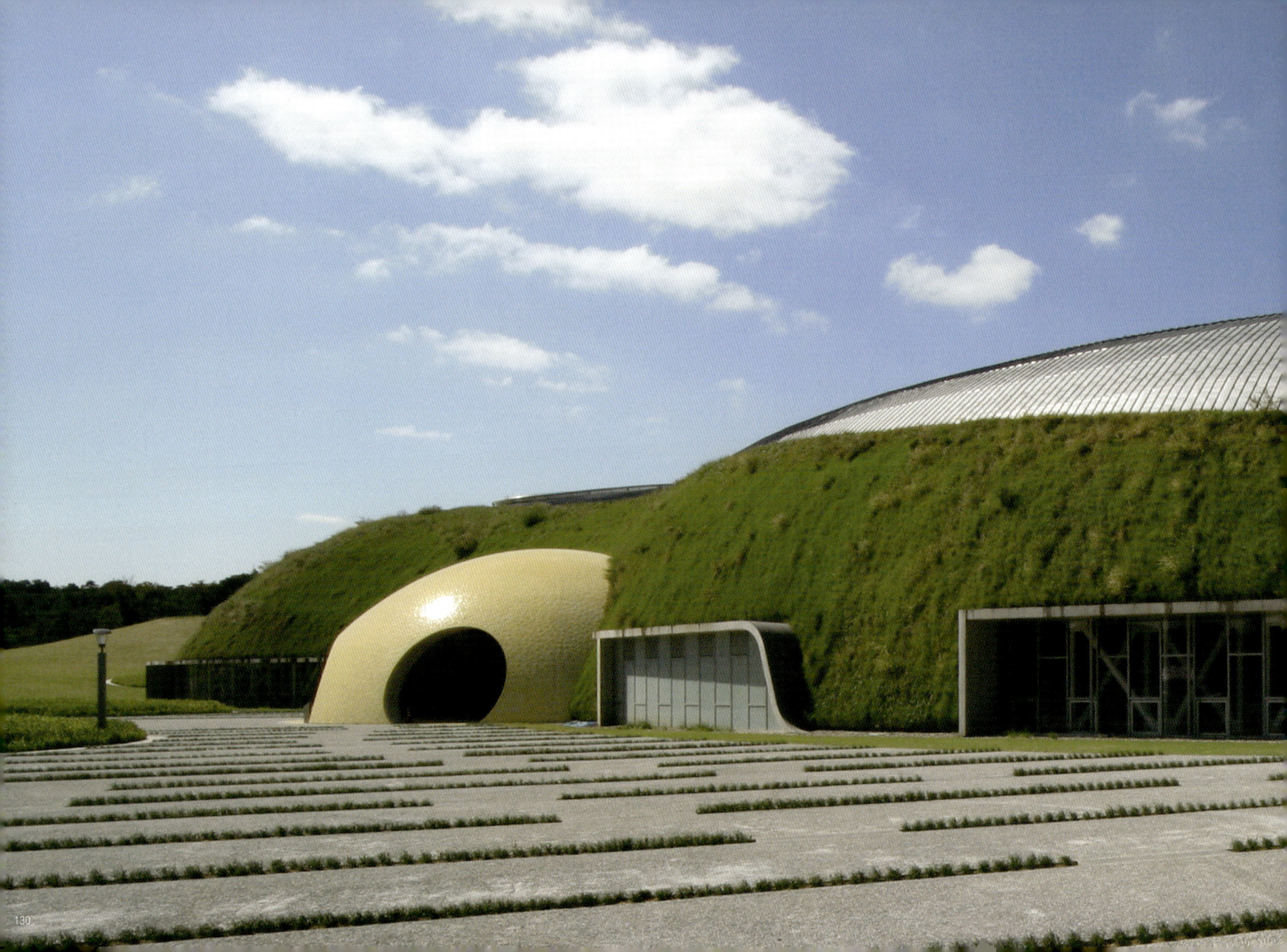

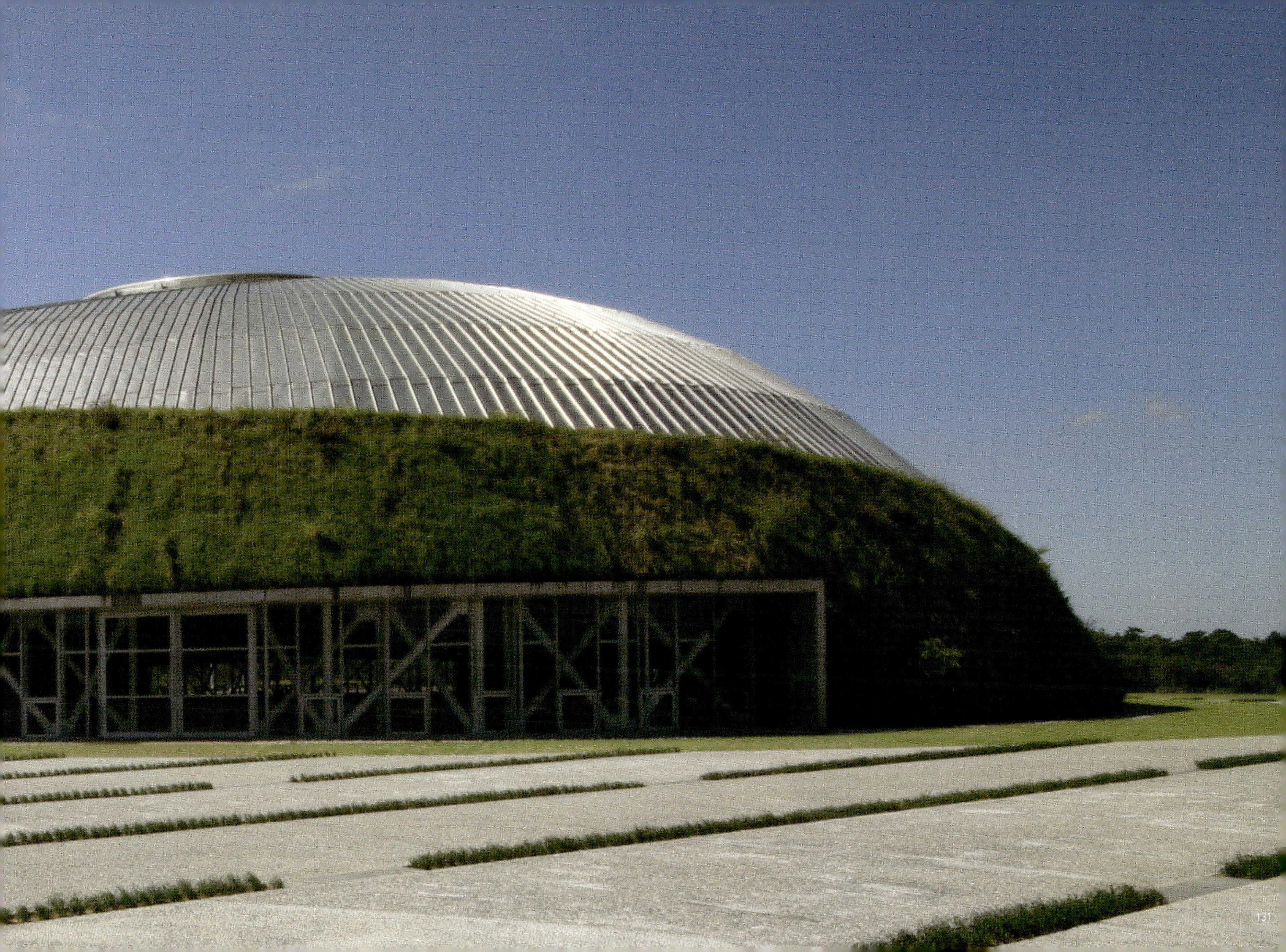

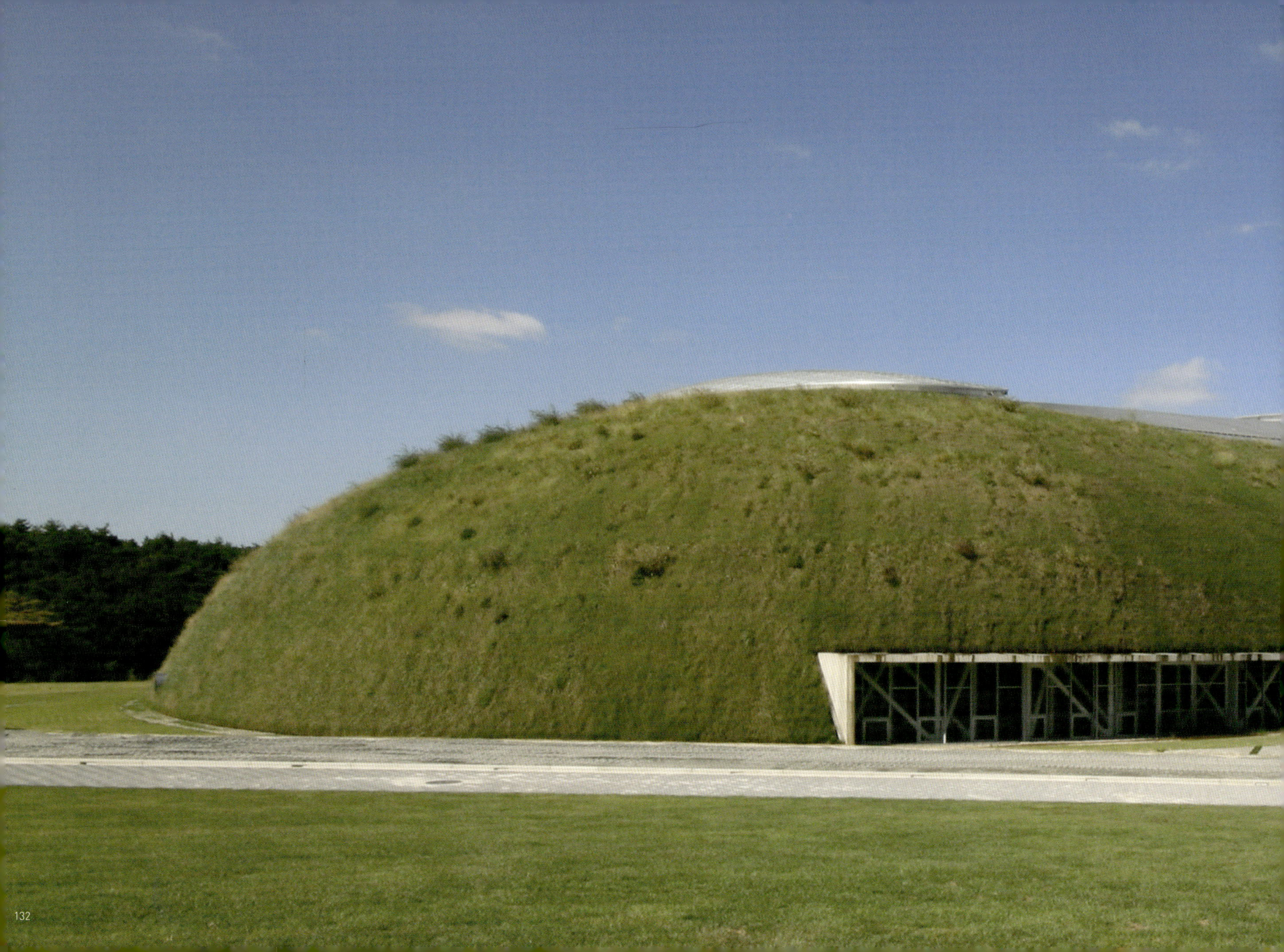

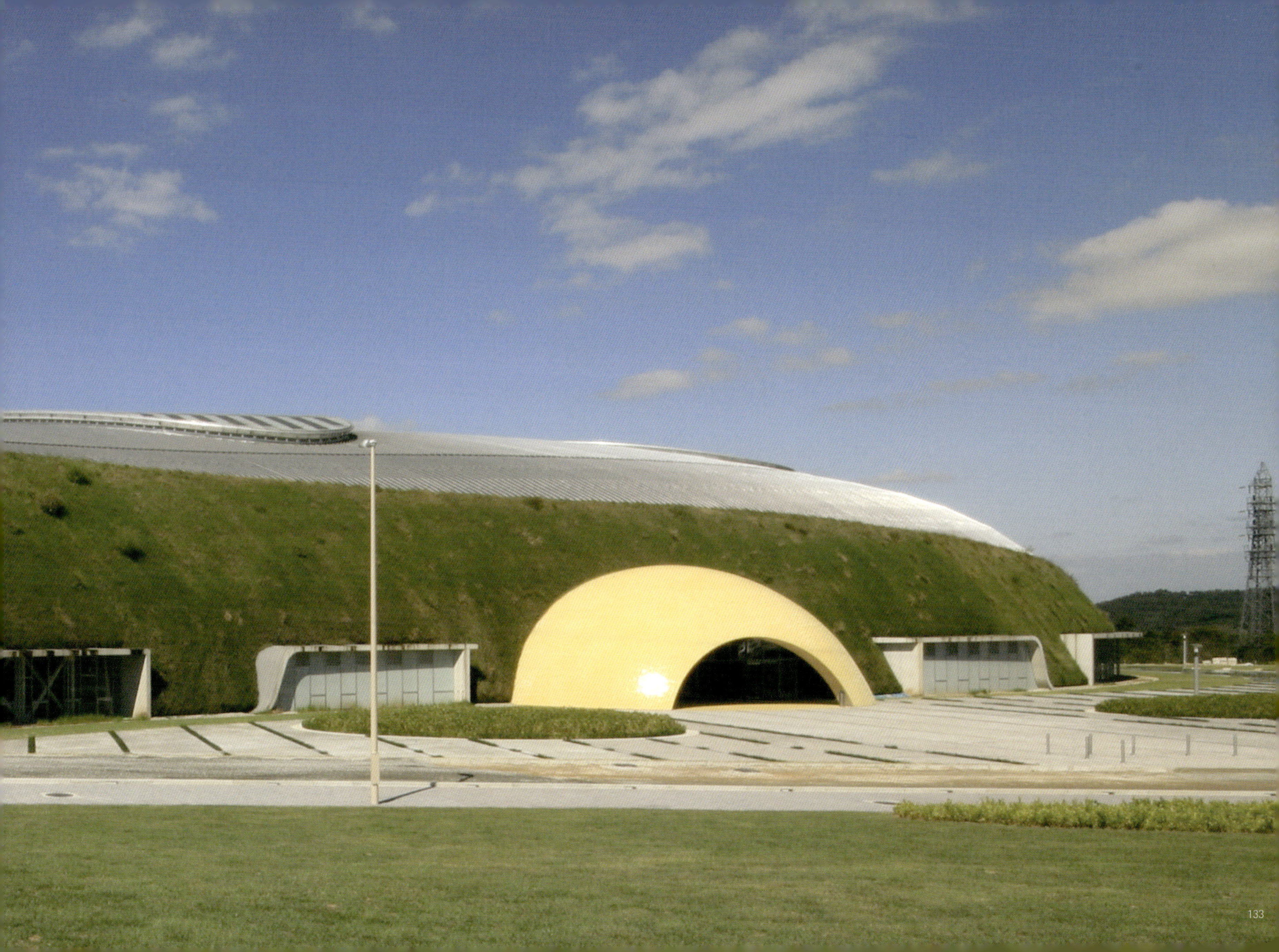

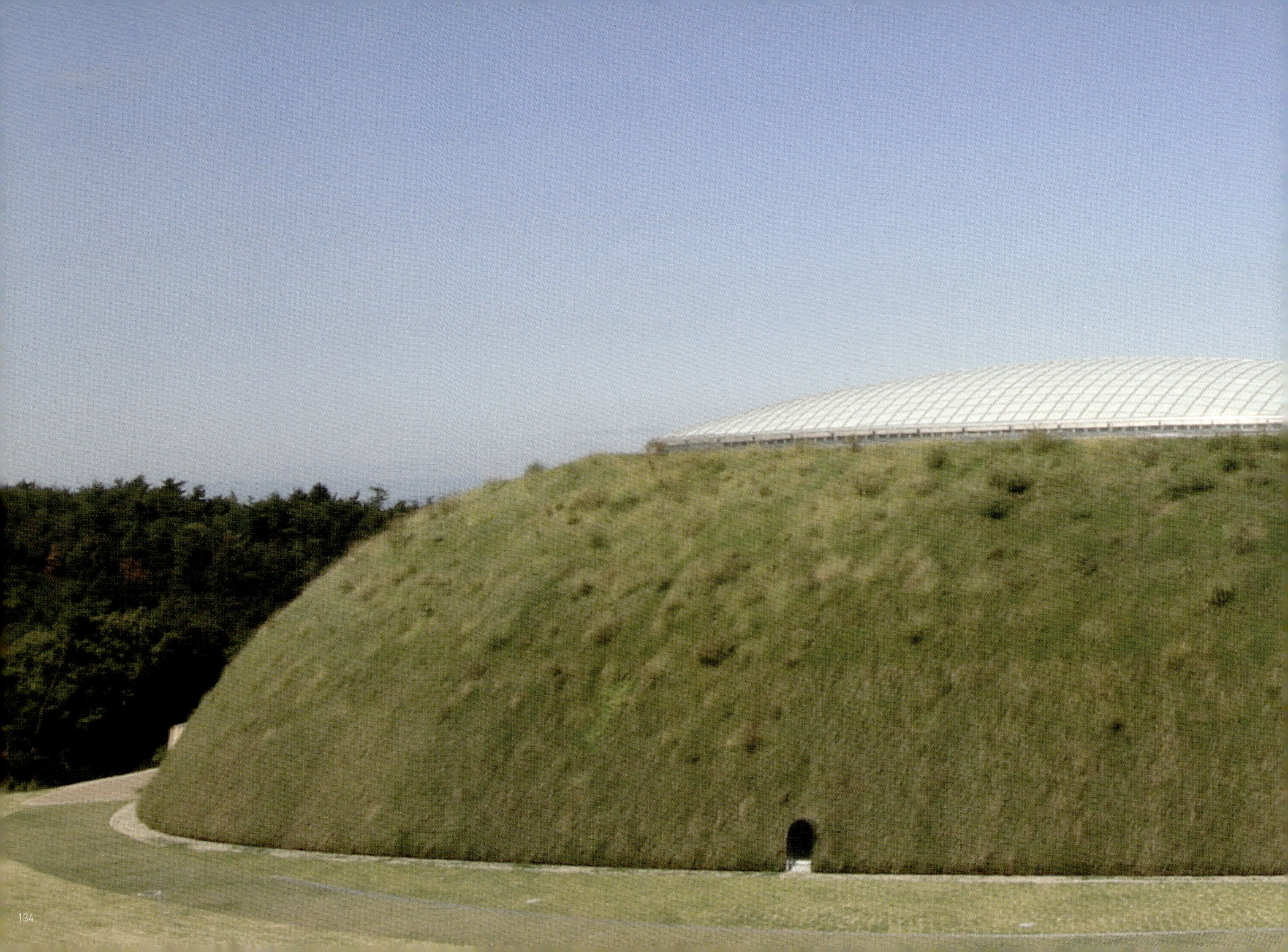

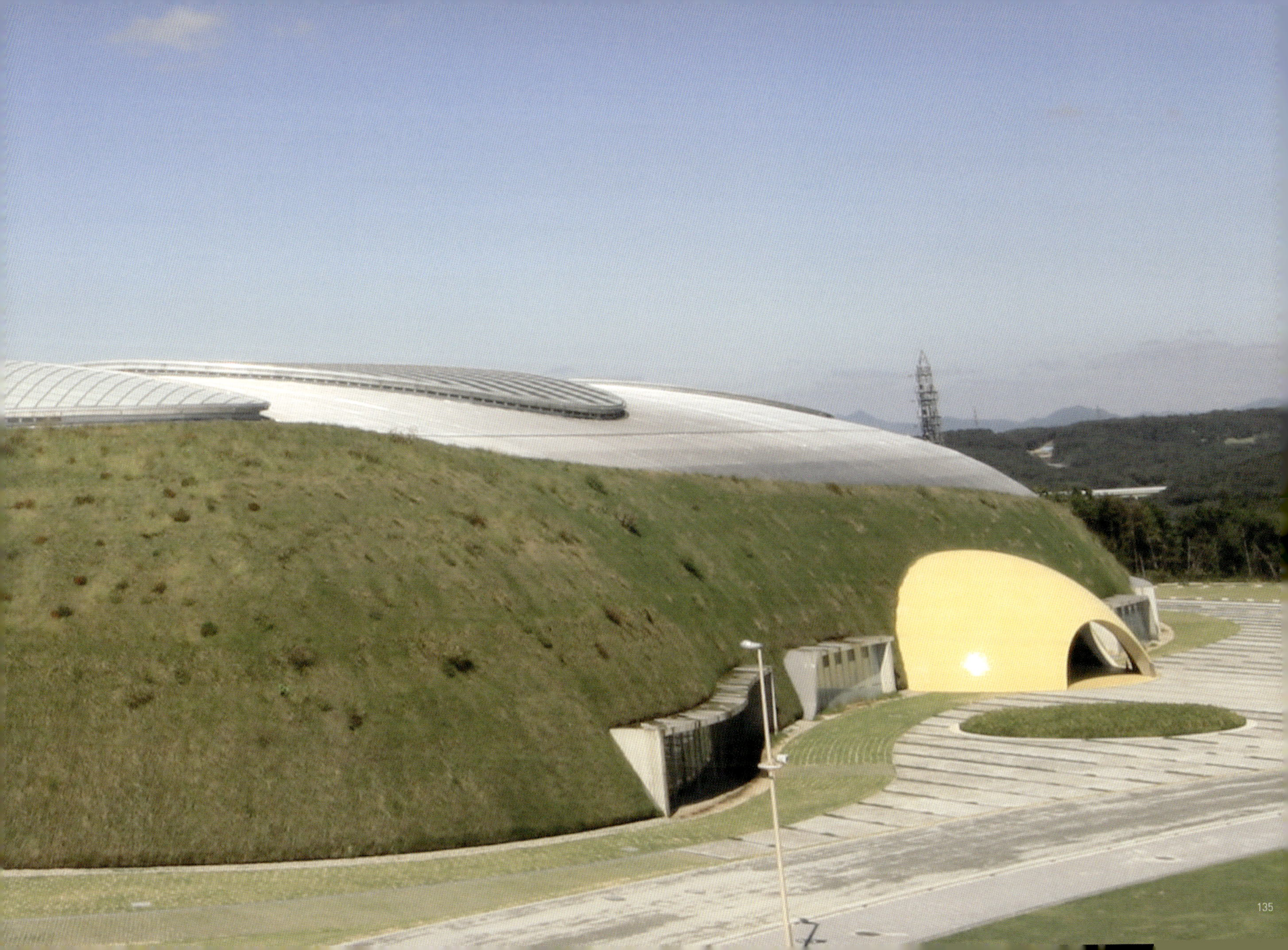

136

BEANS DOME
Slowtecture M Project

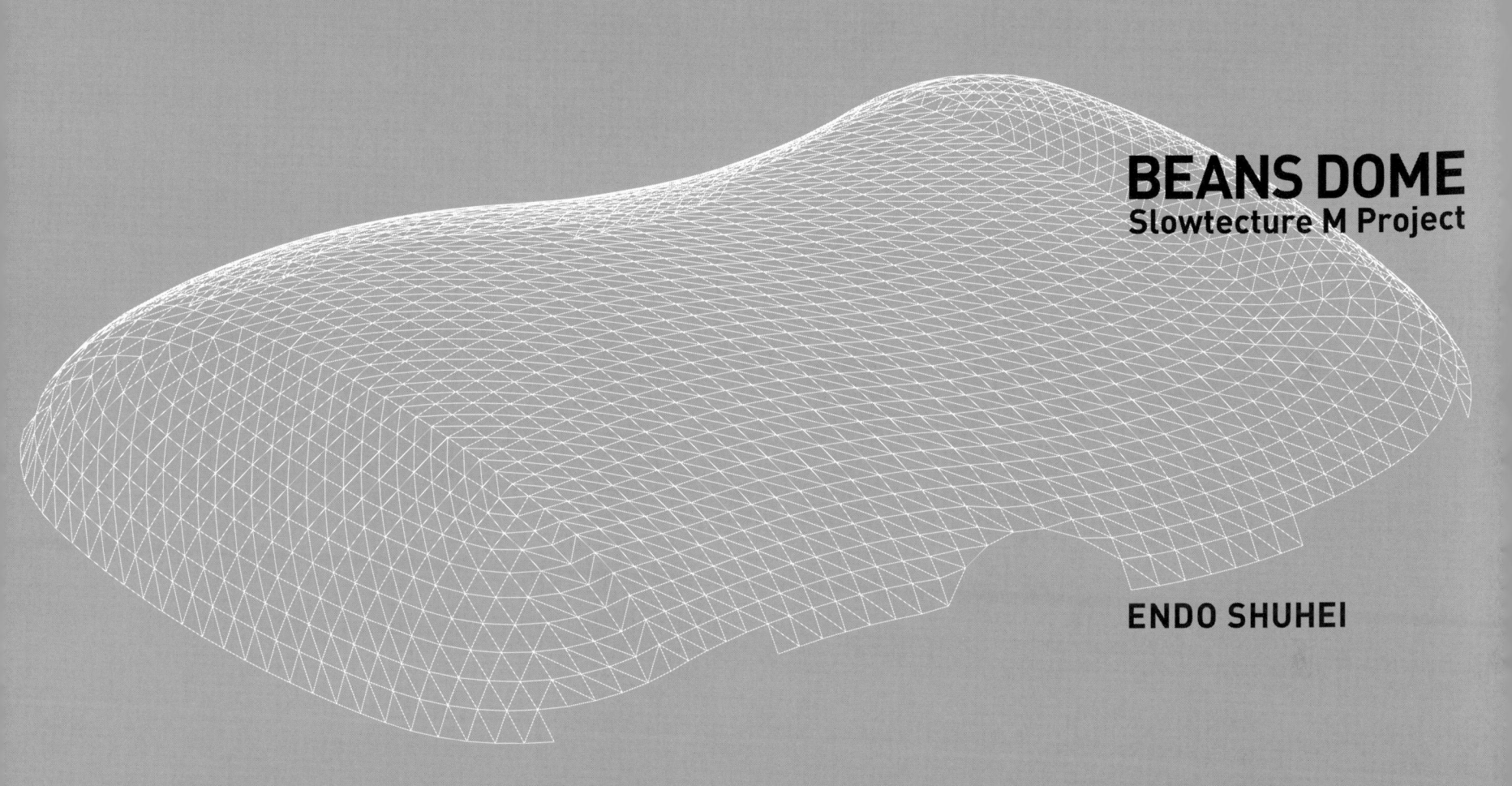

ENDO SHUHEI

スローテクチャーM Pjにおけるメモ　　遠藤秀平

この建築では、ひとつの価値に収斂することにより成立する形式以外の可能性を試みた。つまり、還元主義的象徴の呪縛から解放される形式の具体化である。多くの建築の思考は前提として、あこがれをもって移入されたひとつの方法、つまり20世紀に拡張した抽象化に束縛されてきたといえる。この束縛を離れ、ここでは閉鎖系ではない建築、外部との関連を有していることを求めた。しかし抽象の有効性を全面否定するものではない。

それは自己完結しない形式であり、人工性を前提としながら自然との接点を持続する関係において、あらたな抽象が発見されるのではないかと考える。抽象化とは差異をなくし、そこにみいだされる共通項の拡大である。形による幾何学的結果としての抽象ではなく、関係の連続化／均質化による抽象行為を確認したい。あえて言うならば部分において共有化すること。そして、タイトルとしてのスローとは多様であること。

抽象化

それはひとつの価値体系、幾何学、概念による
変換行為である。
そして均質化することでもある。
結末にはひとつの価値、ひとつの要素、
ひとつの結果が残る。
あえて言うなら一元的共有化。

均質化

それは連続化すること。
ここには意味の連続、形の連続、
価値の連続によりもたらされる。
差異の排除である。

連続化

それは内部と外部、異なる機能、違う目的、
さまざまな価値、人工と自然、
を均質的関係にすること。
つながる関係による均質化。

もうひとつの共有化

これも均質化そして連続化すること。
多くの価値、多くの要素、多くの結果を連続化する。
それは相互の関係接続により連続化、
均質化すること。
形を均質化しない抽象、関係の相対的抽象化。
それをあえていうなら部分の共有化。分有。

Memo: Slowtecture M Pj   Endo Shuhei

This structure is an experiment in possibilities detached from forms established through convergence/contraction to unitary values. It is, in other words, the realization of a form freed from the bounds of reductionist symbolism. The thinking behind many structures is obsessed with a single method, shackled to abstraction, an expansive mode of thought in the twentieth century. Here I sought to leave those shackles behind to achieve a structure that is not a closed system, that has a connection with the outside world. But I do not totally deny the validity of abstraction. It may possible for new abstractions to be discovered in forms that are not self contained, in relationships sustained through points of contact with nature, even if they are artificial. Abstraction eliminates difference and expands the range of shared elements. But I wish to affirm not abstraction as a geometric outcome though form but, rather, the act of abstraction through the sequencing and homogenizing of relationships. Here, sharing is partial. My use of "slow" in the title is deliberately polyvalent and ambiguous.

Abstraction

The action of conversion by means of a single value system, geometry, or concept.
The result is then homogenized.
At the end, there is only on value, one element, one result.
This is a one-dimensional sharing.

Homogenization

Sequencing.
Brought about through sequences of meanings, forms, and values.
It excludes differences.

Sequencing

Making homogenous the relationships between internal and external, different functions or purposes, various values, the natural and the artificial.
Homogenization occurs through a linking relationship.

sharing

Also homogenization and sequencing.
Sequencing many values, elements, and results.
Abstraction without homogenizing forms; relative abstraction of relationships.
Sharing of parts, not the whole.

BEANS DOME Slowtecture M Project
PLAN S=1/1000

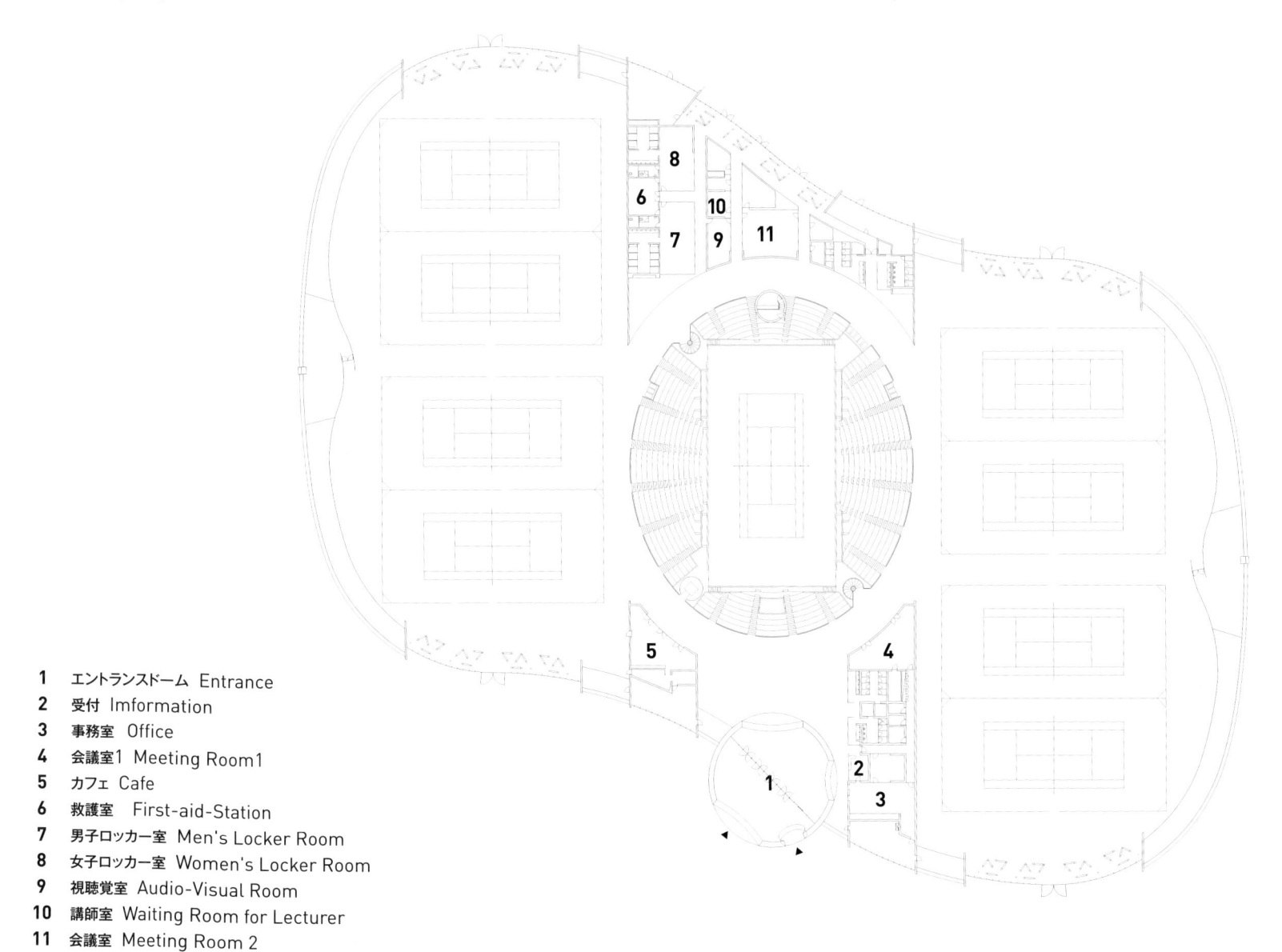

1 エントランスドーム Entrance
2 受付 Imformation
3 事務室 Office
4 会議室1 Meeting Room1
5 カフェ Cafe
6 救護室 First-aid-Station
7 男子ロッカー室 Men's Locker Room
8 女子ロッカー室 Women's Locker Room
9 視聴覚室 Audio-Visual Room
10 講師室 Waiting Room for Lecturer
11 会議室 Meeting Room 2

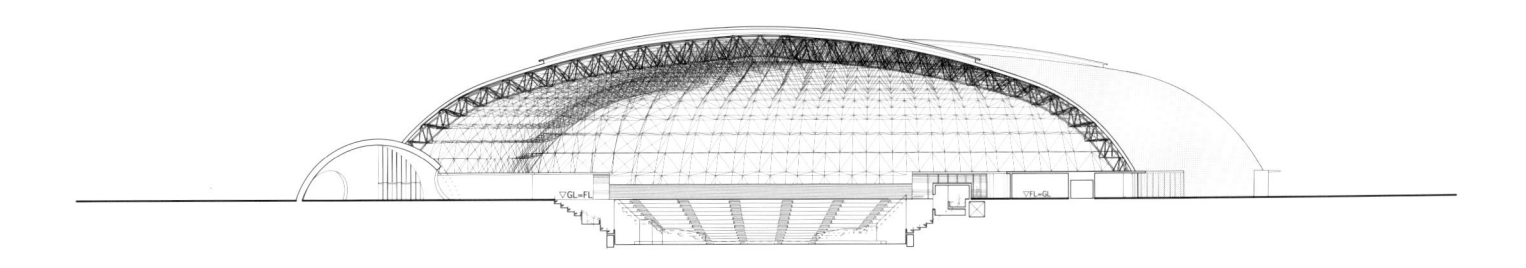

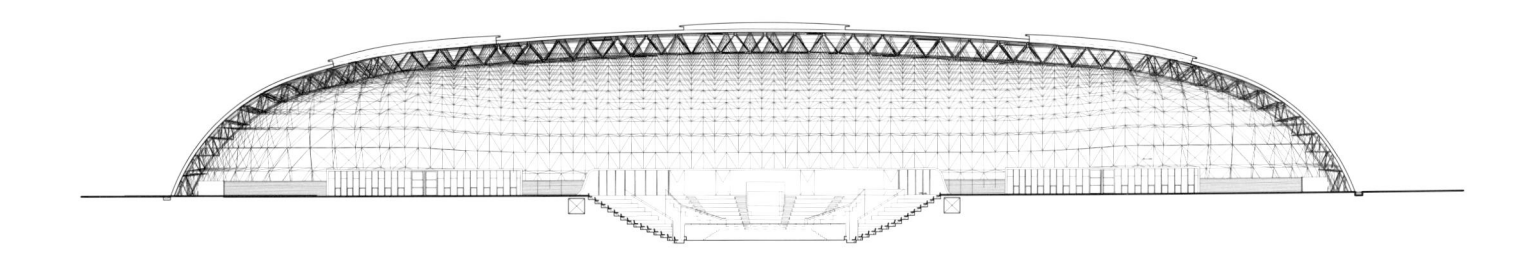

BEANS DOME Slowtecture M Project
SECTION S=1/1000

EAST

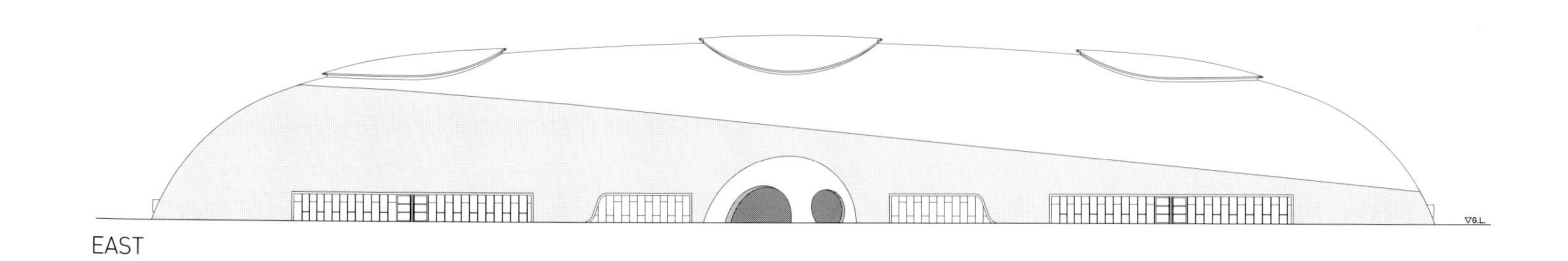

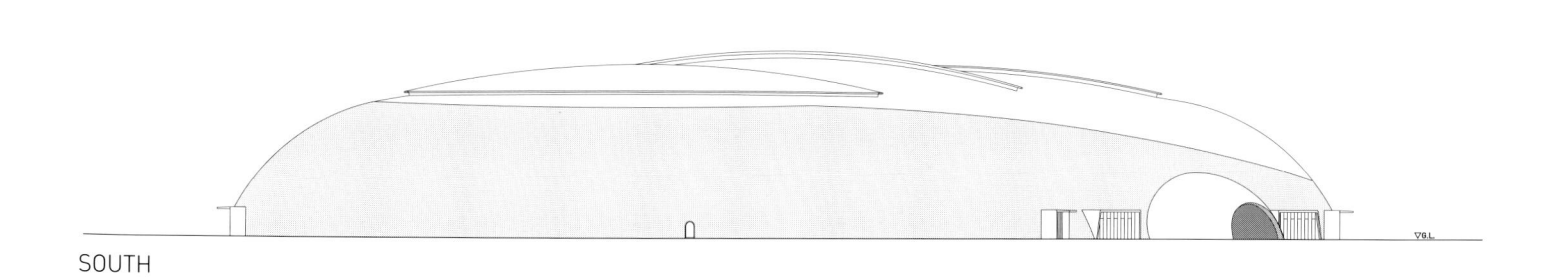

SOUTH

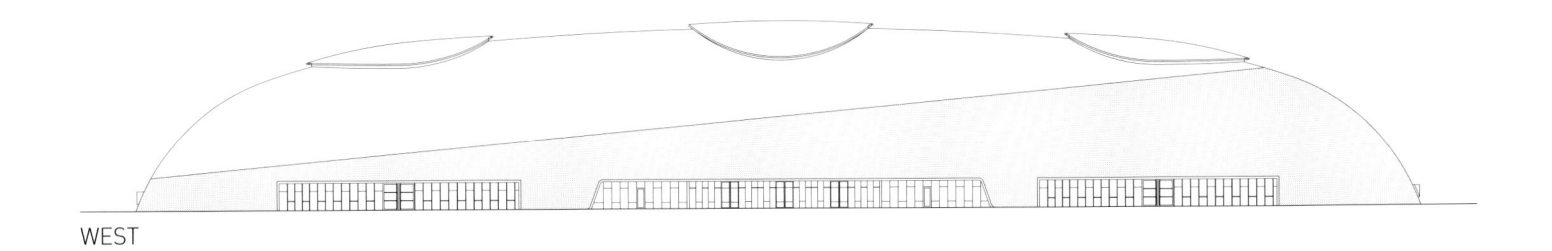

BEANS DOME Slowtecture M Project
ELEVATION S=1/1000

WEST

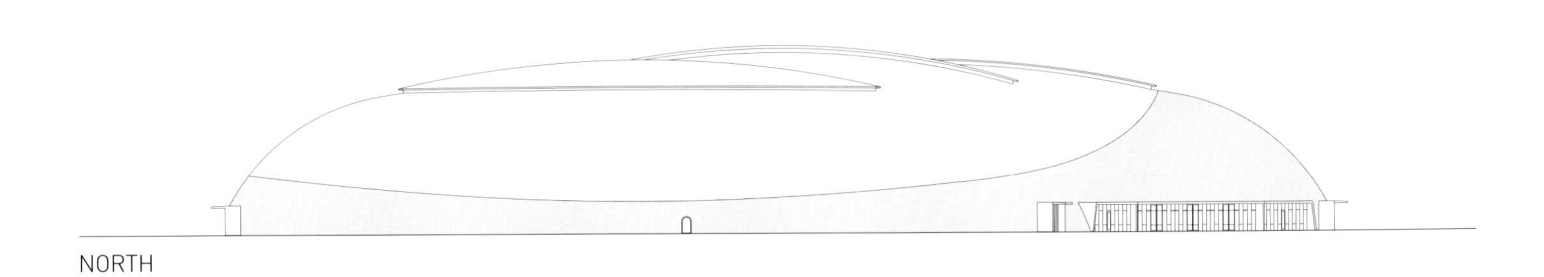

NORTH

- 住所
  兵庫県三木市志染町窟屋

- 発注者
  兵庫県

- 建築規模
  敷地面積　1,124,000㎡（兵庫県三木総合防災公園）
  建築面積　16,167㎡
  延床面積　16,167㎡
  構　造　RC造・鉄骨造
  構造形式　立体トラス
  基　礎　PC杭
  最高軒高　22.85 m

- 工程
  設計期間　2003.9～2005.3
  工事期間　2005.11～2007.3

- 設計
  建　築　遠藤秀平建築研究所／遠藤秀平・藤岡あおい・堀江渉
  設　備　設備技研
  構　造　デザイン・構造研究所／大氏正嗣・稲田竜也
  ランドスケープ　鳳コンサルタント
  サ イ ン　辰巳明久
  案 内 板　フジワキデザイン／藤脇慎吾・小川陽平
  アドバイザー　栗山和三

- 監理
  建　築　遠藤秀平建築研究所
  　　　　遠藤秀平・藤岡あおい・中村重陽・田中麻美子
  設　備　GE設備／松本秀治・山田広樹
  構　造　デザイン・構造研究所／大氏正嗣・稲田竜也

- 兵庫県担当者
  林忠正、岩田修三、大西徹、芹生良、永田佳幸、首藤健一、
  国見益生、木村正博
  佐野正夫、山本逸二、井上道大、小池敏之
  近藤健二、植野一明
  谷郷勘二
  二宗誠治

- 施工
  建　築　鹿島・安藤・アイサワ・丸正・平尾 JV
  電　気　東洋電気工事株式会社
  機　械　播丹実業株式会社

アイサワ工業(株)
(株)青井黒板製作所
(株)葵商会
安藤建設(株)
(株)イシマル
(株)板文
井上板金工業(株)
H・M・Oワークス社
栄輝産業(株)
エスケー化研(株)
(株)エービーシー商会
(株)オオツカ
(株)大林環境技術研究所
(株)岡田商事
(有)尾上運送
鹿島建設(株)
鹿島道路(株)
片岡建材
(株)加藤組
(株)加門組
川田工業(株)
関西トクヤマ販売(株)
計測技研
原頭工業(株)
建築環境技研
琴丘産業(株)
斉藤産業(株)
山大興業(株)
(有)サンメイク
清水工業(株)
JFEシビル(株)
ジェコス(株)
(株)住化分析センター
神姫警備保障(株)
鈴木設計一級建築士事務所
スチールエンジ(株)
西部電工(株)
(株)宣成社
(株)第一工芸
(株)大栄
大興物産(株)
太陽工業(株)
竹迫組
(株)竹延
田平ガラス
田村左官工業(株)
(株)テン
(株)東海
道清木材
東陶エンジニアリング(株)
(株)ニチベイ
日本機電(株)
日本体育施設(株)
(株)日本ネットワークサポート
永井鋼業(株)
(株)中村ポンプ
(株)ナカミツ建工
(株)沼測量
パナソニックSSマーケティング(株)
浜中工業(株)
(株)ハロー
美術工芸研究所
(株)ビゾン
(株)姫路メタルアート
(株)兵庫機工
(株)平尾工務店
(株)藤井商店
(株)フジワラ
(有)朴木工務店
(株)松本商事
MAX KENZO(株)
マルイチ(株)
丸正建設(株)
(株)ミコー総合開発
ミズノ(株)
(株)ミック
三菱電機(株)
三輪運輸工業(株)
美和ロック(株)
(株)モネー
森川壁材(株)
(有)モリトシブラン
(株)ユニオン
(株)ユニバーサル金属製作所
横河工事(株)
吉井金物(株)

遠藤秀平
1960　生まれ
1986　京都市立芸術大学大学院修了
1988　遠藤秀平建築研究所設立
2007～　神戸大学大学院教授

Endo Shuhei
1960　Born in Japan
1986　Obtained a master's degree at Kyoto City University of Art
1988　Established Shuhei Endo Architect Institute
2007～　Professor of Kobe University

URL　www.paramodern.com

遠藤秀平／ビーンズドーム
2007年11月21日　第1刷発行©

編著者：遠藤秀平
テキスト：三宅理一
発行者：鹿島光一
発行所：鹿島出版会
〒100-6006 東京都千代田区霞が関3丁目2番5号霞が関ビル6階
電話03-5510-5400　振替00160-2-180883
カバー＋デザイン：フジワキデザイン
写真：天野憲一
英訳：ラス.S.マクレリー. ザ・ワード・ワークス
印刷・製本：三美印刷

ENDO SHUHEI / BEANS DOME　Slowtecture M Project
First Published 21 November, 2007©
Editor&Writer: Endo Shuhei
Text: Miyake Riichi
Publisher: Kajima Institute Publishing Co., Ltd.
100-6006 6F 3-2-5 Kasumigaseki Chiyoda-ku Tokyo, Japan
Cover + Design: FUJIWAKI DESIGN
Photograph: Amano Kenichi
English translation: Ruth S.McCreery. The Word Works, Ltd.
Print & Bind: SANBI Printing Co., Ltd.

無断転載を禁じます。落丁・乱丁本はお取替えいたします。
ISBN978-4-306-04491-3 C3052　Printed in Japan

本書の内容に関するご意見・ご感想は下記までお寄せください。
URL:http://www.kajima-publishing.co.jp　E-mail:info@kajima-publishing.co.jp